Mobilization Day

Mobilization Day

Americans Debate Militarism, 1914–1924

Roger Possner

Algora Publishing
New York

Library of Congress Cataloging-in-Publication Data —

Names: Possner, Roger, 1942- author.
Title: Mobilization Day : Americans debate militarism, 1914-1924 / Roger Possner.
Other titles: Americans debate militarism, 1914-1924
Description: New York : Algora Publishing, [2019] | Includes bibliographical references and index. | Summary: "America has a fine tradition, mostly forgotten, of opposition to military values and large military forces. This study of the debate from 1914-1928 documents major events of the period and shows how militarists and anti-militarists contended to persuade Americans which policies were best to preserve national security."— Provided by publisher.
Identifiers: LCCN 2019026972 (print) | LCCN 2019026973 (ebook) | ISBN 9781628944013 (trade paperback) | ISBN 9781628944020 (hardback) | ISBN 9781628944037 (pdf)
Subjects: LCSH: Peace movements—United States—History—20th century. | Militarism—United States—History—20th century. | United States—Military policy—Public opinion. | Pacifism—United States—History—20th century. | World War, 1914-1918—United States—Public opinion. | War—Public opinion. | United States—Politics and government—1913-1921. | United States—Politics and government—1921-1923. | United States—Politics and government—1923-1929. | Public opinion—United States.
Classification: LCC JZ5584.U6 P67 2019 (print) | LCC JZ5584.U6 (ebook) | DDC 327.1/72097309041—dc23
LC record available at https://lccn.loc.gov/2019026972
LC ebook record available at https://lccn.loc.gov/2019026973

Printed in the United States

To my dear daughter Carmen

Table of Contents

Preface

This book is a political history of the controversies between advocates of a strong military and their opponents. On the advocacy side were the leadership of the Army and Navy, their allies and supporters in Congress and organizations such as the National Security League and the Navy League. Their opponents included a few maverick military men, some (mostly Progressive) senators and congressmen and groups like the American Union against Militarism and the Committee on Militarism on Education. This opposition often considered supporters of a strong defense to be militarists, which the accused of course strongly denied. German militarism was seen by both sides as the major cause of the recently ended World War, so no one would accept any imputation of any degree of militarism.

I became interested in the history of militarism as I was beginning my PhD studies in the fall of 2002. When a professor predicted that the US would invade Iraq early the next year I (very respectfully) disagreed. I said that I thought that there was not sufficient reason to risk an open-ended commitment when the removal of Saddam Hussein seemed like it could be accomplished by other forms of pressure.

The professor replied with a skeptical glance at me and proceeded to other matters.

There had been protests against the Gulf War of 1991, but there were hardly any against this new attack on Iraq. Undoubtedly this was mostly due to the impact of the events of September 11, 2001. If the political leadership claimed that America was in imminent danger of attack then protest would not be well received by most Americans. Still, the use of the military when other options were being pursued and were nearing a successful conclusion said something about American attitudes towards the use of armed force.

So I thought that the study of the history of the way Americans saw the role of the military in the international arena might be interesting. I discovered that militarism was a live issue in American politics and society from the end of the Spanish-American war until at least the attack on Pearl Harbor in 1941. It was an issue in presidential elections, particularly in 1924, the year that the US Army sponsored Mobilization Day, a national test of readiness for invasion and war.

Mobilization Day tells the story of the fight between supporters of a strong military and their opponents. I believe this history has relevance to our time. Anti-militarists had questions about national security policy, such as who is our enemy? How will our armed forces protect us from this enemy? Is armed force the best guarantee of national security? Though the supporters of the military were passionate about their beliefs as well, these questions were never answered. They do not have good answers today but might have better ones if the questions were pressed as they were in 1920s America. I also think that the contrast with today's attitudes is glaring. Today military spending is hardly ever questioned and neither is projection of US military forces to over 100 countries around the world. In other ways the situation in the nineteen-twenties is similar to today. In 1918 and in 2018 there was and is no nation capable of or interested in invading us.

My research began by looking for books and articles on militarism. From these materials I learned of the people and organizations involved in controversies about militarism and the military policies that were being debated. Most of the research was done online, using the resources of the University of California/Riverside, in particular historical newspapers and periodicals, in 2008 and 2009. At that time full-text books from colleges and universities were still downloadable through Google Books, which was very helpful. I also used the Readers Guide to Periodical Literature to locate articles on microfilm, particularly after there was little full-text available for periodical articles published after 1922.

There is no other book on militarism and anti-militarism in early 20th-century America, except for my earlier work, *The Rise of Militarism in the Progressive Era, 1900–1914* (McFarland, 2009). The Library of Congress catalog shows six books dealing with militarism during the Cold War and afterwards, and one other book discussing pre-World War I attitudes towards naval power in the United States and Germany.

Introduction

Militarism as an issue in American society and politics has a history, which dates from the aftermath of the 1898 Spanish-American War. In my previous book on militarism in America, *The Rise of Militarism in the Progressive Era, 1900–1914*, I showed how the War Department and the Army encouraged the growth of support for the armed forces during the time between the Spanish-American War and the First World War. Some of the ways they did this were by promoting military education in schools and colleges, by encouraging attendance at military maneuvers, expanding military recruiting, and supporting the national marksmanship contests that were a popular spectator sport in early twentieth-century America.

I define militarism as the prevalence of military sentiment among a people, or a tendency to regard military efficiency as the paramount interest of the state. A people that have such a sentiment admire military values, such as hierarchy, obedience and extreme nationalism. The ways in which controversies about militarism played out were different for the Army and the Navy. There was no real possibility of maintaining a large standing army. However, Universal Military Training (UMT) for all young men would be an excellent way to greatly increase readiness and spread military values. A large Navy, however, was definitely acceptable to most Americans, who saw it as a defense against invasion, a concept regularly ridiculed by anti-militarists.

Many Americans, myself included, were taught in primary and secondary school that America followed the same war and peace pattern throughout the twentieth century. After a war, our country rapidly demobilized, gave no thought to preparing for war and isolated ourselves from great power conflict. When the next crisis requiring military action arose, we were completely unprepared for it. With a burst of patriotic fervor we quickly armed ourselves, fought, and defeated our enemies. Then the cycle began again.

As I show in this book, that is not the way it was. We have had a navy second to none since at least 1920. The authorized strength of the Army quadrupled after the Spanish-American War and more than doubled after World War I. Throughout the 1920s the War Department counted on the millions of trained World War veterans to come back to the colors in an emergency. Though the plan to parade these men through city and village streets in a National Mobilization Day observance was not as popular as the War Department had hoped, millions did march—at least on the first observance in 1924. As far as isolating ourselves from great power issues, isolationism did not become a force in American politics until the mid–1930s. And, soon after his election in 1928, President Herbert Hoover gave a speech in which he presented, as a problem, the fact that America had the largest military budget in the world.

Militarism was the major issue in the 1900 Presidential campaign, due mostly to the continuing Philippine-American War. With President McKinley's re-election in a crushing Republican victory, militarism disappeared as a political issue, but the run-up to American entry into World War I revived it. Such groups as the American Union against Militarism and the Women's International League for Peace and Freedom organized in opposition to rearmament after 1914, while the National Security League and the Navy League worked tirelessly to build support for a stronger military. Repression during the war stilled the voices of the anti-militarists, but did not completely silence them. Severe punishment was meted out to critics of the war and the repression continued after 1918. Victims were not only supporters of the Central Powers, but also the Communists who had taken Russia out of the war and their sympathizers here. As the 1920s wore on, antimilitarists regained their energy and began to challenge military values. A political contest developed, as groups favoring and opposing the growth of American military power struggled for influence over public opinion and public policies.

Outline of the Book

In the first chapter events between August 1914 and December 1915 are examined, to show how ideas about militarism and preparedness for possible military action developed. What one group called preparedness another called militarism; positions for and against strengthening military forces and values were stated and the battle of ideas was joined. Chapter 2 describes events in the pivotal year of 1916. Woodrow Wilson was re-elected; both he and his opponent claimed to support preparedness. Three months after the election Germany declared it would return to unrestricted submarine warfare. Two months after the declaration, the United States joined the war on the side of the Allies. The pro-military chorus rose to a roar and drowned out the antis with the declaration of war on April 17, 1917, but their victory was neither complete nor permanent. Chapter 3 describes postwar thinking about war and militarism, from observers such as politicians, journalists and historians. The main issues were what was the role of militarism in causing the war and where was militarism located in the postwar world

Chapter 4 deals with the Red Scare that followed the First World War. In order to make repression of radicals easier many wartime measures, such as the Espionage Act, were kept in force. The repression extended to socialists like Eugene Debs and union leaders such as the International Workers of the World's Big Bill Haywood. Congress would not officially end the war declared in April 1917 until early 1921. This chapter also describes the 1920 presidential candidate General Leonard Wood's campaign for the Republican nomination. Naturally an enthusiastic supporter of the military, he was the only presidential candidate ever who was an active-duty military officer and campaigned in uniform. He enthusiastically supported attacks upon radicals, but as the campaign progressed into the spring of 1920 the anti-radical movement seemed to wither away. Although Wood entered the convention leading in delegates, Warren Harding left Chicago as the Republican nominee.

The next chapter, "American Legion: neither Masses nor Classes," deals with a new and highly important postwar supporter of military values and a strong defense, the American Legion. The Legion creed was strong on obedience, patriotism, and "100% Americanism"—individual liberties came in seventh on the Legion's list of desiderata. Occasional offers from Legion posts to take up arms against the enemies of the nation were wisely turned down by the government.

Chapter 6 shows how the Army and Navy evaluated their war experiences and what they thought they would need to defend the nation, now that the War to End War had ended. It would turn out that they would want bigger forces than the public or the Congress would agree to and this disagreement would continue until December 7, 1941.

In Chapter 7 Harding and his Secretary of State, Charles Evans Hughes, surprise the world at the 1922 Washington Naval Conference by calling for deep reductions in naval armaments. US Navy admirals were strongly opposed, but the Conference reached a historic agreement that they had to live with, though they didn't like what they called the "treaty navy." Supporters of the armed forces were heartened, though, by the response to the September 1924 Mobilization Day event described in Chapter 8. This was a sort of armed forces day with massive civilian participation planned and encouraged. The organizers wanted all men between the ages of 18 and 35 to parade in American towns and cities, and millions did so on the appointed day. This response worried opponents of militarism, but... support for military values reached a high-water mark here and began to recede. Chapter 9 summarizes the debates and looks to the future of controversy about militarism.

1. Militarism: Armored and Brainless? 1914–1915

"All armor and no brains," Walter G. Fuller's description of Jingo, the anti-preparedness dinosaur, 1916.

As Europe entered its second year of war, America remained firmly neutral. The President called upon citizens to exercise impartiality in thought as well as action. Woodrow Wilson's expectations of impartiality were not met. People and organizations began to make cases for or against participation in the war. The debate was often couched in terms of "preparedness," without stating which side the nation might join. There were few, however, who believed that America would enter the war on the side of Imperial Germany. The whole history, culture, language and institutions of the United States inclined towards. Great Britain. Many German-Americans, of course, supported Kaiser Wilhelm II's government and armies. But even they did not contemplate American troops crossing the Atlantic to fight alongside Germany. The main objective of those who did support the German cause was to prevent the USA from allying itself with the British. They pushed for the United States to be—and to remain—neutral no matter what. Maintaining neutrality, however, was to become more and more difficult as Germany's leaders came to believe that a victorious strategy must include unlimited use of a new weapon of war—the submarine.

TR and Righteous Wars

Ex-President Theodore Roosevelt had few, if any, neutral bones in his body. He idolized the heroes of the American Civil War, and the first of the many books that he wrote was a naval history of the War of 1812. As Assistant Secretary of the Navy, in 1898, he took it upon himself, in the absence of the Secretary, to mobilize the Navy for war following the sinking of the battleship *Maine* in Havana harbor. Soon after, he resigned from the government, formed the volunteer cavalry regiment which became known as the Rough Riders, and led his troopers in the famous charge to the top of San Juan Hill.

In the fall of 1914 Roosevelt spoke out in favor of universal military training, stating that the country needed the "virile strength of manliness which accepts as the ideal the stern, unflinching performance of duty...righteousness with force." TR and others calling for a stronger military initially met with little sympathy from the Wilson Administration. The President was uninterested and he was, according to Roosevelt, "flanked by a pacifist Secretary of State (William Jennings Bryan) and a Secretary of the Navy (Josephus Daniels) more interested in moral power than sea power." These characterizations were not entirely unfair. Thrice-defeated Democratic presidential candidate Bryan, though not really a pacifist, spent most of his time as Secretary of State negotiating arbitration treaties with 24 foreign countries. He would resign in 1915 because he thought American neutrality was not being properly maintained. Josephus Daniels was indeed interested in what he saw as moral behavior. He had outlawed alcohol on Navy vessels in 1914 and was to outlaw prostitution around naval bases in 1917. He was no pacifist, however, and served as Secretary of the Navy though the First World War and to the end of the Wilson Administration, vigorously supporting the interests of the Navy

Nevertheless, in late 1914 Wilson was not only uninterested in developing the military; he saw a definite downside. He believed that if the nation began to arm itself it would become like the European combatants and lose the moral high ground. He was also convinced that the American people were not militaristic and would remain that way.[1]

Roosevelt naturally disagreed. A collection of his magazine articles was published in early 1915, under the title *America and the World War.* In it, TR disavowed any notion of choosing sides in the war. This did not square very well with his emphasis on the fate of Belgium and Luxembourg as victims of attack. The experience of these two countries demonstrated to him the futility of treaties as a defense against aggression. Both countries had been declared neutral by treaties signed in 1832 and 1867, respectively, by Germany, England, and France. If Americans depended on treaties to maintain our rights while a neutral, we could well suffer the same fate as those two countries—invasion and despoliation as in Belgium, or complete subjugation as

[1] John Patrick Finnegan, *Against the Specter of a Dragon: The Campaign for American Military Preparedness, 1914–1917*, Westport, Connecticut, Greenwood Press, 1974, 25.

in Luxembourg. The only treaties that applied to America were The Hague and Geneva conventions, which defined the status of neutral nations and how it is maintained. All these treaties were "scraps of paper" to nations bent on aggression. Roosevelt believed that neutral nations, such as the United States, should have protested at the German treatment of Belgium, but he also believed that any such protest was useless unless backed by force. How or whether American force might be applied in case of a violation of neutrality he did not indicate.

A Crime against the Nation

He did, however, outline a hypothetical case about events that might happen if, in the aftermath of the current war, some foreign power decided it was in their interest to take and fortify Magdalena Bay in the Baja California province of Mexico or St. Thomas in the Virgin Islands:

> No arbitration treaties, or peace treaties, of the kind recently negotiated at Washington by the bushelful, and no tepid goodwill of neutral powers, would help us in even the smallest degree. If our fleet were conquered New York and San Francisco would be seized and probably each would be destroyed, as Louvain was destroyed unless it were put to ransom as Brussels has been put to ransom [The Germans forced the payment of an indemnity, which they called a war tax, of $40 million after the occupation of Brussels. A further payment of $100 million was demanded in September 1914, but the Germans relented after objections by the American Minister that this demand was contrary to international law.] Under such circumstances outside powers would undoubtedly remain neutral exactly as we have remained neutral as regards Belgium. Under such conditions my own view is very strongly that the national interest would be best served by refusing the payment of all ransom and accepting the destruction of the cities and then continuing the war until by our own strength and indomitable will we had exacted ample atonement from our foes.
>
> This would be a terrible price to pay for unpreparedness and those responsible for the unpreparedness would thereby be proved guilty of a crime against the nation.[2]

The ex-President titled Chapter VIII of his book "Self-Defense without Militarism," and for the rest of the book he was at pains to deny that any and all measures that he advocated could possibly be thought of as militaris-

[2] Theodore Roosevelt, *America and the World War*, New York, Charles Scribner's Sons, 1915, 12.

tic. He opened Chapter VIII by lumping together a passage by Secretary of State Bryan and a statement by an admirer of Bryan, a "typical ultra-pacifist or peace-at-any-price man." Secretary Bryan had said that he thought that America should state that it did not believe in war and would be willing to submit any dispute it had with other nations to arbitration. The unnamed admirer of Bryan pointed out that China did not engage in foreign wars and survived to the present day while the Roman and Athenian empires were long gone and the German Empire was but 35 years old. TR wrote that if anyone believed China to be an example worth imitating, they should advocate trying to "Chinafy the United States," though this would mean believing that the "average inhabitant...of North or South America occupies a lower moral, intellectual and physical status than the average coolie."

Roosevelt ridiculed the idea of arbitration by considering what would have happened had we submitted the major disputes in our history to arbitrators. He seems to have thought it would not be possible for the United States to ever win before an arbitration tribunal. Thus, he wrote that had we been consistent users of arbitration Cuba would still be Spanish, there would be no Panama Canal, Texas, Arizona and California would still be Mexican, and we would still be a colony of Great Britain. He considered it unfair and evasive of Bryan to be in favor of arbitration but unwilling to admit that he wanted us to still be a colony of Great Britain and to model ourselves on the Chinese.[3]

As a model for a peaceful U.S. president, TR offered himself. He professed to believe that "No man could possibly be more anxious for peace than I am. I ask those individuals who think of me as a firebrand to remember that during the seven and one-half years that I was President not a shot was fired at any soldier of a hostile nation by any American soldier or sailor and there was not so much as a threat of war." This ignores the shots fired at Filipino nationalists during the Philippine-American War (then called the Philippine Insurrection and declared to be over in 1902, though fighting continued for many years after.) He also stated that no shot was fired at any Colombian by an American as Panama rose up against the "alien yoke" of Columbia. This is true, but ignores the facts that we instigated the Panamanian uprising, supplied it with arms, and sent warships to the area in support. Our interest of course was not in the liberty of Panama but in a government that would cede control of the land needed to build an isthmian canal, which the Colombians had refused to do.[4]

---

[3] Ibid., 130–131.
[4] Ibid., 134.

> I do not believe in a large standing army. Most emphatically I do not believe in militarism. Most emphatically I do not believe in any policy of aggression by us. But I do believe that no man is really fit to be the free citizen of a free republic unless he is able to bear arms and at need to serve with efficiency in the efficient army of the republic. This is no new thing with me. For years I have believed that the young men of the country should know how to use a rifle and should have a short period of military training which would make them quickly capable of defending the country in case of need.[5]

As to how marksmanship and military training should be organized, Roosevelt thought the Swiss had done the best job and we should look to them for pointers. In complete agreement with military (and some civilian) leaders, he thought that such training benefited young men in their nonmilitary working lives. It would make better men out of them; improve their "... health and spirits. The service is a holiday, and a holiday of the best, because of the most useful type."[6] Switzerland would probably have been unique if men required to do military training viewed it as a holiday, but whether most Swiss enjoyed military training is unknowable. TR was undoubtedly correct in stating that upon the outbreak of the war, the Swiss mobilized forces in a projection of Swiss territory between Germany and France and no foreign troops had set foot on any part of Switzerland. There is, however, no evidence that either country saw any need to violate Swiss neutrality or had any plan to do so.

Universal military service modeled on the Swiss system would do for the army, but our navy could not be small and expandable—we needed a naval force to defend our coasts and territories. T.R. believed that the leadership of the navy should tell the government what force structure was necessary, and the civilian leadership that would pass on the admirals' plans must keep in mind some basic facts about naval power. First and foremost, they should understand that the fleet was an offensive weapon, meant to confront enemy fleets. Roosevelt was well aware of the value of submarines, destroyers, minefields and airships, but as a convinced disciple of Alfred Thayer Mahan he believed the fleet of battleships was the crux of naval power. The entire navy was "the right arm of the United States and is emphatically the peacemaker. Woe to our country if we permit that right arm to become palsied or even flabby and inefficient!"[7]

---

[5] Ibid., 136.
[6] Ibid., 138.
[7] Ibid, 173.

Applied Pacifism

TR returned to refuting charges of militarism in the concluding chapters of *America and the World War*. He evidently decided to go on the offensive and confront the opponents of preparedness, whom he referred to as "ultra-pacifists": "...in the last half-century all the losses among our men caused by militarism, as they call it, that is, by the arms of an enemy in consequence of our going to war, have been far less than the loss caused among these same soldiers by applied pacifism, that is, by our government having yielded to the wishes of the pacifists and declined in advance to make any preparations for war." He was here referring to the period 1865 to 1915, in which the only time we went to war was against various Indian tribes and against the Spaniards in 1898. The 1898 war was the only declared war and our navy in being was more than powerful enough to obliterate the Spanish fleet in Manila Bay. Our Army was indeed tiny, but with the addition of a quarter million volunteers was able to quickly defeat the Spanish forces in Cuba and Puerto Rico while suffering 287 combat deaths. Perhaps these facts made Roosevelt think his case for more preparedness was not strong enough. This may be why he brought up the number of deaths suffered in industrial concerns controlled by Andrew Carnegie, well known as a committed pacifist. He asserted that the number of such deaths must be larger than the war deaths sustained by the U.S. during Carnegie's promotion of world peace. Did this mean we should oppose "necessary industry?" Obviously not; so neither should we oppose "righteous wars" on the grounds that they too caused deaths.

There were other problems with "ultra-pacifists." About one hundred years ago, one of them, Aurelio Bertela, claimed that Europe had reached such a state of perfection that there would be no more wars. Many others before and since had made similar predictions. All had been false and all would be false until there was some sort of organization, which disposed of force to back up its efforts to maintain peace. There was also the matter of whether or not the ultra-pacifists bête noir, militarism, even existed in the United States. TR claimed it did not, and wrote that to "inveigh against militarism in the United States is about as useful to inveigh against eating horse flesh in honor of Odin." Very likely this comparison was obscure even in 1914. It seems to refer to a ritualistic practice of the long dead and inactive religion of the Vikings.

TR acknowledged that some of his opponents called him a militarist because he supported Universal Military Training (UMT) as per Switzerland. He responded that "The plan I advocate would be a corrective of every evil that we associate with the name of militarism. It would tend for order and self-respect among our people. Not the smallest evil among the many evils that exist in America is due to militarism. Save in the crisis of the Civil War there has been no militarism in the United States and the only militarist president we have had is Abraham Lincoln."[8]

Conscienceless Jingoes

Then too, the question of which nation is militaristic and which is not depends on what role its armed forces are expected to play. Reverend Franklin Monroe Sprague (1841–1926) in his 1915 book explained that England's navy, the largest in the world, was for defending the sea lanes and the empire. It was for self-defense. Germany's army, on the other hand, the largest in the world, was for invading other countries and thus was intended for aggression. Germany was militarist, England was not. Besides, "England's insular position and possessions required all her dreadnoughts for defense, while Germany's armies are ten times what are needed for defense. In view of England's coasts and colonies to be protected as compared with Germany, England is not as well equipped with dreadnoughts as Germany."[9] As for America, "Our country, like any other, has its conscienceless jingoes. They are not, however, those who while deploring war, favor reasonable armaments for defense. So long as a predatory nation is allowed to attack and reduce another nation to vassalage, so long will it be the only safe and sane policy for every nation to provide armaments for defense. This is not militarism, it is self-preservation."[10] There was also the attitude of soldiers towards their enemies. Those who were fighting to establish or maintain "great principles", as American soldiers in the Revolutionary War or the Civil War," would act "without malice but with kindly feeling towards the enemy." The Reverend contrasted these kindly soldiers with the German Army's "harsh and oppressive" rule in Alsace-Lorraine after the Franco-Prussian War. Their brutality was a consequence, Sprague thought, of German militarism.[11]

Reverend Sprague and Theodore Roosevelt did not in 1915 call for direct intervention by the United States in the war. They agreed, however, that Germany was militaristic and America, though peaceful, should look to its defenses. Sir Norman Angell was not so sure. Angell (1873–1967) was well-known for his 1913 pamphlet *The Great Illusion*. The illusion of the title was that nations could benefit by war. He theorized that there could be no economic gain for a nation as a whole by conquering other countries and

---

[8] Ibid., 261

[9] Sprague, Franklin Monroe, *Made In Germany*, Boston: The Pilgrim Press, 1915, 54.

[10] Ibid., 99.

[11] Ibid., 54.

appropriating their resources. The costs of defeating, occupying and ruling a hostile population would outweigh any economic advantages obtained. Angell's 1915 book, *America and the New World-State,* argued that it was impossible to separate America from the world in general and Europe in particular. America and Europe were so deeply connected economically, socially spiritually and intellectually that separation was not only impossible, but would do serious damage. But now that European nations were at war what was America to do? Fight with the Allies, fight with the Germans, attempt to stay out of it entirely or...?

Norman Angell had a long career as a peace activist. Born in Croydon, England, he was educated as an economist. Angell spent the years 1890 to 1898 in America, where he worked as a cowboy, prospector and newspaper reporter. His work on behalf of peace, especially the publication of *The Great Illusion 1933*, earned him the 1933 Nobel Peace Prize.[12]

America was already preparing for war. Expansion of the army and navy was being planned. Angell thought that America could instead engage in an "intervention...that should not be military...but mediatory and moral." He admitted that no nation had attempted such a thing. His proposal was that America should become a sort of world policeman. The role of police in a national society, as Angell saw it, was mainly protection of the citizenry against criminals who would use force against them to injure or despoil them. If a dispute threatened war, the United States could, in

> ...the general council of conciliation, namely, say this: We shall throw our weight against any Power that refuses to civilization at least an opportunity of examining and finding out what the facts of a dispute are. After due examination we may reserve the right to withdraw from any further interference between that Power and its antagonist. But at least we pledge ourselves to secure that, by throwing the weight of such non-military influence as we may have on the side of the weaker...America should become the center of a definite organization of the world state that has already cut athwart all frontiers and crossed all seas.[13]

Norman Angell was aware that most of those who thought and wrote about war and peace would find his proposal dubious if not ridiculous. "That man's fighting instincts are ineradicable, that he does not act by 'reason,' and cannot be guided by 'logic,' that wars are the result of forces beyond the control of makers of theories, is a position which the average believer in ortho-

[12] This and the following quotes are from "Sir Norman Angell," https://www.britannica.com/biography/Norman-Angell, January 29, 2009, accessed 4/16/2017.

[13] Sir Norman Angell. *America and the New World State; a Plea for American Leadership.* New York and London, G..P. Putnam & son, 1915, 63.

dox political doctrine that the great majority hardly esteem it worthwhile to defend any other." If that were indeed the reality, then what would those believers conclude?

The conclusion, say the militarists, is that you should give him as many destructive arms as possible, so that his capacity for damage while in his condition of blind rage should be as great as possible...There are some militarist writers who seem to imagine that they can evade the consequences of their own conclusion by pleading, not that all parties should be highly armed, but only that we should be so armed ourselves.

Logic and reason told Sir Norman the proper conclusion was that no one should be highly armed.[14]

Among the doubters was a reviewer for *The Literary Digest*, who wrote that there were two kinds of policy proposals. Angell's *The Great Illusion* was a destructive proposal—it "flung onto the scrap heap all the old theories of Metternich, Palmerston and Bismarck with regard to war and the necessity of standing armies, navies and military establishments of whatsoever kind." *America and the New World State*, however, was different. It proposed to construct a new international system, inspired and led by America, which would try to prevent war. While *The Literary Digest* reviewer didn't state that Angell's ideas were ridiculous, they were at best unrealistic: "While we may admire the enthusiasm of Mr. Angell and are interested in his theory for a new world policy for America, we are bound to consider his scheme as impracticable as would be a movement for the abolition of police, judges, law courts and jails."[15]

Since Angell was a citizen both of the U.S.A. and Great Britain, he had policy proposals for both. His suggestions for Britain were intended for the British and the French. He organized the Union of Democratic Control, with which he and his supporters hoped to influence the peace settlement that would eventually end the war. War aims of the Allies would be a major problem, Angell asserted. The enemy could not be German nationalism, expansionism or even militarism:

> ...the Allies have gone into this war for the purpose of destroying Prussian militarism, and freeing the world from the menace of German world domination. [Angell] shows the folly of believing that bad faith, cruelty in war, greed for world markets, aspiration for world domination...are the particular product of German civilization, and have never made their appearance in any other nation of the world...it is impossible to suppress German nationalism...Germany, even crushed tempo-

[14] Ibid., 103–104.

[15] Angell, Norman. "America and the New World State." *The Literary Digest*, vol. 50 April-June 1915, 1164.

rarily, will quickly rise again...Any such idea is only going to result in the increase of militarism in Europe.

Rather, Angell proposed that international organizations oversee a post-war settlement that had some of the features proposed by Woodrow Wilson in the Fourteen Points and elsewhere, such as no transfers of territory without plebiscites, no secret treaties and "establishment of a League of Powers and creation of an International Council." These bodies would attempt to settle disputes and end balance of power politics.[16]

The Reverend Newell Dwight Hillis took a much sterner view of Germany. He stated in his 1915 book that he would let the German historian and politician Heinrich von Treitschke (1834–1896) define militarism, "Lest an American overstate the case." Letting Treitschke define it did not include direct quotations, but Hillis wrote that the German held that "...the nation should be looked upon as a vast military engine; that its ruler should be the commander of the army; that his cabinet should be under generals; that the whole nation should march with the concentered aim of an armed regiment; that the real 'sin against the Holy Ghost' was the sin of military impotence; that such an army should take all the territory it wants and needs and explain afterwards." The Reverend added that Carl Schurz, perhaps the most famous 19th century German-American, criticized the militarism of his native land in "words that literally burn," but again the exact words were not furnished.[17]

In view of all these qualities of Germany, Hillis had some questions to ask. Would all small states be in danger from German militarism? Would every European country have to arm itself to the teeth? And "What is the meaning of the German professor's article in the *North American Review*, written two or three years ago, in which he says that once Germany is victorious the Monroe Doctrine will go and the United States will receive the "thrashing she so richly deserves." ? "[18]

America could not respond by becoming like Germany, because "...the American ideal is not a military machine, but a high quality of manhood... America stands at the other pole of the universe from imperialism and militarism." This was shown by the way America treats neighboring small nations, such as Canada. America had ten times the population of that country, yet all was pacific between them and we had no thought of using force against them. The border was undefended on both sides and was certain to

[16] Gibbons, Dr. Henry Adams, "Europe's Only Salvation," *The Public*, vol. 18 Mar. 26 1915, 313.

[17] Newell Dwight Hillis, *Studies of the Great War, What Each Nation has at Stake*, New York, Fleming H. Revell Co., 1915, 246.

[18] Ibid., 247.

stay that way. Beyond saying America was not at all like Germany, however, Hillis had a proposal and a hope for the future. The proposal was for German-Americans to organize so as to speak with one voice "...to ask the Fatherland now to present its cause to arbitrators." With the appalling numbers of men killed and wounded and the war developing into a bloody stalemate, "Some of the most thoughtful men in this land believe that the destiny of Germany rests now with the leaders of the six million German-Americans in our country." Even if those leaders did nothing, however, Hillis had the faith appropriate to a Congregationalist minister: "The great Vine of Liberty was planted by Divine Hands in the Eden garden. Just now the storm roars through the branches of the tree of life. But the storm will die out. Better days are coming."[19]

A pamphlet by a George Oglethorpe Ferguson, opposing Dr. Hillis' views, analyzed German militarism in a very different manner; in fact it analyzed it out of existence. The author claimed that the opposition was not between German militarism and Americanism, but between "Germanism-Englishism and Americanism." The discussion begins by defining militarism as "...a policy of national defense, based upon the necessities arising from the situation and environment of a nation." Germany is surrounded by states that have been hostile to her for hundreds of years. The "Militarism" of Germany is mainly a system of education that prepares boys to be efficient soldiers and productive citizens: "...German Militarism is a carefully thought out and wrought out system of national defense and development in its many diversified departments according to the requirements and necessities of geographic position, so as to ensure a harmonious autonomy. Any nation that has less Militarism than this is a nation of weaklings."

Dr. Hillis is directly disputed at several points. The six million German-Americans are not refugees from oppression but seekers after greater economic opportunity. Some, like Carl Schurz, came here because they could not get "political preferment." (Schurz came to America after the failure of the 1848 revolutionary movement in Germany.) They remain admiring of Germany and the Kaiser for the most part. Germany is not the brutally repressive regime that some think it is, and responsible criticism of the Kaiser is permitted. The consequences of extreme newspaper criticism can be dire:

> When liberty of the press and free speech run riot to license in humiliating caricature and stigmatic denunciation of our Presidents, we have a martyred Garfield and a martyred McKinley. That part of the press representing the Stalwart wing of the Republican Party assassinated Garfield. The venom of unusual party strife reeking in newspapers

[19] Ibid., 261.

> controlled by disappointed politicians assassinated McKinley[20] [Garfield was assassinated by a disappointed—and likely insane—office seeker. McKinley was assassinated by a committed anarchist.]

Sea Militarism

So, if German militarism was defined as self-defense, was there any other kind? Indeed there was:

> Is it not passing strange that Dr. Hillis makes no reference to English Militarism...? What is English history as regards her Militarism on the seas? England being an insular nation, that is, in her original possessions, found it just as important and essential to build up a colossal Sea Militarism as Germany from her position inland found it necessary to build up equally powerful land militarism. With this colossal naval power England has plowed the seas, bullying and ravaging other nations...when India and Egypt and South Africa protested against the steal of their country and revolted at their impressed servitude, England, with unspeakable fury, tyranny and cruelty, poured her shot and shell among the helpless men, women and children in terrible slaughter and—a la Mahomet—said 'Follow our Lord and Mater the King or take the sword'[21]

It was not only Germany and England that were not what they might seem. There was also America. In the final section, headed "Americanism", the author lays out his argument that America is not the respecter of rights and liberties that Dr. Hillis said it was. Ferguson's "evidence" for this was a series of court decisions against citizens and corporations: "...under the apparently inoffensive plea of regulating the business of these citizens and corporations, passed laws of nullification and repudiation, the sequence of which actually enabled them [local, state and federal governments] to plunder and graft at will." Ferguson seemed to think that, due to this loss of our freedom, we were in no position to criticize: "Ah! Dr. Hillis, before we throw stones at our neighbor across the ocean, let us first get out of our own glass house; before we stretch our hands across the sea to pull the beams from Germany's eyes; let us pick the moats [*sic*] out of our own eyes."[22]

Harvard military historian Prof. R.M. Johnston (1867–1920) also wrote about English sea militarism in *Arms and the Race*: "Now from the beginning of the seventeenth century until today England has maintained a sea militarism

[20] George Oglethorpe Ferguson, *An Answer to the Rev. Newell Dwight Hillis" Sermon Recently*, Wash. D.C., 1915, 3-5.

[21] Ibid, 6.

[22] Ibid., 16.

of an extreme character. For it has during most of this time rejected equality with its opponents and attempted, with general success, to maintain superiority and supremacy." However, Johnston differed sharply with Ferguson about the uses to which the British navy was put. There was no England "plowing the seas to bully and ravage, because "...this sea power that for a century and a half dominated all the world and created the greatest empire yet seen, never provoked the fears and jealousy that were felt for the eighteenth-century army. For a fleet arises from commerce. Its home is the ocean. It neither helps the despot nor threatens the citizen." Johnston went on to state that the American citizen was willing to add and fund a battleship, but not a regiment of soldiers. In the rest of his book the Professor worked hard to convince the American public that modern conditions demanded that the United States make it a priority to increase and improve its Army.[23]

Whether it should do so was debated from the viewpoints of Theodore Roosevelt and Henry Ford in the November 25, 1915 issue of *The Christian Century*. The lead editorial stated that America was in a unique situation. President Wilson was calling for increasing our army and navy to ensure "the aggressive protection of our land against any potential enemy." This was unprecedented in peacetime America, especially since the President did not claim we were in any immediate danger. Were we to do as he recommended, we would be like the nations of Europe who have been maintaining large military establishments in war and peace for more than a hundred years. It was also unprecedented because of the current state of Christianity. The editorialist thought that scholarship of the past two centuries on the historical Jesus gave a clearer picture of the moral values of the Christ, such that it was now clear that "war is the antithesis and contradiction and archenemy of the Kingdom of God." The United States, however was in a very different position than were England, France and Germany:

> These nations, nominally Christian like our own, were far embarked on a policy of militarism, re-enforced by all their traditions, before ever the modern insight into the moral ideals of Jesus was awakened...So that when, on this dark day of international chaos and hatred, it is proposed that the United States arouse itself from its helpless Unpreparedness and put on the whole armor of militarism, the proposal strikes and the very quick of the Christian conscience that has been growing in the Church throughout the years."

[23] R.M. Johnston, *Arms and the Race*, New York, Century Co., 1915, 20-21.

What the outcome of the challenge would be the editorial did not predict. It did call for a religious revival and for the active participation of Christians in the debates and movements of the following presidential election year.[24]

Henry Ford's Militaristic Parasites

A statement by Henry Ford followed the editorial. The industrialist began with an emphatic statement that

> I have prospered much and I am ready to give much to end this wasteful 'preparation.' Not by building palaces of peace [the Peace Palace, which houses the International Court of Justice in The Hague, was opened in August, 1913], not by inspiring fearful peace by powerful armament, but by teaching the men, women and children of America that war does not threaten us, that war will not reach us, that the fullness of peace is their inheritance, not the burden of militarism with its heavy hand that curbs liberty and its foul sustenance on the blood, the labor and the toil-earned happiness and good of the worker.

Exactly how this was to done, Ford did not know. But he believed that an effective peace movement must be worldwide, for "...there can be no peace while there remains one set of these militaristic parasites who encourage war."

As he had stated, Henry Ford knew how to make money. The root of the problem of war was, as he saw it, that other people knew how to make money by manufacturing the implements of war. They were few, but the many took no action to oppose them. When international competition grew into conflict, over colonial claims for instance, war was threatened. Such competition was seen by many observers as a contributing factor to the outbreak of war in August 1914. Ford proposed a businessman's solution: "If Germany, as many of her opponents claim, wanted colonies, she could have secured a very extensive place in the sun by direct purchase—a business transaction—for a fraction of the terrific cost she is now paying in warfare." Ford naturally favored business transactions as problem solvers—except those deals made by armament manufacturers. He was, of course, not naïve. He knew that throughout history "...the overpowering unanswerable weapon of wealth has been on the side of slaughter..."[25]

His condemnation of those whom he saw as responsible for the war was visceral:

[24] "Religion in the Coming Political Campaign," *The Christian Century*, vol. XXXII no. 47 (Nov. 25, 1915), 786.

[25] "Henry Ford on Universal Peace," *The Christian Century*, vol. XXXII no. 47 (Nov. 25, 1915), 788.

> If these men who brought on the war were insane, we could comprehend the cause of the war. But when we think that all is done coldly, deliberately by these militaristic parasites, and that millions of men are torn from the life that is theirs by right of birth, and driven to slaughter by the system of murder that envelops these nations, we are crushed by the enormous crime.

It was totally unnecessary for the United States to participate in this criminal enterprise. Preparedness was a fraud. We had not and would not be invaded, no matter how many "paper invasions" were successful in newspaper stories:

The advice of militarists as to the need of a vast army and navy is about the same as the advice of a group of professional gamblers would be in the framing of civil laws. The only difference is the military men would gamble with human lives and the peace and plead for national honor when they mean "personal glorification" or "blood money."

Even though the money already spent on preparedness had not caused us to be in a war, it was still a waste on several levels. The young men now in the military, totaling about 145,000 were in the prime of life, yet produced nothing of value. In fact, their upkeep was a cost to the nation: "That is the curse of Europe. A million non-producers swagger around living upon the workers." In 1908 forest fires burned over 2 million acres in Michigan. A non-existent threat of invasion kept these young men from performing useful services during the disaster. And, just at the time these young men could be learning a trade so as to contribute to society for the rest of their lives, they were learning "...the ideas, the aims and the self-vindicating but false apologies of murderous militarism." [Perhaps Ford was referring to the early 1900s scares about war with Japan.]

Ford believed that American workers would not tolerate the militarism that had infested Europe. Yet he had hopes for European nations: "The present war's end, will, I believe and hope, see the end of the military spirit and the military castes in all Europe; the death of the military party in Germany; and those very workers who are today performing wonders of arms against the whole of Europe under the eyes of an emperor and a Fatherland may be the very ones who will end that reign of militarism."[26]

Apostles of Timidity

Theodore Roosevelt did not bother to discuss militarism any more. He strenuously objected that America had wasted almost a year "...keeping our-

[26] Ibid., 789.

selves unprepared, expressing the hope that if we thus preserved immunity from hatred by keeping our selves beneath contempt, we might create a situation where he [President Wilson] would be employed as a go-between, a man to fetch and carry among the warring powers when the time for peace negotiations arrived." The initiation and conduct of the war convinced TR that Germany was the "antithesis" of democracy. Americans claimed that their democracy was superior to any autocracy, including the German. It was all very well, he wrote, to make such claims in "windy Fourth of July speeches," but fine words were not nearly enough. Action, in the form of a vigorous program of national defense, was required. Opponents of such a program, "Every professional pacifist, every representative of commercialized greed, every apostle of timidity, every sinister creature who betrays his country by pandering to the anti-American feeling that masquerades under some species of hyphenated Americanism" [read: "professional German-Americans"] were working against our democracy.

We had taken no action against Germany when it had violated multiple provisions of the Hague conventions. We should expect no one to take our part if we were the victims of such mistreatment:

> The United States has—and deserves to have—only one friend in the world. This is the United States...We need a first-class Navy, in size and efficiency second among the nations of the world [conceding first place to the Royal Navy]. We need a small but highly efficient professional Army of at least a couple of hundred thousand men. Then, and above all, we need to have every young man in the United States trained so that in the event of the country being assailed he shall at once be available to render with reasonable efficiency military service to the land to which he owes everything. This will be carrying out the democratic ideal."[27]

This would have been the destruction of the democratic ideal, according to Dr. Frederic Lynch (1867–1934); Secretary of the Church Peace Union [founded 1914 by Andrew Carnegie, now the Carnegie Council for Ethics in International Affairs.]:

> A part of the program of this ardent group of militarists on which they lay great stress is the introduction into our schools and colleges of instruction of military training and instruction in shooting. Do the parents realize what that means? If they do not, let them go to the psychologists. It means that all our boys are to grow up with their imaginations turned towards war. It means that they are to grow up in the

[27] Roosevelt, Theodore. "Theodore Roosevelt on Preparedness," *The Christian Century*, vol. XXXII no. 47 (Nov. 25, 1915), 790.

> atmosphere of the camp. It means they are to learn martial music, martial terms and martial principles...For when boys are trained to shoot you have got to train them to shoot at something. As a matter of fact, in military training human forms are used as targets. Professor Vernon Lee Kellogg, of Leland Stanford University, says in *Beyond War* that he found soldiers in the California woods shooting at targets made in the form of men and remarkably resembling Japanese. That is what military drill is going to mean, mothers and fathers. It is going to change the whole character, the whole idealism of the next generation. It is going to give us a new type of American—the military, Prussian, type instead of the industrial, democratic type. Again, let us never forget that *militarism is the eternal foe of democracy.* Every increase of army or navy is a blow in the face of democracy...It is time for the United States to take warning. Every battleship, every soldier means so much more autocracy, so much less democracy. Militarism and democracy cannot exist together. There has lately arisen in the United States a group of men who are leaving no stone unturned to urge the United States to follow in the footsteps of the Old World and base its civilization on armaments, guns, a vast navy and a huge army. They are endeavoring to turn the minds of our people from industrialism and that high idealism that has marked the growth of our people, to militarism and preparations for war...They want...our people trained to shoot their brothers and some are systematically urging the introduction of military drill into our schools and colleges.[28]

Lynch believed that the "group of men" behind increased war preparations drew its members from four sources. The first was military and naval officers and retired officers who supported such organizations as the Navy League and Uncle Sam's Safety League, which were encouraging public backing for preparedness. "The second class is composed of those who profit by war and the preparation for war—manufacturers of powder, guns, armaments and the builders of battleships...after the revelations in Europe which have shown how feverishly this class of men worked to bring on this present war—willing to plunge Europe into this hell for a few dollars—there can be no doubt of their activity here." Third, there were politicians who were enthusiastically supporting preparedness in order to oppose and hopefully harm, President Wilson, who was favoring a more neutral go-slow policy. Last were those who were taking advantage of fears about war and invasion: "Forgetting that it is militarism and trust in armament that has precipitated

[28] Frederick Lynch, *The Last War, a Study of Things Present and Things to Come*, New York, Fleming H. Revell Co., 1915, 102

the present war in Europe, they would have us arm against the danger of invasion by Germany, should she prove victorious."[29]

George Harvey's Altar of Misstatement

Roosevelt had claimed that we had done nothing about violations of the Hague Conventions, but what were the responsibilities of the signatories? According to George Harvey, editor of the North American Review, there were essentially none. He pointed out that Germany had given an ultimatum to Belgium, stating that Germany would invade if the Belgians did not accede to its terms. When Belgium rejected the ultimatum it became a belligerent, no longer neutral. Other acts of the German armed forces, such as destroying historical monuments and demanding excessive indemnities of the Belgians, may well have been war crimes, according to Harvey. However, the treaty had no mechanism for a neutral such as the United States, to take action on anything. Moreover, Harvey asserted that President Roosevelt had given up any conceivable right or duty to intervene, by having his diplomats insert the following reservation to the 1907 Hague Convention: "Nothing contained in this Convention shall be so construed as to require the United States to depart from its traditional policy of not intruding upon, interfering with or entangling itself in the political questions of policy or internal administration of any foreign state." Harvey wrote that this was inserted to protect the Monroe Doctrine, which pledged American non-interference in Europe in return for European non-interference in our hemisphere:

Surely Mr. Roosevelt must have been aware of this when he 'ordered the signature of the United States to these Conventions' and no less surely now he must realize that the assumption by this Government of an obligation as the guarantor of the neutrality or independence of any foreign state would involve complete abandonment of the Monroe Doctrine—a consummation which he, of all men, would be the last to desire or concede.

Harvey's final salvo at TR came after he quoted him as stating that our failure to act in Belgium's defense put us at a "dreadful disadvantage" whenever we would have complaints about infringements of our rights: "This is our Colonel at his best; none other would have the audacity to marry altruism with self-interest at the altar of misstatement."[30]

Theodore Roosevelt was a frequent target of Harvey, but this did not mean Harvey was a supporter of Germany and Austria-Hungary. He made this clear in a March 1915 editorial in the *North American Review*, in an open

[29] Ibid., 105–109.

[30] Harvey, George, "The Government and the War," *North American Review*, vol. 201 (May 1915), 651-2

"Letter to the Times," addressed to its editor, Lord Northcliffe. The editorial had extended quotes from Treitschke and other advocates of loud and aggressive German nationalism and imperialism. It was the very nature of the German state and its radical difference from England and the United States that was at the root of the war: "To our minds, then, the real issue is not, as your people seem to think, mere militarism; it is the hideous conception of which militarism is but one of many manifestations, it is despotism itself..." Harvey reassured Northcliffe that although America was neutral "... in the name of the nation, but not in our heart of hearts. We are for the England which has been gradually freeing the world [likely a reference to white settler colonies granted self-government, Canada, Australia, South Africa] while Germany was planning to enslave it." His editorial concluded by assuring Northcliffe that the day would come when America would not "...fail to do its full part" to support England.[31]

If militarism was a consequence of despotic government, did that mean that it could not happen in the United States, no matter how large our Army? Yes, according to Lindley M. Garrison (`1864–1932), a New Jersey lawyer who was President Wilson's Secretary of War in his first term, because

> Militarism in the sense of having the military force interfere in the slightest with the conduct of government by our civil authorities, is not conceivable in this country, is not urged by anyone and is not feared even by those who use the word in that sense to prevent proper consideration and to confuse the public mind. Militarism in the sense of the absolute necessity of proper military precautions and military preparations is the subject for consideration; it is the imperative question for decision; and it needs stout hearts and sound minds to decide it. We are surely not so deluded as to believe that we can reach by intuition what others can acquire only by training and experience. We are surely not so sacrilegious or irreverent as to believe that Providence has unjustly discriminated in our favor and against the other peoples of the world.[32]

Militarism Eclipses Feminism

War, militarism and preparedness had, according to George Harvey, quite taken over the national discussion in 1915: "Militarism has for the time eclipsed Feminism. War news in the press has forced suffrage news into sec-

[31] Harvey, George, "A Letter to the *Times*," *North American Review*, vol. 201 (March 1915), 338.

[32] Garrison, Lindley M., "The Problem of National Defense," *North American Review*, vol. 201 (June 1915), 839.

ond place. 'Relief for Belgium' usurps the prominence of 'Votes for Women.' " Harvey wrote that the outbreak of a general European war was seen by backers of women's suffrage [women were granted the right to vote in the 19th Amendment to the Constitution, ratified in August 1920] as proof that men were incapable of restraining their aggressive impulses: "Therefore this unequalled calamity to the human race is a stupendous object lesson in the need for equal suffrage." Harvey was doubtful. His reading of history was that women rulers were just as willing to go to war as men were. He granted that women rarely engaged in combat, but thought that the record showed that that they usually encouraged men to go to war and were likely to scorn those who did not: "At least in the human species she is as militant as he. There is no sex in militarism." But women did not have the vote now. If they did, would they vote for measures against war? Would they support anti-war, anti-military candidates? Again, Harvey had doubts. He seemed to have a great deal of confidence when predicting electoral outcomes, though. He believed that women would be the minority of voters, for several reasons. Some women stated opposition to votes for women, thinking it improper or not supported by religion. Many more women than men would be unable to vote because of "illness, or domestic cares." So,

> The two sexes being of about equal numbers, then, the male voters would in all probability form a marked majority, so that if the question of militarism or non-militarism were to be decided be decided by a trial of voting strength between the two sexes, the former would prevail. To say that the votes of the women plus those of the non-militant men would be a majority is to assume that all the women's votes would be against militarism, for which in either history or current conditions there is absolutely no warrant." Harvey granted that none of this bore on the question of whether the vote for women was a good idea, an issue in which he did not seem to be greatly interested.[33]

Military men naturally favored preparedness and none were more vocal than former Army Chief of Staff Leonard Wood. Wood's career in the United States Army was highly unusual. Born in 1860, he was the son of a doctor in the Union Army. He wanted a military career, but being unable to secure an appointment to West Point or Annapolis, he graduated from Harvard Medical School in 1883 and accepted an appointment as an Army contract surgeon in 1885. It wasn't long before he demonstrated more aptitude for military command than for medicine. In 1886 he participated in an epic 3,000 mile

[33] Harvey, George, "Women and the War," *North American Review*, vol. 201 (March 1915), 344-347.

pursuit of Geronimo's Apache band, and was awarded a Medal of Honor for his bravery and leadership under grueling conditions.

An assignment to Washington brought Wood into contact with many important people, most especially Assistant Secretary of the Navy Theodore Roosevelt. As they both had an interest in manly ,sports they became friends and boxed, wrestled, and fenced together. They continued their association in the Spanish-American War, when Colonel Wood commanded the 1st Volunteer Cavalry Brigade, the famous Rough Riders, with Lieutenant Colonel Roosevelt as his second-in-command. During the war he was promoted to brigadier general.[34]

Wood was an efficient commander and inspired much loyalty in his subordinates, but was not popular with the Army establishment. His beginning as a medical officer, rapid promotions over more senior men, and his brusque, outspoken manner offended many high ranking officers. He reached the top in 1910, when he was appointed to be Army Chief of Staff for a four year term. After 1913, though, he was to be frustrated at every turn. The combat command he wanted badly was denied him in the First World War, by the Democratic administration of Woodrow Wilson and by his enemies in the leadership of the Army.

General Wood spoke and wrote prolifically about preparedness and universal military training. In 1915 Princeton University Press published three of Wood's lectures on these topics. The University's president, John Grier Hibben, wanted to make it clear in his introduction to the book that "General Wood is a soldier and yet a man of peace. He hates militarism but believes in a reasonable preparedness and naturally shrinks from the task of leading forth the devoted but inexperienced young men of our land to be slaughtered at the hands of experienced and seasoned troops. He desires peace with honor, but would not sacrifice honor for the sake of a comfortable ease and security of peace."[35]

Speaking for himself, the General defined militarism as "...the condition which may be described as one under which the military element dominates the nation's policy." And, although he didn't claim to hate militarism, "Nothing could be more unfortunate than the establishment of such a condition in this country or elsewhere as development along normal lines is concerned." His method of avoiding militarism was the same as Theodore Roosevelt's—adoption of a system of UMT similar to that of Switzerland. TR seemed to think that young Swiss men would view regular military training as a break

[34] David Pietruska. *1920. the Year of Six Presidents*, New York, Carroll & Graf Publishers, 2007, 168.

[35] Leonard Wood, *The Military Obligation of Citizenship*, Princeton, Princeton University Press, 1915, iv.

in the routine, almost like a holiday. Wood did not claim this for it, but did think the results would be as positive as TR thought:

> ...all of this training is accomplished without any interference worthy of consideration with the youth's educational and industrial career. In fact, he is better physically, morally and better as a citizen, because of his training. He has learned to respect the flag of his country and to have a proper regard for the rights of others, and he has built up in him an appreciation of the obligation to serve his country in time of war.

Proof of the benefits was shown by the "...criminal rate of Switzerland, which is only a fraction of our own."[36]

Deadly Holidays

Wood wrote that war was not as much of a killer as working for a living, joining Roosevelt in comparing workplace and war casualties. He cited statistics that revealed there were around 450,000 industrial accidents in the United States every year, around 80,000 of them fatal. This was much higher than the annual average killed and wounded in the first two years of the American Civil War. He stated that of course these statistics were not reasons to be warlike or uncaring about the costs of war, but noted that there was no public demand to lower these kinds of numbers. Earning one's daily bread had its costs, as did maintaining the "...institutions which have been handed down to us..." This was not all. Fourth of July holiday accidents had claimed a total of 1,800 lives and wounded more than 30,000 during a ten-year period from 1901 to 1910. The General wrote that the number killed was equal to battle deaths in the Indian wars, the Spanish-American War and the Philippine-American War.[37]

Leonard Wood and Theodore Roosevelt were tireless and effective proponents for preparedness and UMT. They were vigorously opposed by the Woman's Peace Party (WPP) and the American Union against Militarism. These groups and others like them, including many religious and politically left organizations, saw no need for a bigger military, since they were against involving the United States in a war in Europe. First in opposition was the WPP, which was founded by leading feminists such as Florence Garrison Villard and Jane Addams. They believed that they would be able to further progressive reform by organizing to oppose militarism and war.[38]

[36] Ibid., 36-37.
[37] Ibid., 69.
[38] David M. Kennedy, *Over Here: the First World War and American Society*, New York, Oxford University Press, 1980, 30.

Addams was one of the most famous women in the world, founder of social work as a profession and a leader of the Progressive Party. She was one of a small group of women who met at The Hague [the Netherlands was neutral in World War I] in February 1915 to discuss the war which had been raging for six months. They decided to invite women from all nations, neutral and belligerent, to The Hague in April, for an International Congress of Women. The purpose was to deliberate upon and hopefully agree to a set of resolutions drafted at the February meeting. Jane Addams was president of the Congress and she wrote about the relationship between militarism and democracy: "War itself destroys democracy wherever it thrives and tends to entrench militarism. If the object of the war is to down militarism, it must be clear that the very prolongation of the war entrenches the military ideal not only in Russia and Germany, but in more democratic nations as well."[39] An Englishman might believe that the very object of the war was to crush Prussian militarism: "It seems clear, however, that while the crushing process goes on militarism is firmly lodged in men's minds and that no body of men is seriously trying to discover how far militarism is being crushed by this war or how far civil forces are merely becoming exhausted and the methods of negotiation discredited."[40]

The American Union against Militarism (AUM,) established in 1915, was first named the Anti-Militarism Committee, then the Anti-Preparedness Committee, and finally the American Union against Militarism.[41] Called the "most formidable and intelligent of the anti-preparedness lobbies," the AUM located its headquarters in Washington and selected the "uncommonly gifted" Charles Hallinan, a Chicago publicist, as its executive director. It collected money, distributed its leaflets, and put together a speaker's bureau. Some well-known figures joined, including Rabbi Steven Wise, writer and editor Max Eastman, and Congressman Oscar Callaway. Supporters of preparedness usually supported universal military training and pointed to the model that Switzerland had adopted as the best exemplar. The AUM reprinted a pamphlet that described what they saw as critical differences in the defense needs of Switzerland and the United States. The author, George William Nasmyth, agreed that Switzerland was not militaristic. However, he cited the statements of the Swiss socialists at an international congress as evidence that the officer corps of the Swiss Army was the same as the officer corps of any other country— anti-democratic and always eager for more and

[39] Jane Addams, *Women at the Hague: the International Congress of Women and its Results*, New York, Macmillan Co., 1915, 77.

[40] Ibid., 78.

[41] http://www.swarthmore.edu/library/peace/DG001-025/DG004AUAM.html, accessed 5/30/09, American Union against Militarism, records 1915–1922.

better weapons. And, there was little scope for aggressive militarism if you were a small nation surrounded by large empires. It would be "ludicrous"[42] to start something, if not dangerous and possibly suicidal. As far as equality of the sacrifice one made to serve, Nasmyth wrote that there was none:

> ...for the poor man it means a definite interruption of his economic life, the stopping of his earnings, postponement of the time when he can afford to marry, an interruption of his difficult task of gaining a foothold in his trade or small business...but for the rich man, military service offers a career, an entrance into the ranks of society, the opening of positions in the government service and educational advantages of technical training in the officers colleges.

General Wood had written that the army was the most democratic institution in America. Nasmyth demurred: "Those who believe that class distinctions can be broken down and democracy created by regimenting men into masses and forcing them to drill together have missed the central idea of democracy, which is based on the principle[s] of voluntary cooperation, of equality of opportunity and the abolition of caste privileges."[43]

Caste privileges of officers and their mindset made armies not only undemocratic but the "most formidable enemy of democracy." We were fortunate in America to have had very little militarism in our past. Nasmyth quotes Lord Bryce, probably the most eminent non-American historian of America of his time that luckily "...the country was free from a pernicious military caste which worked such frightful evil in Europe, being indeed driven to desire opportunities for practicing the work for which the profession exists." Proponents of universal military training claimed it would improve discipline among the young men of America and make them better citizens. Regarding discipline, Nasmyth thought self-discipline was what was required, not discipline imposed from without. A person who has been trained to obey orders instantly and without question will unhesitatingly carry out orders to "...sink the Lusitania or destroy the city of Louvain. [The British passenger liner the *Lusitania* had been sunk by a German submarine on May 27, 1915, killing 1,200 including 128 Americans.[44] The Belgian university town of Louvain was burned by the German Army in August 1914. German troops executed civilians and destroyed a world-famous library, which contained many irreplaceable medieval manuscripts.[45]] This is especially the case if

[42] George William Nasmyth. *Universal Military Service and Democracy*, Washington D.C., American Union against Militarism, 1917, 8.
[43] Ibid., 9.
[44] Michael S. Neiberg. *The Path to War*, New York, Oxford University Press, 2016, 67.
[45] Ibid., 30.

universal military training is a long standing policy and has become traditional and accepted without question."[46]

Mechanical Methods of Militarism

Nasmyth quickly disposed of the final two benefits claimed for UMT, unifying the nation and strengthening patriotism. There was no historical evidence that compelling military service was a unifier. The experience of the European empires of Russia, Austria-Hungary and Turkey showed otherwise: "America needs unity, a national consciousness and a national will, but no reactionary, militaristic, obsolete old world instrument such as conscription can unify the American people." As for patriotism, a true patriotism would dedicate America to a cause such as Norman Angell's League to Enforce Peace, rather than follow "...the path of conscription, of fear and servile obedience and the mechanical methods of militarism."[47]

Everyone knew that preparedness meant being ready for war. Individuals and groups that favored readiness, such as the National Security League (NSL), supported measures to increase the size of the military and the military training available to citizens. The League's founder was New York lawyer S. Stanwood Menken, who had been in Britain in August 1914 and had witnessed the House of Commons debate that led to the declaration of war. When home he sent out a letter to influential men of affairs in New York, inviting their support for a congressional investigation of the nation's defenses. In December a committee of those willing to help met in New York, electing Menken as their leader and formally constituting the National Security League, which began to press Congress about defense. Woodrow Wilson remained unconvinced. In a message to Congress he stated that he opposed building up the Navy because it was not yet certain what kind of navy would be needed. To rearm now might close off "opportunities of friendship and disinterested service which should make us ashamed of any thought of hostility or fearful preparation for trouble."[48]

The NSL got heavy financial support from banking and corporate circles and did not publicly support either side in the European war; it saw itself as promoting "patriotic education and national sentiment and service."[49] By the summer of 1916 $160,000 had been collected to support the League's work. Important figures such as publisher George Haven Putnam, New York May-

[46] Ibid., 10.

[47] Ibid., 11–12.

[48] Finnegan, *Against the Specter*, 28.

[49] David M. Kennedy, *Over Here: the First World War and American Society*, New York, Oxford University Press, 1980, 31

or John Purroy Mitchel and former Secretary of War Henry Stimson, were active members. Seventy branches were formed in cities across the nation by autumn 1915. It had both prominent Republicans and Democrats as members, and it supported President Wilson as he began to call for augmenting the nation's military strength in that same autumn of 1915. Though the NSL was the most influential exponent of preparedness, there were many others. They included the Navy League, the Army League, the American Defense Society, the Aero Club, the Council on National Defense and a proposed umbrella organization, the Conference Committee on Preparedness.[50]

Securely Wrapped in the American Flag

Some who questioned the League's positions did so on the grounds of what they thought an effective national defense policy should be. Writing in *Pearson's Magazine* in 1915, Alan Benson claimed that Stanwood Menken was a jingo. This was because Menken was calling for a big increase in the U.S. battleship fleet. According to Benson, battleships were an offensive weapon, used to project power. If we only wanted to defend ourselves, Benson wrote, then we should invest in submarines and minefields—these would prevent aggression from an enemy fleet of battleships. Mines and submarines had already proven effective in the war in Europe. Battleships were offensive weapons, meant for intimidation and conquest. While it would be expensive to protect our long coastlines with mines and submarines, it would be even more expensive to build a battleship fleet powerful enough to defeat any and all comers:

> As a witness against themselves, I present Mr. S. Stanwood Menken, President of the National Security League. The league is one of the ultra-patriotic associations that, securely wrapped in the American flag, is trying to make the oceans bristle with our guns. I quote from an interview with Mr. Menken published in the *New York Times* on July 17, 1915: 'The league is much encouraged by the public statement of the Secretary of the Navy that he believes in preparedness for war, but the fact remains that the modern battleship is still the all-important unit of every fleet and so far as it has hitherto been shown, all improvements in aeroplanes, submarines and other subsidiary forces are subordinate to it.' Think of the impudence required to make such statements almost twelve months after the beginning of the present war! Before the war, such statements seemed true. So far as defense is concerned, everybody now knows they are not true.[51]

[50] Finnegan, *Against the Specter*, 100.

[51] Alan Benson, "The Navy We Need", *Pearson's Magazine*, Sept. 1915, 292.

Benson here was probably referring to the considerable effectiveness so far shown by British minefields and German submarines against enemy operations.

Menken's letter about Benson's article appeared in the October issue of *Pearson's*. Menken wrote that the League had determined that Congressional critics of the nation's defenses had understated the seriousness of its deficiencies. He quoted his own recent remarks in a speech given in Philadelphia, during which he stated that our policy must be to

> ...provide the maximum of preparedness at a minimum of expense both in MEN and MONEY. We in the League do not attempt to define what is necessary for the defense of the United States, our function being to provoke inquiry—not to define methods. Under present military conditions it would seem the question of methods is one for the scientific naval and military men, trained in the service, aided by economists, organizers and social workers, rather than for any individual.[52]

Most likely Menken did not fear that "scientific naval men" would be uninterested in more and better battleships.

Benson did not seem to be convinced that those advocating more battleships would be content if things did not go their way. This was because, as he wrote in a December 1915 article, those advocates were motivated by more than patriotism:

> However much they may protest their patriotism, the militarists cannot escape the fact that some of them would derive hundreds of millions of profits from a plunge into preparedness, while the capitalist class as a whole craves great military establishments with which to force its way more deeply into the markets of the world...their pretensions are belied by the kind of weapons they advocate...It is more than strange that men who talk so much about defense are so little interested in purely defensive measures and eagerly alert only when the instruments of offensive warfare are considered.[53]

Benson claimed Thomas Edison as an ally. The great inventor was selected by President Wilson to chair a committee tasked with making recommendations for modernizing the nation's defenses. In a public statement Edison said he was opposed to a large standing army. He advocated training of more officers for both the army and navy, so that the navy ships and army divisions could be competently led and fully manned. He further recommended that the nation should build the capacity to supply war materiel—but not actual-

[52] S. Stanwood Menken, "A letter from S. Stanwood Menken, President of the National Security League", *Pearson's* magazine, Oct. 1915, 335.

[53] Alan Benson, "Unmasking the Big Navy Promoters," *Pearson's Magazine*, Dec. 1915, 565.

ly produce the munitions until they are needed. All in all, Benson considered Edison's ideas to fit in well with his call for defenses like submarines and minefields. So far, though, Edison's ideas had found little favor.

A Useless Member of the New York Legislature

In his previous *Pearson's Magazine* article Benson had estimated the cost of laying extensive minefields to protect our coasts. The cost would be considerable, since the mines would need to be laid fifty feet apart. This would be much less expensive, however, than building a dominant battleship fleet. According to Benson, after reading his article a reporter for a Washington newspaper went to the Navy Department to ask why mines and submarines would not be as good, if not better, defenses than battleships. Secretary of the Navy Josephus Daniels was not in, so Assistant Secretary Franklin D. Roosevelt responded to the inquiry. FDR did not think mines would be practical. He noted that laying three lines of mines along 2,000 miles of coast would b would be very expensive. It would also be time-consuming and tricky—it was difficult to keep mines tethered in some areas due to variable winds and ocean currents. Benson's reaction to Roosevelt's statements was scornful, bordering on hostile. He wrote that the Assistant Secretary "...speaks with the stolid obstinacy of a sea-dog. Though he is but 33 years old, was educated to be a lawyer, and a few years ago, was nothing but a rather useless member of the New York legislature." Since Roosevelt had no background in naval affairs, Benson claimed he was only "parroting" what he heard from senior naval officers at Washington clubs like the Army and Navy Club and the exclusive Metropolitan Club. FDR belonged to both.[54]

Benson produced some figures. He estimated the cost of purchasing and installing three lines of mines along the 2,000 miles of the eastern U.S. coast to be $254 million. He noted that it was planned to spend $500 million on building ships for the Navy including 10 new battleships, over the next five years. We would still be second to Great Britain and probably about even with Germany in the strength of our fleet, as we were now. Or, we could have minefields that would defend against any number of battleships any enemy could send against us.[55]

Benson believed that those who advocated building battleships for defense were not disinterested patriots:

> However much they may protest their patriotism. The militarists cannot escape the fact that some of them would derive hundreds of mil-

[54] Ibid., 568..
[55] Ibid., 569.

> lions of profits from a plunge into preparedness, while the capitalist class as a whole craves great military establishments with which to force its way into the markets of the world...It is more than passing strange that men who talk so much about defense are so little interested in purely defensive measures and are eagerly alert when the instruments of offensive warfare are considered.[56]

While Franklin Roosevelt was not accused of money-grubbing, according to Benson he revealed the true motives of the battleship advocates in naval budget battles. In a newspaper article published October 15, 1915, Roosevelt wrote that

> Strictly speaking, if national defense applies strictly to an armed landing on our Atlantic or Pacific shores, no navy at all is necessary. (*The truth is coming out!*) But if defense means also the protection of the vast interests of the United States as a world nation, its commerce, its increasing population and resources...then and only then does a navy become necessary.

Benson's reaction to FDR's article was "There are the cards on the table. To get a big navy these gentlemen try to frighten you with the specter of an invasion, but what they really want is a big navy with which to force into foreign markets American goods which are needed at home and could be consumed at home if our workingmen were paid enough wages to enable them to buy the things they have made."[57]

Conclusions

By the end of 1915 many facets of the war vs. peace debate had been exposed. Self-defense was considered a right by most observers, but some who opposed increasing the size of America's military establishment claimed that there was no threat that justified increased preparations for war. Our borders were safe and no one had made a serious threat or incursion upon our territory in over a hundred years. There was nothing threatening looming on the horizon either, but that could change if we began an arms buildup. Nations with commercial and colonial interests in our hemisphere could well take note

The words "Prussian" and "militarism" usually went together. Germany, after all, had invaded Belgium and France, not the other way around. So, was a country militaristic if it was an aggressor, if it relied upon military force to resolve issues? This seems reasonable, but who decides who the aggressor is?

[56] Ibid., 565.
[57] Ibid., 570.

Every country who has crossed the border of another with its military says it was provoked, that the other country was about to attack it, that its very survival was at stake, et cetera and so forth. Most neutral countries probably won't believe the invaders protestations, but the invader's citizens, allies and some neutrals will. There were also people and nations that were not happy with Britannia ruling the waves, considering this to be "sea militarism."

A non-aggressive militarist isn't very likely, but perhaps the sine qua non for militarism is a considerable military establishment. Most European nations had a good sized army and many had conscription laws. The coastal nations had navies, though Great Britain had by far the most powerful. The United States had a large and modern navy and a considerable building program. The American army was a small volunteer force but was about to be expanded. No matter what side of the war and peace debate one was on, there was general agreement that American history had no militarism in it.

The response to the European crisis, however, could bring militarism in its wake. One of the ways this could happen, according to peace advocates, was if we adopted some sort of universal military training scheme. The protests of advocates of such training, such as Theodore Roosevelt and General Wood, that it built character and not militarism, were not credited by those opposed, like Jane Addams and Dr. David Starr Jordan. Universal military training became an issue with the outbreak of the war in 1914 and would arise again after the Armistice.

2. Peace, War and Peace, 1916–1918

Nineteen-sixteen was the last year of peace, and an election year. President Wilson would run against former New York Governor and current Supreme Court Justice Charles Evans Hughes. Both would campaign on preparedness and condemn and deny militarism. Both would claim to be neutral; neither could be said to be impartial as regards the causes of Germany and Great Britain. By this time there were very few partisans of Germany willing to state their views publicly. Both Germany and Great Britain had infringed upon the rights of neutrals. Only Germany, however, sank ships carrying civilians from neutral nations. The sinking of the *Lusitania* was the most horrific incident, but there had been and would be others. In the end, unrestricted submarine warfare by Germany would bring about America's entry into the war.

Nineteen-sixteen saw events in the war and in Mexico that affected the preparedness debates. In February the Germans announced that they would again use their submarines to sink merchant vessels engaged in trade with Great Britain, even if these carried civilian passengers. This reversed their position taken after the sinking of the *Lusitania* in 1915 when they had espoused a policy of not attacking vessels carrying civilian passengers. On March 27 a German submarine torpedoed the British Channel ferry *Sussex*, killing dozens of civilians. Several Americans were injured; none were killed. President Wilson was more firm with the Germans this time than he had been over the sinking of the *Lusitania*. In May 1916 Germany returned to the previous policy, promising they would not attack merchant or passenger vessels. This commitment was known as the Sussex Pledge.[58] The continuing issue of sub-

[58] Neiberg, *Path to War*, 104, 109.

marine attacks on ships carrying Americans provided preparedness advocates with support for their claims that we needed a bigger and better navy.

Also in 1916 turmoil along the southern U.S. border increased dramatically. Mexico had been in crisis since the overthrow of long-time dictator Porfirio Diaz in 1911. Factions armed themselves and a civil war spread to most parts of the country. Rebels led by Pancho Villa were operating in the northern Mexican province of Chihuahua and there were border and cross-border incidents involving American casualties in 1915 and 1916. Finally, Villa ordered a raid on Columbus, New Mexico, which took place on March 9, 1916. Eighteen Americans were killed and the American public was outraged. The President ordered a punitive expedition to cross the border, disperse Villa's fighters, and bring Villa himself back for trial in the United States. The expedition, led by General John J. Pershing, managed to force a few small skirmishes with Villa's troops, but did not defeat or capture him. The performance of the National Guard units in the American force left much to be desired and that was used to support the claims of those who wanted to expand and improve the regular army.[59]

Pretending Patriots

Not everyone thought we needed a bigger army and navy. On January 4, 1916, Congressman Isaac Ruth Sherwood (1835–1925), an Ohio Democrat, was granted 50 minutes to address the House on the subject of national defense. Sherwood was a veteran of the Civil War, serving in many campaigns and rising from private to brevet brigadier general. He made clear in his speech that he was not a "peace at any price" man, but he was one to ask questions. He believed that submarine attacks were the most brutal form of warfare ever invented. If Americans were killed by such attacks, however, our response should be to break off diplomatic relations with the attacking nation. Why, then, were we building a "brood of submarines," if not to become brutalizers ourselves? And, why was the House asked to pass bills increasing expenditures for "idle armies or top-heavy navies"?: "Up to date none of the advocates of preparedness have given Congress or the people one valid reason why we should squander any more hard-earned tax money on militarism. Not one of this whole array of pretending patriots have pointed to an enemy hostile to the United States or liable to attack the United States." Sherwood said everyone in the administration and the armed forces could be quoted as saying, less than a year before, that we were secure from attack and our defenses were adequate. Since then the opposing forces in the

[59] Ibid., 165, 167.

war had killed each other off in massive numbers. They were weaker than they were before, so how could we be in more danger now than we were then? If we were in no real danger, then who was pushing us to prepare for war at such great expense?[60] The Congressman quoted *La Follette's Magazine*, with the answer:

> They are the Morgans, the Rockefellers, the Schwabs, the Garys, the DuPonts and their prototypes, who are back of the 38 corporations benefiting most from war orders, the stocks of which have increased more than a thousand million dollars above their highest value before the war. They are the dollar-scarred heroes who organized the Navy League of the United States. Shades of Lincoln! What a band of patriots, with their business connections covering every financial and industrial center in the United States! Owning newspapers, periodicals and magazines and controlling through business relations the editorial good will of many others, they will be able to render powerful but disinterested aid in the great propaganda for preparedness now flooding the country.[61]

We had never had a large standing army while we were at peace, but if we established such an army it would lead us down

> ...the devious path of world-power exploitation. Militarism and imperialism are a couplet of devious devils that will carry the American people on the down grade speedily. You cannot separate militarism from imperialism. To use an unclerical expression, they are the twin devils of rapacity and moral decay—useless one without the other. Like the Siamese twins of long-term memory they are coursed with the same blood, and if you cut the umbilical cord both will languish and die (applause)."
>
> ....
>
> Here is what George Allen England says about this humbug scare, misnamed preparedness: "The whole thing is perfectly obvious. Seizing upon the European butchery as an excuse, the armament makers and militarists are determined to drive this country over the brink if they can. They remain indifferent to all truisms such as that preparedness has not prevented but has always induced war. There is money in this thing for them, so down with old-age pensions, educational expansion, improvements of all kinds and hurrah for Moloch. Militarism

[60] Isaac Ruth Sherwood, "National Defense," *Congressional Record*, vol. 53 part 1, Jan. 4, 1916, 459.

[61] Ibid.

> is a quick cut to millions. Moloch, militarism, murder, massacre—I think that sums it all up with neatness and dispatch" (applause.)[62]

The Congressman continued speaking about the tax burden that would be imposed on the American people to pay for an expanded army and navy. We already had a powerful navy. Though it might be second to that of Great Britain, it was first by a large margin in the Western Hemisphere and more than adequate for defense of the United States. He estimated that, should taxes be increased by enough to pay for the expansions requested, America would be expending 70% of its budget on the military, which was a higher rate than any of the warring nations. He was adamantly opposed to naval expansion, but did not favor keeping the same size army—he wanted it reduced by half, to 50,000 men. The savings thus realized could be used to establish a system of old-age pensions: "As a matter of national defense it would be a cognate inspiration to every worker."[63] He concluded his speech by stating,

> I hope the time is coming and is near at hand when all this brass-toned hysteria over militarism and ocean domination will cease...Let us pray, and labor with our prayers, that this hour of military hysteria will speedily pass, and that the sword and the man on horseback will never frustrate the true mission and destiny of our beloved America—peace, progress and prosperity under the supreme guidance of constitutional law (Applause.)[64]

Sherwood was a Democrat, and had high praise for Woodrow Wilson in opening his remarks. He considered that Wilson's diplomacy and adherence to neutrality to be correct and necessary, but as can be seen from his statements above he was unequivocally opposed to expanding the army and navy. Preparedness was militarism in disguise and could only lead to disaster. The President did not agree. In a speech in New York the evening of January 27, 1916 he outlined what he meant by preparedness and why American preparedness had nothing to do with militarism.

He began by saying that there are some differences between America and other countries. America had absolutely no desire to gain territory by war. We had always had room to grow, and, busy with our own affairs, no need to intervene in the affairs of others. On the rare occasions when we did intervene abroad, it was not to conquer, but to liberate. As an example, he offered the case of Cuba: "The world sneered when we set out upon the liberation of Cuba, but the world sneers no longer. The world now knows, what it was

[62] Ibid.
[63] Ibid., 462.
[64] Ibid., 463.

then loath to believe, that a nation can sacrifice its own interests and its own blood for the sake of the liberty and the happiness of another people." Then, in what seems now to be an oddly tentative manner, he said

> Whether by one process or another, we have made ourselves in some sort the champions of free government and national sovereignty in both continents of this hemisphere; so that there are certain obligations that every American knows that we have undertaken [probably a reference to the Monroe Doctrine]. The first and primary obligation is the maintenance of the integrity of our own sovereignty. That goes as of course. There is also the maintenance of our liberty to develop our political institutions without hindrance; and last of all the obligation and determination to stand as the strong brother to all those in this hemisphere who mean to maintain the same principles and follow the same ideals of liberty[65] [definitely a reference to the Monroe Doctrine].

Preparing a Great Machine

The President discussed other issues; tariffs, immigration, the changes in the world economy and world order that might come after the war. He professed no knowledge as to what the future would hold, but was certain about some things that it would *not* hold:

It goes without saying, though apparently it is necessary to say it to some excited persons, that one thing this country will never endure is a system that can be called militarism. But militarism consists in this, gentlemen: it consists in preparing a great machine whose only use is for war and giving it no use on which to expend itself. Men who are in charge of edged tools and bidden to prepare them for exact and scientific use grow very impatient if they are not allowed to use them, and I do not believe the creation of such an instrument is an insurance of peace.

What sort of instrument did Wilson want, then? He proposed an army that would be used in two ways. The first way would be for purposes of peace. He did not elaborate on this first use, but presumably meant maintaining peace by keeping our defenses strong. The second was for a scheme of "industrial and vocational education, combined with

> ...training in the mechanism and care and use of arms, in the sanitation of camps, in the simpler forms of organization and maneuver, as will make these same men, at one and the same time, industrially efficient and immediately serviceable for national defense. The point about such a system will be that its emphasis will lie on the industrial and

[65] Woodrow Wilson, *National Preparedness*, Washington D.C., Government Printing Office, 1916, 5.

> civil side of life, and like all the rest of America, the use of force will only be in the background and as a last resort. Men will think first of their families and their daily work, of their service in the economic ranks of their country, of their efficiency as artisans, and only last of all of their serviceability to the nation as soldiers and men-at-arms.

Wilson estimated that the country needed half a million such "trained citizens," and the training would be done by the US Army. He said he thought there were methods and details to accomplish this that his Administration had not considered and he would be glad to learn about them from anyone willing to offer suggestions.[66]

The United States Senate was hearing a lot of details about military training that January of 1916. General M.M. Macomb, commanding the Army's War College, testified about the Hays and Chamberlain bills, both of which dealt with military training for civilians. Both bills, and others being considered, were very detailed and accompanied by charts and tables. In regard to the Chamberlain bill, the General was asked if the bill would institute universal military service. He replied that it would, which he thought right and proper. In fact, if we acted in a timely fashion we could carry "...it into effect without making a heavy drain upon the country, amounting to militarism, we can form the framework for giving us what we need with certainty and can do so in time of peace." By "heavy drain" he may have meant conscription. Resistance to the draft had been widespread in the Civil War, including bloody riots in New York City in 1863. General Macomb may have thought that universal military training would make conscription unnecessary.[67]

The committee chair noted that some critics objected to universal training on the grounds that it would stimulate a military spirit in the country. Not a problem, said the General—as long as it was the right kind of military spirit, one that was a "...spirit of self-preservation...The people can perfectly well provide for defense and as soon as they realize what it means will provide for it. It does not mean militarism and it does not mean a military spirit throughout the country subversive of proper regard to the superiority of the civil power over the military."[68]

Also in January 1916 the National Security League sponsored and organized a "National Security Congress" which convened in New York. The league was organized in 1915 to support rapid expansion of America's armed

[66] Ibid., 7-8.

[67] United States Congress, Senate Committee on Military Affairs, *Preparedness for National Defense, hearings before the Committee on Military Affairs, United States Senate, Sixty-Fourth Congress, first session, on bills for the reorganization of the Army and for the creation of a reserve army*, Washington D.C., 1916, 410.

[68] Ibid., 412.

forces. The opening address at the Congress was by the League's founder and moving spirit, attorney S. Stanwood Menken (1870–1954). He addressed the question of national defense in near-apocalyptic terms, stating that we must be a united people "...who demand national defense, knowing that their own existence and all they cherish depend upon it and that failure or inefficiency will imperil the liberties of America and of the institutions (Applause.)... We are talking in terms of national existence and for world civilization." Menken claimed to be totally non-partisan and completely neutral as to the opposing sides of the European War. As he admitted, the League had been highly critical of the Wilson Administration in the past, but the President's recent support for a much larger Army was warmly praised. Plans for the Navy, however, were seen as highly inadequate. It was also regretted that there was no provision for universal military service, a measure the League promoted vigorously.

The Scientific Man Trained in Arms

There were high-ranking retired military and naval men supporting the League and some active duty officers addressed the conference. Menken stated that "From the first we have insisted that the solution of the question was a matter for the scientific man trained in arms, guided by those who had full understanding of the spirit of our people." Presumably Menken and the League knew who the scientific men and the guides were, or might even be able to supply them.[69] Menken also knew who opposed his positions, and why they did so:

> The present Congressional situation is particularly menacing, owing to the fact that the majority leader [Claude Kitchen, D., North Carolina] on the floor of the House of Representatives is opposed to the recommendations of the [President] and finds support in the position taken by Mr. William Jennings Bryan. Mr. Bryan's view is, according to his supporters, based upon sentiment. To my own mind, it is merely another proof of his notorious inability for direct or hard thinking on any matter. This has been shown before in his advocacy of fiat money under attractive disguise [free coinage of silver], his lack of recognition of the stern dignity of the United States and by his general tendency to pander to popular demands. Men of this type always attract a following in politics or on the lecture platform, because of a failure of many people to differentiate between soft promises and hard principles... The forces opposed to [us], like all other groups of opportunists, have

[69] Menken, S. Stanwood, "Opening Address," *Proceedings of the National security congress under the auspices of the National security league, Washington, January 20-22, 1916*, New York, National Security League, Inc., 8.

> nothing to lose and everything to gain by defeating the Administration's plans, as they are on the outs politically without credit even in their own party and they will not scruple to indulge in the treasonable practice of endangering the country if by so doing they can advance their own fortunes.[70]

Another speaker at the congress was Yale professor of political economy Henry C. Emery (1872–1924.) He said the American people had two fears about preparedness, the first being fear of the economic impacts of preparedness. This fear had no real basis: "If the American people were willing to sacrifice, say, two things, chewing gum and going to the movies, we could maintain an army so big that nobody would dare to look at us from across the way." In fact, Emery claimed that compulsory military training and industrial efficiency went hand-in-hand in Germany and would do so in the United States. Unfortunately there was

...a certain hoodlum period in the life of an average young man of this country...that dangerous period from when they get out of school, before they get into the responsibilities of life, when the most attractive thing is to sit around in pool parlors or make loud talk in barber shops or engage their activities in every way that is offensive to everyone save themselves (Laughter.) If young men did military training instead of idling and annoying their elders, they would learn discipline and be prepared to be good employees and good citizens.

Preparedness, in fact, was "preparedness for peace,"[71] not for war.

The Last Refuge of a Pacifist

The second fear described by Professor Emery was the fear of militarism, and he set out to define his term. He said that as Dr. Johnson defined patriotism as the last refuge of a scoundrel, he might define militarism as the "last refuge of a pacifist." He averred that this was not a serious definition, however. His real definition was that militarism existed when the

> ...State finds its highest and best expression in its militant organization to protect its rights, to defend itself from its enemies, to conquer what they may need for their development. Practically, this carries with it the establishment of a military caste which is socially superior to any other class in the community, the establishment of the sanctity of the military code, which is different from the civilian code, the exemption of the military class from the rules of the civilian code, and finally the assumption that military efficiency is all that is necessary for any of

[70] Ibid., 11.

[71] Ibid., 108.

> the activities of life. That, it seems to me, is a fair description of what militarism really is. Now, are we afraid of that kind of militarism in this country? Is there any danger of our being Prussianized?

Eight paragraphs later in the transcript of his speech Emery answered his own question firmly: "No, gentlemen, do not fear this spectre. On that steep road which leads to the supremacy of civilian authority and the sanctity of individual rights, from Runnymede to Gettysburg, we have come too high. We shall not fall [great applause]."[72]

Other speakers agreed that American preparations for war were not militaristic. In fact, military training had benefits above and beyond those provided to the armed forces. Dr. David Jayne Hill (1850–1932), academic and former ambassador to Germany, stated that "...it is in no respect a drift towards militarism to say that every able-bodied young man in our country should first be well-instructed in the meaning and value of our free institutions...it would elevate and ennoble the tone of the present and coming generations of American youth."[73] Former Secretary of War Luke E. Wright said that "We hear a great deal about Prussian militarism and of course I would not for a moment favor that stern and rigorous discipline that the Prussian subject goes through..." The right kind of training for an American young man, however, "...would give him physical stamina that would prolong his life many times one year...above all, he would be taught habits of respect for constituted authority, which our youth so sadly lack. He would be taught order and discipline."[74] New York's Mayor John Purroy Mitchell claimed that he was "...as much opposed to militarism, as Europe knows it, as the most ardent pacifist, but I do believe that citizenship in a democracy carries with it a fundamental obligation; that mild and brief citizen training for a few weeks each year, during adolescence and early manhood, is the minimum necessary to realize the condition of a trained citizenship in arms."[75]

Other Americans opposed to "militarism as Europe knows it" wrote articles for the monthly *American Defense*, which debuted in January 1916. Contributing editors included such well-known writers as Hamlin Garland, Rex Beach, Owen Wister and Irwin S. Cobb. Other contributors included generals, congressmen and academics. John Grier Hibben, President of Princeton University, wrote that

> ...the ability to defend ourselves will never lead to aggressive and insolent militarism. The spirit of militarism can never be due to mere

[72] Ibid., 111.
[73] Ibid., 28.
[74] Ibid., 95.
[75] Ibid. 198.

> preparedness, but is created by a warped mind and a heart of greed and ambition. Militarism is not determined by chance or circumstances, but by the definite policy of a state seeking world power and world domination...I have sufficient confidence in the spirit of our nation, in our traditions of Justice, our moral integrity, in the sincerity of our moral pledges, in the freedom from the mania of imperial conquest and territorial acquisition, so that I have no fear that our nation will ever be betrayed by the false ambition of militarism to wage an unjust and unrighteous war in an unworthy cause.

In short, "preparedness is preparedness against war, not for war."[76] Former Ambassador to Germany David Jayne Hill also saw no possibility of militarism in preparedness, done in moderation. "Over-armament" could be a cause of war, but a "reasonable means of defense, governed by a pacific policy, would certainly make for peace. The curse of militarism lies in the accumulation of force for the sake of domination. But armament for the defense of national rights is not militarism. It is a contribution to the reign of law and justice in the world."[77]

War for Our Daily Bread

Another contributor to *American Defense*, popular novelist Harold MacGrath, was even more scornful of former Secretary of State William Jennings Bryan than Theodore Roosevelt, who called Bryan an "ultra-pacifist." MacGrath's article "The Ostrich or the Bulldog?" was illustrated with photos of Bryan and a bulldog. Making his opinion of Bryan more clear, MacGrath referred to him as "a colossal failure [as Secretary of State,]...profoundly ignorant...neither observant nor receptive." He illustrated the last characterization by claiming that "...he is the pattern of man who would go into the Waldorf and drink his coffee out of a saucer because he would not observe that the other diners were drinking theirs out of the cup. More, he would hold that his way was right and the other way wrong." MacGrath wrote that civilization is the "evolution of force." He equated all human effort with warfare, but Bryan did not understand the way of the world:

> It is war to get our bread, to eat it, for always another hand is reaching for it. And that we may eat our bread depends upon our strength to keep it long enough. War in commerce, war in finance, war in art if you must have it. War in the human body, the white corpuscle against

[76] John Grier Hibben, "Preparedness against War," *American Defense*, Vol. 1 # 2 (Feb. 1916), 46.

[77] David Jayne Hill, "A Defensible Program of National Defense," *American Defense*, Vol. 1 #2 (Feb. 1916), 56.

> disease. War from the first breath until the last ...Bryan would have us abolish the force which protects our bread. By a few unctuous phrases, a few raisings of picturesque eyebrows, Bryan will abolish war. And so might Charlie Chaplin.[78]

In February 1916, Henry Ford got the attention of the nation with a full-page paid advertisement in many of the leading newspapers. He quoted the President Wilson's January 27 speech in New York, in which the President said the country was not in danger of foreign invasion. Ford emphatically agreed. We were imperiled, but not by foreigners:

> Our danger is internal. We are confronted by the danger of militarism. The very burden that caused thousands of men of all races to come to the United States in search of a haven of peace, to escape the toils of militaristic government, now is being preached throughout the land by men, by newspapers, by magazines, moving pictures and in fact by every means of intelligence. Conscription, the base of militarism, is advocated openly.

Ford stated that those who were advocating strengthening the military were wrapping themselves in the flag and claiming our national honor was at stake. He believed that the Navy League had started the agitation for preparedness and then attacked those, including serving Secretary of the Navy Josephus Daniels, that they thought insufficiently active in building up the military. Ford cited speeches made by Representative Clyde Tavenner on the House floor, which charged that the Navy League was organized and controlled by "war traffickers," by which he meant arms manufacturers.[79]

The Wall Street War Trust

One of the speeches by Representative Tavenner (D., Illinois) that Ford cited was given on December 15, 1915. Tavenner began by quoting some stock-price figures. Since the beginning of the war the price of a Bethlehem Steel share had risen from $40 to $474. Bethlehem Steel was a major supplier to companies manufacturing arms for the Army and Navy. The arms manufacturers and their suppliers were members of what the Congressman considered to be the "Wall Street war trust." Tavenner said that although war

---

[78] Harold MacGrath, "The Ostrich or the Bulldog?," *American Defense*, Vol. 1 #3 (March 1916), 70.

[79] Henry Ford, "Concerning Preparedness," as reprinted in *Leading Opinions both For and Against National Defense, a Symposium of Opinions Collected and Arranged by Hiram Maxim, A Handbook and Guide for Debaters and Public Speakers, Presenting both Sides of the Question with Absolute Impartiality*, New York, Hearst's International Library Co., 1916, 73.

caused great suffering and privation, for the management and ownership of these companies it meant huge profits.[80]

The Representative cited some figures for national expenditure for the military and stated that it now amounted to 67% of the nation's budget. He saw the rate of increase as unsustainable and claimed that if it continued families would not earn enough money to provide the basics for a decent life. He favored taking the profits out of supplying arms, by having the federal government take over the manufacture of armaments. He stated that the country was more endangered by "Wall Street war trust" profiteering than by any foreign military forces. Representative Tavenner was well prepared to defend his position from attack:

> Mr. Miller of Delaware: The gentleman is speaking of the additional taxation to be placed upon the people on account of the expenditure for the Army and the Navy. He has introduced into this Congress five bills which, if enacted into law, would add an additional $1,165,000, with respect to the Rock Island Arsenal in his own district.
>
> Mr. Tavenner: Yes.
>
> Mr. Miller of Delaware. May I ask him in that connection if the War Department or the General Staff has asked for any of this or whether it has been recommended in any report?
>
> Mr. Tavenner. No. I will answer that by saying that the War Department would rather give contracts to the J.P. Morgan controlled war trust, though at the Rock Island Arsenal we have manufactured certain materials 54% cheaper than the prices we were paying private manufacturers. If you were going to buy $20,000,000 of an article, would you pay 54% more for that article than you could manufacture it for yourself?

Continuing with his speech and with his contention that removing the profit motive from arms manufacturing would make the world more peaceful, he stated that

> Practically all the peace societies of the world which do not have on their board of directors or in their memberships stockholders in the private war trafficking firms, have declared in favor of the nationalization of munitions of war, on the theory that if private profit and private graft are taken out of militarism the incentive for at least that portion of the systematic agitation for increased military appropriations inau-

[80] Clyde Howard Tavenner, "The Navy League Unmasked, Speech" Washington D.C., Government Printing Office, 2.

> gurated by those who directly or indirectly profit from the sale of war materials will have been removed and an important step taken in the direction of peace.[81]

Much of Tavenner's speech was taken up by listing the corporations that sold armor plate and other war materiel to the government. He noted that the price per ton of armor plate that they charged was almost twice the amount that the government paid for armor plate produced by federal arsenals. These companies and their managers and boards of directors were active in the founding of the Navy League. The League also had retired admirals and ex-Secretaries of the Navy as members. The League did not ignore current office holders, for it used its resources to "...banquet Secretaries of the Navy and Members of Congress, hire speakers and carry on the elaborate campaign for 'preparedness' which the Navy League has been carrying on most earnestly for the last 13 years and which promises now to bear fruit in the form of staggering increases in Army and Navy appropriations."[82]

Patriotism Runs to Metal

Congressman Tavenner made special mention of Col. Robert M. Thompson:

> "Now I come down to the officers of the Navy League today. The president of the league, Col. Robert M. Thompson, the gentleman who was unkind enough to threaten to sue me, but not kind enough to do it [applause on the Democratic side] is chairman of the board of directors of the International Nickel Co., the business of which, according to the *Wall Street Journal*, has been very much improved by the war."

Nickel was an essential ingredient in the process of hardening steel for armor plate. These and other metals were necessary for the production of war materiel and the corporations mining and refining them stood to make very large profits:

> "As we proceed to analyze the various groups of founders, life members, honorary vice-presidents and contributors to the Navy League covering its entire existence of 13 years, the conviction will be gradually driven home to us that patriotism runs to metal, and that the Navy League is the magnet that draws together the men who make money handling metal in some form or other and who want to make more money. After these basic facts are established in our minds it will not appear strange, but quite the logical thing, that our friend, Col.

[81] Ibid., 5-6.
[82] Ibid., 12.

> Robert M. Thompson, the president of the New York Metal Exchange, should be the president of the Navy League.[83] If the people wish to insure themselves against all forms of government by armor plate, cannon and munitions makers, there is but one way they can do it and that is by *taking private profit out of war and preparation for war by having the government manufacture its own materials for the Army and Navy*... Behind the war trust is the most powerful group of men in the United States, if not in the world. Its control is in the same group of money kings that rule the insurance companies, the great banks, express companies, telegraph companies, railroads and steamship lines. To realize the colossal power of the capitalists behind the steel, armor, ammunition and shipbuilding companies and recall the desperate ends to which more than one investigation has revealed that they will go to satisfy their sordid greed for gold, and then to contemplate that the United States in war means more dollars to this group, is enough to justify the most optimistic man to tremble for the peace of this patriotic and Christian people."[84]

Henry Ford took a back seat to no one in his condemnation of the munitions industry. In his full-page newspaper ad he cited as evidence for the arms manufacturers venality the fact that they had no problem with supplying arms to both sides of a conflict. A good example was Mexico, where war materiel was flowing to all who could pay for it. The press played an important role, by highlighting charges of war crimes against the Germans and not giving the same attention to their denials of culpability. We were able to sell munitions to the British and French, but the blockade of Germany by the Royal Navy prevented trade with the Germans or the Austrians. The press told the American people that "...one of the warring factions [the Allies] was bleeding to crush [Prussian] militarism. Yet in the same pages the assumption of this beginning of militarism is declared to be the duty of the United States" The whole thing was an "attempt to work up an artificial hysteria as a preliminary to inoculation with the rabies of war," Even when retired military men like General Nelson Miles and active-duty officers like Admiral Victor Blue stated firmly that no invasion here was possible the beat went on. The Dardanelles Campaign, the attempt by Britain to land troops on the Gallipoli Peninsula and thus command the entry to the Black Sea, failed with horrendous casualties. We were at least as competent as the Ottoman Turks to defend our shores. And who would the invader be? All the European nations at war were becoming exhausted by the carnage already suffered. They were hardly able to cross the Atlantic and take on a strong new opponent.

[83] Ibid., 20.
[84] Ibid., 26.

Ford urged all citizens to let their Congressmen and Senators know that they were opposed to increasing the appropriations for the military. A sentence or two was enough, just so it was made clear that no money should be spent to defeat "ghost invaders." In sum, "There have been fine words about preparedness and militarism being totally different, but Europe knows today the only difference is in spelling."[85]

It might be expected that the Navy League would object to Henry Ford's description of them and their activities. Their objection took the form of a $100,000 libel suit. Naturally their definition of militarism was quite different from Ford's: "So at what point may the limit be laid down between militarism as a national necessity and militarism as a national menace?"[86] The League came down on the side of necessity.

Other observers agreed with Ford that war industries were behind much, if not all, of the push for preparedness. This had not been so at the outbreak of war, however:

> "Directly the war broke out we all exclaimed, 'This is what comes from armament. Europe is paying the price of its militarism.' A few jingo voices were instantly raised to demand armament on this continent, but they were pretty sternly repressed in the general chorus of thanking our stars that we had so few guns or soldiers. Our plain common sense had read us too clearly the lesson of that spontaneous combustion of militarism to make us care to repeat the experiment on our own soil.
>
> "Those who would profit from a military buildup were eager to do so, but the word militarism had a terrific black eye. So we set to work to invent a new term. That word is the hybrid 'preparedness'...The difference between militarism and preparedness, we told ourselves, was the difference between offense and defense—serenely oblivious of that having been what every nation in Europe had been telling itself for the past three decades."[87]

A Pugnacious Pacifist

Some who disagreed with Henry Ford did so strongly and financed it themselves, just as he had done. One such was Hudson Maxim, inventor of smokeless powder and brother of Hiram Maxim, inventor of the machine

[85] Henry Ford, op. cit., 75.

[86] J.W. Sullivan, "War and the Wage Workers," *American Defense*, Vol. 1 #4 (April 1916), 123.

[87] Seymour Deming, *From Doomsday to Kingdom Come*, Boston, Smart and Maynard, 1916, 74-75.

gun. He distributed free of charge a 160-page book called *Leading Opinions, both for and against national defense; A symposium of opinions of eminent leaders of American thought on the subject of our needs for national defense, collected and arranged by Hudson Maxim; A handbook and guide for debaters and public speakers, presenting both sides of the question with absolute impartiality*. The book included Henry Ford's advertisement and Maxim's response to it, which began by describing the conquering hordes of Attila the Hun. Maxim acknowledged that Attila rode 1500 years ago, but, still,

> ...men and women were not so thick in the path of the human game hunters as they would be in the path of the Huns that Henry Ford is inviting into this country...he attacks everyone who is trying to safeguard this country against invasion and the red hell of war, and I am one of those against whom he delivers a broadside of misrepresentation and abuse. But I am in good company. Colonel Robert M. Thompson, the Navy League, munition makers in general and armor plate makers in particular have also been smitten by the mailed fist of this pugnacious pacifist.[88]

Maxim wrote that he believed that we were now in an age of specialization. It would be foolish to have your lawyer try to remove your appendix or send your plumber to represent you in court. It was obvious that the most qualified experts on military affairs were generals and admirals. Maxim professed to be puzzled why Henry Ford, who had built his business by specialization, would not want military experts' advice to decide what was needed to defend the country. As to Ford's charge that munitions manufacturers promoted war to make money, Maxim was willing to be reasonable. No one could deny that munitions manufacturers made much more money in wartime. In times of peace army and navy budgets and expenditures were low. Cost cutting was the norm. Once war was declared or danger was imminent it was a sellers' market. The government wanted all the war materiel it could get and wanted it fast, price being of little consequence.[89]

However, so what? Modern military needed not only munitions, but tons of clothing, mountains of food, horses, telephones, airplanes—and automobiles. All manufacturers and suppliers of raw materials would make more money. Were they war promoters as well? Not as far as Hudson Maxim was concerned. The whole idea of arms manufacturers' ruthless profit-seeking as a cause of war was so ridiculous to him that he claimed to suspect the motives of Ford:

[88] *Leading Opinions*, op. cit., 141

[89] Ibid., 142.

> Is Henry Ford playing the fool or knave? If Henry Ford should succeed, in his propaganda against national defense, in defeating or impeding that movement, and if he were judged by the harm he would do, he would be one of the most evil monsters that ever afflicted mankind. He would bring a greater calamity upon this country than Attila the Hun brought upon Europe. As a traitor to his country, in my opinion he would make Benedict Arnold look like a patriot.[90]

Concluding his evaluation of Henry Ford and true patriotism, Maxim stated that he had recently established Maxim Munitions, Inc. His inventions had many military applications, but he had never before been involved in manufacturing for the armed forces. He intended to sell arms to the opponents of the Central Powers and to the United States. If the USA declared war, then he would sell all that the government wanted to them. He would not feel guilty about making any profit from what he saw as an essential contribution to national defenses.[91]

Possible Wars

Ford however had more than one way to get his message across. He entered the April 1916 Michigan Republican Primary—and won. This was a wakeup call for other candidates, about the strength of anti-war sentiment. No candidate of either party advocated an immediate entry into the war, but some wanted bigger, better and faster rearmament programs than others. And some like Theodore Roosevelt had made fiery speeches about Prussian barbarism and America's obligation to stop it. According to an editorial in *The Nation*, things were changing. Ford's victory and other news from the Midwest showed that a

> ...feeling against a militarist policy is growing so strong that there is even talk out West of starting a new party, with peace and anti-militarism as its chief issues. And for such a party ample financial backing could easily be assured. Now, does anyone suppose that such a political stirring could go unnoticed by the keen politician at Oyster Bay [i.e. Theodore Roosevelt]? What, a fund of millions ready to found a peace party which might tempt away from him thousands of his old Progressive following, who believed him sincere in his humane cries of 1912? Something must evidently be done. And so we get the authorized announcement that Mr. Roosevelt hates war more than any man living and desires nothing so ardently as to round out his services in

[90] Ibid., 143.
[91] Ibid., 150.

> the cause of peace. His press agents are printing lists of wars which he might have waged, but did not, when he was President.[92]

Wars that never happened were a topic of the very next editorial in *The Nation*. The editorialist picked out several incidents in the past where the United States laid down the law to European powers, at times when we had little or no army or navy to back up our strong language. Our diplomatic notes, sometimes couched in the "roughest" terms, did not provoke war. This was because, while our military may be small in peacetime, we had great resources in men, industry and national spirit that enabled us to mobilize quickly and forcefully. "The record of our diplomatic relations with other countries will be scanned in vain for evidence that any one of them ever set out to pick a quarrel with the United States. Many of them have been at great pains to avoid a quarrel with us. And the question of our actually disposable military force has scarcely entered into our foreign controversies." *The Nation* acknowledged that what was true in the past may well not be true in the future, but still advocates of a strong force-in-being had no history to support their claims.[93]

Preparedness had not only individual opponents like Henry Ford. Groups began to form to fight what they saw as militarism and a drift towards war. One such group, the Anti-Preparedness Committee, planned an April 1916 mass meeting in New York. It claimed inspiration for a proposed tour of American cities from a speech by President Wilson in St. Louis in February 3, 1916:

> When President Wilson spoke in St. Louis on his recent tour advocating unusual naval and military preparedness, he put it up to those who differed with him to hire large halls and put their case before the public. The challenge was taken up by the Anti-Preparedness Committee, and on April 6, at Carnegie Hall in New York, it held the first mass meeting in a cross-country series. The 'truth about preparedness' and 'democracy against militarism' were its slogans.[94]

The Committee was needling the President. In his St. Louis speech, he had stated

> There is no politics in national defense, ladies and gentlemen. I would be sorry to see men of different parties differ about anything but the details of this great question; and I do not anticipate any essential differences. Some men do not see anything. Some men look straight in the face of the facts and see nothing but atmospheric air. Some men are so

[92] "Strange Friends of Peace," *The Nation*, Vol. 102 no. 2651 (April 20, 1916), 428.
[93] Ibid.
[94] "Swinging Around the Circle against Militarism," *The Survey* (April 22, 1916), 95.

> hopelessly and contentedly provincial that they cannot see the rest of the world; but they do not constitute a large or influential minority even. You must listen to them with indulgence, and then absolutely ignore them. They have a right to talk, but they have no right to affect our conduct. Indeed, if I were in your place I would encourage them to talk. *Nothing chills folly like exposure to the air, and these gentlemen ought to be encouraged to hire large halls, and the more people they can get to hear them the safer the country will be*[95] [italics mine.]

The keynote address at Carnegie Hall was by Lillian D. Wald, of the Henry Street Settlement. Ms. Wald was chair of the American Union against Militarism (AUM), the new name of the Anti-Preparedness Committee. She claimed patriotism for opponents of preparedness like herself:

> I hardly dare hope that I can convey with any degree of accuracy the causes for the uneasiness, nay, the causes of sorrow and unhappiness of men and women who see in the military propaganda of the day a great peril to the America that has the passionate love of its true patriots...under the seemingly reasonable term of preparedness militarism has invaded us from every side and even marched into our schools, threatening by legislative enactment, where exhortation has failed to establish conscription there. Extraordinary and unprecedented measures have been taken to promote a public demand for military and naval expansion and these have brought in their train hysteria and the camp followers of self-interest...Because preparedness has been used as a synonym for militarism, the emergency committee deemed it right to come out against that kind of preparedness, and to employ their influence in urging that people understand that it is in reality militarism that is being pressed upon us...the committee as such has not even suggested or has it stood at any time for disarmament or for peace-at-any-price...[96]

Fear has Dethroned Reason

Lillian Wald continued by noting that

> Were it not significant of the extent of the influence of military clamor one might find humor in some of its manifestations. Fear has dethroned reason, and people are "seein' things at night." In all sincerity one man declared that at two o'clock in the morning he *saw* a company of Germans drilling in Van Cortlandt Park. Months ago many of us

[95] Woodrow Wilson, "Address at the St. Louis Coliseum in St. Louis Missouri," February 3, 1916, http://www.presidency.ucsb.edu/ws/index.php?pid=117297.

[96] "Swinging Around the Circle against Militarism," *The Survey* (April 22, 1916), 95.

> were asked to give up our country homes for our "wounded soldiers," and blankets and sheets have long been packed in chests ready for use. Yesterday I was told by a Boston friend that ladies there are registering their automobiles as available to "carry the maidens inland" if necessary.

She concluded her speech by stating that

> The committee has found, however, that great numbers of the citizens everywhere have expressed their fear, not of an invading army, but of the danger that is close upon us and in our midst. In the East and the West, the North and the South, public-spirited men and women, good and true citizens of the great American republic, have voiced their desire to be united with those who stand for democracy as against militarism. To accomplish this is the committee's essential purpose and propaganda."[97] [In 1916 "propaganda" could refer to any effort to persuade. It was not yet used to refer only to an enemy's falsities.]

An important part of the A.U.M.'s "propaganda" was its platform:
Platform of the American Union Against Militarism

To Fight Militarism

- By demanding honesty and efficiency in our present army and navy, while opposing increased armament with its inevitable challenge to a coalition of nations against us.
- By establishing government production of munitions
- By keeping military training out of the public schools and fighting the idea of military and industrial conscription.

To Build Towards World Federation

- By declaring our national intention never to acquire territory by aggression
- By exposing the exploitation of weaker nations by commercial interests operating under our own or foreign flags.
- By establishing a joint government commission, representing Japan, China and the United States, to devise a solution to the issues involving America and the Orient
- By promoting a conference, official or unofficial, of the twenty-one American republics, to devise a means, other than military, for preserving the republican form of government in the western hemisphere

[97] Ibid.

- By creating institutions which shall provide the machinery for the judicial settlement of international disputes.[98]

The audience at Carnegie Hall heard perspectives other than Lillian Wald's on national defense. Congressman Oscar Calloway of Texas, a member of the House Naval Affairs Committee, expressed

> ...the large skepticism of the central states with respect to the trepidations of the seaboard. "I ain't any pacifist. I come from Texas and you don't raise them there. But when I meet a man coming down the street with a Winchester and two six shooters and a brace of brass knucks, I know he's not a brave man; I know him for a braggard and a bully. Nobody is afraid of a man like that and don't want to have any business with him either. Nobody is afraid of a nation like that and don't want to have any business with it either [*sic*]."

Other speakers included representative of labor, farmers and the clergy. The Rev. A.A. Berle (father of A.A. Berle Jr., noted member of FDR's "brains trust") spoke in opposition to a proposal included in the Chamberlin bill before Congress, that men who had served six years in the army would be admitted, upon the recommendation of three officers, to civilian employment in the War Department, or other civil branch of the government. This means, he said, that men who have served in the army would automatically be "railroaded" into the civil service, and he regarded the legislation as nothing less than "a deliberate conspiracy to militarize the civil service of the United States."[99]

Jingo, the Dinosaur of Militarism

After the Carnegie Hall event the tour of major American cities began. Two days before the speakers arrived at each stop, advance men prepared the way. They brought along visual aids, one of which was a large model of a rather sleepy-seeming dinosaur, somewhat like a stegosaurus with armor-like bony plates along its spine. Walter G. Fuller, one of the workers on the model, thought that there was

> ...no more proper and appropriate symbol of militarism...What could be more like the heavy, stumbling, brutal foolery which is destroying Europe than those old monsters of the past, the armored dinosaurs? These beasts, all armor plate and no brains, had no more intelligent way of living than 'adequate preparedness.' All their difficulties were met by piling on more and more armor, until at last they sank by their

[98] Ibid.
[99] Ibid.

own clumsy weight into the marshlands, such as one might expect to find at low tide at Oyster Bay" [Oyster Bay was the ancestral estate of Theodore Roosevelt's family.]

Here was an animal unable to do even a little intelligent thinking. Its brain cavity in proportion to the size of its body was more diminutive than that of any other vertebrate. Like the militarist, therefore, it was unable to conceive of any intelligent foreign policy. Moreover, its vision was limited. Its eyes were small and could only look in a sideways direction. It could not look ahead.

It is also considered likely that the dinosaur had no funny bone.

It is thought by those who have studied these creatures that at one time there were at least fourteen different species of armored dinosaurs roaming about the face of the earth. This fact has a peculiar significance, since there are just that number of "patriotic" societies in this country now urging dinosaurian preparedness upon us. Increasing bulk and development of the armor caused the dinosaur to lose celerity of movement; he became a sluggish, slow-moving creature of low mentality. Whereas his contemporaries in the animal kingdom, whose minds did not run so much on 'preparedness', kept their wits about them and decided upon some workable plan to live and let live, with the result that modern man and the armored dinosaur now meet one another only in museums.

So it will be with great nations.

The free peoples who refuse to take upon themselves the badge of militarism are destined to march far along the road of human progress and civilization, while the cringing, goose-stepping, eternally saluting taxpayers of the militarist top-boot will have 'prepared' themselves off the face of the earth.

Someday, not very far distant, happy civilians will come to look at models of the fighting men of today all dressed up—gas respirators, steel helmets, trench boots and the rest of it—in the chambers of militarist horrors which will everywhere be a part of the national museums of the future.[100]

The tour went first to Buffalo, then Cleveland and Detroit:

At Detroit the tour came into its own. The local opera house was packed and a crowd of 2,000 stood in the street for two hours and listened to the

[100] Ibid., 37.

speakers who came outside. Mr. and Mrs. Henry Ford occupied an inconspicuous corner in a box. At a reference to the vote which Mr. Ford had received in the Michigan presidential primaries, the unwilling 'candidate' was compelled to rise and bow to the cheers of his neighbors.

From Detroit the tour moved on to several more cities, ending in Pittsburgh. The [unnamed] reporter covering the tour for *The Survey* magazine thought that "Where no large local business groups have been interested in the war trades, the audience drew on all factors of the population. Elsewhere, where preparedness has been actively agitated the audience was a group of protestants drawn from the wage earning population,"[101] He also cited the hostility of the local press in some cities.

Splendid Anti-Militarist Traditions

Perhaps influenced by the AUM's cities tour, President Wilson met with a delegation of its members on May 20, 1916. The delegation brought with them a list of questions that they asked the President to respond to:

1. Could the President assure the American public that there would be no break with the "splendid anti-militarist traditions of our past"? These included no large standing army, no peacetime conscription and heavy reliance upon volunteers for military service. President Wilson said in response that he believed there were "reasonable" preparations which could be made without violating national traditions, "For the traditions of the country have not been those of military helplessness, though they have been those of anti-militarism."

2. Did the President agree that "...much of the so-called preparedness movement is rooted in motives sinister and even sordid?" Wilson made no comment on the motives of preparedness advocates.

3. What were the President's views on compulsory military service? He said that he was not opposed to the mass of the nation learning how to use arms, but was opposed to the establishment of a large army that was controlled by a few men for their own purposes. That was the "militarism of Europe" and he wanted no part of it. How large the army should be was a "point of practical necessity."

4. How large did the President think the navy should be? The delegates believed that the President had been "...incorrectly pictured as demanding the greatest navy in the world." Wilson replied that the tasks required of our navy had increased "tremendously." He hoped that the additional forces

[101] Ibid., 96.

needed would not be seen as unreasonable, and that in an effort to avoid militarism we would not get the navy we needed to protect our interests.[102]

During the meeting some AUM delegates asked the President to elaborate on certain points. During the discussion about naval expansion a delegate commented that he was in London during the Venezuelan crisis of 1895, when the US and Great Britain were at loggerheads over British naval demonstrations over Venezuelan non-payment of debts. The delegate "...had heard it said that if America had a great navy President Cleveland's message would have been regarded as bullying and unquestionably would have led to war." Wilson replied, "But this is not the year 1895. This is a year of madness...All the world is seeing red." This made it incumbent upon America to keep its head but also meet its responsibilities. These responsibilities now included contributions to the security of the entire Western Hemisphere (i.e., maintenance of the Monroe Doctrine) and in the future, perhaps to the entire "family of nations." Lillian Wald then asked if this would not logically lead to limitless contributions by America. The President replied, "Well, logically, Miss Wald, but I have not the least regard for logic. What I mean by this is in such affairs as we are now discussing the circumstances are the logic." He believed that if the family of nations came together to maintain peace, individual contributions towards maintaining the peace would be made "moderately and not indefinitely." The final questioner wanted to know if the President believed in compulsory military service. Wilson was noncommittal: "I did not say I believed in it. To use the phrase of a friend of mine, my mind is to let on the subject. I would say merely that that was not contrary to American tradition."[103]

A few days after this meeting there was a preparedness parade in New York. Its organizers included some of the most important business leaders in the city. The Executive Committee organizing the "Citizens' Preparedness Parade" met in the Yale Club in New York on May, 3, 1916, to plan for the event. Marchers were organized by trades—carpenters, masons, roofers, etc. They were not to carry any signs of a "critical or political nature," or any sign identifying the business that employed them. No one was to wear a uniform, except National Guardsmen. Each of the 74 trades units in the parade was to be provided a "Mayor's Escort." Their dress was to be formal: cutaway coats and silk top hats. One man at the meeting suggested derbies rather than top hats, perhaps feeling this was more in keeping with what was supposed to be a great upwelling of popular support for preparedness. This was voted down by an "overwhelming majority." The parade was predicted to be the largest

[102] "The President on Militarism," *The Survey*, (May 20, 1916), 198–199.
[103] "President on Defenses," *New York Times*, May 9, 1916, 1.

civilian parade in American history, with more than 200,000 already signed up and no more room for new recruits—in fact, 25,000 potential marchers had already been refused a place in the line of march. It was estimated that it would take at least ten hours for all the units to pass the reviewing stand.[104]

Some total numbers of participants were announced at the meeting. The financial district group was one of the largest: "General Oliver B. Bridgman, who is organizing the Wall Street units for the parade, reported that up till noon yesterday 7,200 Wall Street men had enrolled in the Wall Street battalions. A division of women employees, banks, brokerage houses and other Wall Street institutions is now in the process of organization." Some other group totals were reported. The Sporting Goods and Publishing contingents were 500 each, while Monsignor Connolly reported that of the Clerical division "...several hundred priests and ministers would march to show that a large proportion of the clergy favors adequate national preparedness for any emergency."[105]

General Leonard Wood attended and addressed the meeting. He wished attendees to understand that preparedness was not preparing *for* war, but preparing *against* war:

> We believe in arbitration and we believe in peace and we believe in working for them. But the fact remains that we all know that trouble is all about us. Preparedness is in the last analysis nothing more or less than peace insurance, and if we are to be properly insured it will take money and patience and time to get it. As businessmen you know that in order to compete with an efficient firm your business must also be efficient. What we need to do to apply to this business of preparedness the same broad, sane principles that businessmen apply to their affairs.[106]

Although applications by men to march on the 13 of May 1916 were being rejected, some women could still apply to participate. The *New York Times* thought it was "interesting" that college women and "professional and amateur nurses" could still join units composed of their confreres. This was one of the smaller efforts to gain participation by women. A much larger campaign was headed by Mrs. Lindon Bates, who was chair of the Women's Section of the Movement for National Preparedness, which operated under the auspices of the National Civic Federation. Bates had been the chair of the Women's Section of the American Commission for Relief in Belgium. That organization had dissolved itself in December 1915, and Mrs. Bates was now

---

[104] "General Wood Indorses Citizens' Big Parade," *New York Times*, May 4, 1916, 6
[105] Ibid.
[106] Ibid.

attempting to persuade its former members to move from war relief to war preparedness, or war prevention as General Wood would have had it. The persuasion effort included "allied organizations" of women, making the total of potential female persuadees some 8,000,000.

Mrs. Bates and other leaders of the new Women's Section went on a speaking tour including many of the cities visited by the American Union against Militarism. Their tour, however, was merely "educational." They stated they had no program of preparedness to present, because it was better to leave the details of how best to defend the country to men, who were more knowledgeable about such matters. As to which men in particular, they wanted "army and navy experts" to make the choices, a time-honored tradition in American politics. They also wanted universal military service, the central part of many preparedness programs. This did not include military training in the public schools, though Mrs. Bates wanted "training in matters of health, discipline and conduct which shall make the boys fit for the military camp later." No matter how favoring universal military training might appear, Mrs. Bates wanted everyone to be clear about her organization: "The Women's Section is not a militaristic organization. We deplore militarism and do not want it. We want simply defense of America's ideals and citizenry."[107]

The Greatest Processions of Civilians

The *New York Times* was mightily impressed on May 13, 1916. By their count there were 135,683 marchers, of which 3,287 were women, with Mrs. Bates one of the listed names. Other estimates varied, but it was "perhaps the greatest procession of civilians that the world has ever seen." Apparently the rule against identifying particular companies with signs was observed by the marchers, but many of the trades represented identified themselves elaborately. The jewelry trade certainly did. They "made perhaps the biggest hit of the entire parade." Their contingent appeared to some like a "...great block of solid gold...Every man in line carried a bright gold pennant and wore an equally bright sash, while brilliant brassards, also of gold, circled the right arm of every marcher. On the sashes of every marcher the single sentence was printed in big black letters, "We jewelers urge preparedness."[108]

Some of the units in the parade were quite large. Municipal employees totaled 5,702, lighting companies 10,774, architects 6,600. The wholesale dry goods division had 7,196. They were led by "H.D. Cooper, their marshal, followed by the leading men of the business, marching beside their junior

[107] "Seeks to Rouse Women to Duties in Defense," *New York Times*, May 4, 1916, 6.
[108] "Every Calling in the Line." *New York Times*, May 14, 1916, 1.

clerks and salesmen..." Some of the units had famous people in their midst. The 6,000 men of the engineering division included Thomas Edison. "Mr. Edison was recognized and loudly cheered by the crowds. He marched as a boy of twenty, stepping lightly and smilingly acknowledging the greetings shouted at him." Perhaps the largest division was the bankers and brokers:

> There were 15,000 men in this division, among them some of the most prominent men in the financial district. Instead of American flags they carried red, white and blue pennants, and different subdivisions adopted other distinctions of dress, such as red, white and blue leggins [*sic*]; white spats, colored hatbands and the like. Something more than 100 men in this division wore little Belgian flags in their lapels. This was the only display of a foreign flag in the parade.

One of the smallest divisions was that of clergymen. They totaled 130 ministers and priests of various denominations. There were eight named members of the leadership of the division, including "Rev. Dr. Joseph Silverman, representing the Jewish Church." These marchers were wearing their ecclesiastical dress and "American colors," and so were very noticeable and garnered much applause from the crowds watching. And, "As the clergymen passed the reviewing stand someone shouted 'Hurrah for the Church Militant!' and a great cheer emphasized the exclamation."[109]

The parade route was Fifth Avenue from Twenty-Fourth to Fifty-Eighth Street. General Wood was on the reviewing stand and thought it a "splendid showing...the best example of citizen marching I have seen." Joseph Choate of the National Security League also marveled at the appearance and skill of the marchers: "the parade has exceeded the expectations of the National Security League and me. I am deeply impressed with the splendid physical appearance and apparent intelligence of the men. They would make good soldiers. They have an earnest and brave bearing and show that they do not take their marching as play. They are in deadly earnest. The parade is bound to have a great influence on the country."

Two days after the parade the Sunday sermons were sampled. Of the ten clergy that were quoted eight were strongly in favor of preparedness. It was "less a holiday and more a consecration," "the first step toward international brotherhood and love," "fighting unrighteousness, injustice and all forms of evil and vice," and "[a] splendid display [which] shows how deeply and widespread the demand for preparedness is." Of the two opposing preparedness, Rabbi Stephen Wise was much the better-known. He stated that he did not want to disparage the marchers. He thought that they were motivated by a desire to show unity to the world, so that no potential foreign

[109] Ibid., 2.

aggressor would believe there were divisions among Americans that could be exploited. Still, he felt that the marchers were being deceived. There was no country preparing to invade us or even one that wanted to antagonize us. "But do the paraders understand that their unquestioned patriotism is being capitalized in the interests of a program of militarism, more gravely menacing to the American democracy than foreign foe can ever become?"[110]

Although the rule against displaying signs with company names was apparently strictly observed, this did not mean that the companies who had done all the assembling of their employees went unknown. Page 3 of the May 14, 1916, *New York Times* listed every division in the parade and every company whose employees had marched.[111] And, according to some sources, participation in the parade was not exactly voluntary. In 1916, the six-day work week was standard for most companies. The parade was held on a Saturday. Several weeks before the parade a reporter for *The Survey* obtained a copy of a letter that an unnamed corporation sent its employees. It notified them that if they did not participate in the parade they would have to work a full day—even though this company only worked a half-day on Saturdays. To the reporter this amply demonstrated that "the subsidized newspapers will announce this parade as a great patriotic demonstration of loyal American citizens, etc., in the interest of preparedness, whereas, in reality it will be a parade of, for and by the big commercial interests."[112] That idea may have gained some support from the statement by George T. Wilson, who was one of the leaders of the insurance division in the parade. Wilson was the president of Equitable Insurance and was deeply impressed by the parade. He was chairman of the Insurance Club, which he and other insurance executives were forming to support preparedness. He was also in charge of organizing a dinner to honor the 200 or so business executives who had supervised the 74 divisions participating in the parade. He wanted to enlist these men into a permanent organization like the Insurance Club that would work directly for preparedness. Wilson didn't know any specifics yet about what these new organizations would do, but he had a pretty good idea about who might participate: "Just think, there are 200 men banded together who have practically listed the sentiments of every man in about seventy- two [seventy-four, actually] callings. They can check up not only the name of every man who marched, but they have the name of every man who did not march and why. This is vital information and it would seem a great pity if the men having this information were not held together in a permanent organization."

[110] "City Pulpits Voice Parade's Big Plea," *New York Times*, May 15, 1916, 3.
[111] Ibid., 3.
[112] Henry Saum, "March or be Penalized," *The Public*, vol. XIX no. 944 (May 5, 1916), 416.

A "check-up" on who participated in the parade and who did not indicated the marching may not have been voluntary. Some journals sympathetic to unions claimed participation was in fact compelled: "In New York city on May 13 took place a tremendous demonstration of the dangerous power over citizens held by privileged financial interests...Evidence exists which indicates a large proportion of these were coerced, intimidated or otherwise improperly induced to march. The parade made clear that those who control the livelihood of New York want preparedness."[113]

Making for Harmony

In June both parties held their conventions. The Republicans were first, meeting in Chicago June 7–10, 1916. The first major speech was by the temporary chairman, Senator Warren G. Harding of Ohio. He welcomed the delegates and admonished them that "The country, wearied afresh by a disappointing and distressing Democratic administration, is calling for Republican relief..." In order to provide the relief, Republicans would have to unify. The 1912 convention had been a disaster for the Republicans. President Taft had won re-nomination, but ex-President Roosevelt had not accepted this outcome and ran on the Progressive party ticket. The result was the election of Woodrow Wilson and a Democratic Congress. By 1916, however, the party was reunified enough that there was laughter in the convention hall when Harding observed that "We did not do very well in making for harmony the last time we met."[114]

This time would be different. Republicans thought they had the positions on the issues of war and peace that would bring them victory in November. President Wilson was portrayed as weak and vacillating. In a pointed reference to the President's comment about being too proud to fight, Harding declaimed that

> We have territory to defend, we have independence to preserve, we have lives to safeguard, we have property to protect, we have rights to assert, we have missions of humanity to perform. We proclaim justice and we love peace and we mean to have them—and we are not too proud to fight for them (Loud applause.) Let no one apprehend the curse of militarism in this fair land. We declare unalterably against it. Our free citizenship, walking confidently, absorbed in the triumphs of peace, would tolerate no such blight on American institutions.[115]

[113] "Thoroughly Demonstrated," *The Public*, vol. XIX no. 946 (May 19, 1916), 457.
[114] "Address of the Temporary Chairman, "*Official Report of the Proceedings of the Sixteenth Republican National Convention*," 14.
[115] Ibid. 19.

The delegates began the balloting for the nomination on Friday, June 9, 1916. The first ballot had Hughes in the lead with 258, former Secretary of War Elihu Root, 103, Theodore Roosevelt 81. The rest of the votes were scattered among favorite sons and party favorites. Four hundred ninety-four were required to be nominated. A second ballot followed, with Hughes getting 328, Root 98 and Roosevelt the same 81. The trend was clear, but the hour was late and the convention adjourned until 11am the next morning. Matters undoubtedly having been arranged the night before, on Saturday's third and final ballot Hughes received 950 votes out of 987 possible. The ritual unanimity motions passed and Hughes was their candidate.[116]

There was even less drama in St. Louis June 14, 1916, when the Democratic convention opened. The temporary chair of the convention, former New York Governor Martin Glynn welcomed the delegates. He, like Senator Warren Harding, thought it was impossible that militarism could develop in this country. His denunciation of it was considerably more poetic than Harding's, though:

> Democracy refuses to be frightened by those who pretend to fear that this great land will descend into the abyss of militarism. It knows that militarism can no more thrive in this country than the cockle and the tare can thrive amid the wheat of the husbandman who loves his land... Militarism in the United States is as impossible as the shadow of a ghost in the midday sun.

Glynn observed that after every war America had fought, the soldiers returned to the pursuits of peace:

> From the ranks of democracy they came as silently as Putnam left his plow in answer to the shot heard round the world; and back to democracy they went as silently as the Southern heroes whose horses Grant returned so that they might plow the very fields that had been harrowed by their cannon's wheels (Applause.)"[117]

Militarism is a Spirit

A few days after the Democratic Convention, on June 13, 1916, President Wilson addressed the graduating cadets at West Point. Perhaps with his recent conversation with the American Union against Militarism in mind, he made a statement about preparedness and militarism:

[116] Ibid., 180, 183, 197.

[117] "Address of the Temporary Chairman," *Official Report of the Proceedings of the Democratic National Convention (1916)*, 29.

> You know that the chief thing that is holding many people back from enthusiasm for what is called preparedness is the fear of militarism. I want to say a word to you young gentlemen about militarism. You are not a militarist because you are military. Militarism does not consist in the existence of an Army, not even in the existence of a very great army. Militarism is a spirit. It is a point of view. It is a system. It is a purpose. The purpose of militarism is to use armies for aggression. The spirit of militarism is the opposite of the civilian spirit, the citizen spirit. In a country where militarism prevails the military man looks down upon the civilian, regards him as inferior, thinks of him as intended for his, the military man's, support and use; and just so long as America is America that spirit and point of view is impossible with us. There is as yet in this country, as far as I can discover, no taint of the spirit of militarism.[118]

The President certainly saw no militarism in the provisions of the Hay-Chamberlain bill, officially the Army Reorganization Act, which he signed on June 3, 1916. This bill expanded the Regular Army and provided for federalization of the state national guards. It also provided more money for training, including the "Plattsburgh Movement" summer camps, which gave a military experience to civilian volunteers The legislation was a compromise between hot and lukewarm supporters of army expansion. Among the hottest advocates were the leaders of the National Security League. They had urged the President to veto, not sign, the bill, which they believed was "totally inadequate...sanctions wrong principles and methods, which will make it more difficult to obtain hereafter an adequate system of defense, also that it creates a false sense of security."[119] Much more colorfully, Representative Augustus Gardner said that "For a nation as great as ours to support an army no bigger than we have and propose, is almost as sensible as it would be for Ty Cobb to attempt to hit Walter Johnson's pitching with a sulphur match."[120]

The American Union against Militarism also ridiculed the bill, though on very different grounds. Their main objection was to the provisions of the bill that federalized the state national guards and increased the federal financial support. This, they believed was an invitation to thieving and/or lazy state officials to establish a "political machine" that would waste or misappropriate federal money. Such a machine could "wrap itself in the flag" to lobby for more money on behalf of a state, and how could this flag-wrapped machine be denied? In taking this line the AUM was using some of the debate argu-

[118] "Militarism Impossible Here," *The Democratic Textbook*, New York, Democratic National Committee, 1916, 418.

[119] "Asks Army Bill Veto," *New York Times*, May 28, 1916, 22.

[120] "Army Bill Passes," *New York Times*, May 22, 1916, 22.

ments of US senators who later came to support the compromise of the bill signed by the President, including Senator Chamberlain. The AUM also believed that militia-type units like the state national guards had never constituted effective fighting forces and would never do so. And, there were other problems with the state guards. Exhibit A for the AUM was the actions of the New York State National Guard at the recent Constitutional Convention convened in Albany. There the Guard successfully opposed measures which would forbid military courts trying a civilian when the civil court system was operating. The AUM stated that

> Contrary to our own expectations when we organized last December to resist the worst features of the so-called 'preparedness' agitation, this proposed subsidy to the National Guard has become the single biggest evil in the whole situation. It is militarism incarnate—the soldier caste equipped with gun, unlimited cash, the court-martial and the vote. We do not believe that the sponsors for the subsidy clearly realize how it will look to the American people when they thoroughly understand it.[121]

To Charles Hallinan, Editorial Director (after the war Executive Director) of the AUM, "...the easy victory of the impudent military legislation in the New York Legislature and the unchecked career of the equally impudent, not to say disastrous, army bill in Congress should show us that our old standby will not suffice, that militarism takes constantly new forms not quickly recognized by the untutored Jeffersonian." Hallinan wrote that many had even seen the bill as a pacifist measure. It did not establish a military dictator or dictatorship or a huge new regular army. However, quoting Senator William Borah,

> There is a more modern, a more subtle, a less dangerous, and less suspected method by which modern militarism, under the guise of law and order...supplants the courts and tears down the guarantees of personal liberty. It subordinates the civil to the military authority as happened in the New York [constitutional] convention. Modern militarism dictates from the gallery here, through its persistent and well-organised lobby, what appropriations shall be made in its interest and on its behalf...[122]

> [A] ...widespread distrust of something called militarism which is commonly embodied in the bogey of a large standing army [was clearly outmoded]. For what the new law chiefly does is multiply enormously the new centers of militarist infection. It is not an emergency measure,

[121] "Pacifists Turn Fire on National Guard," *New York Times*, May 19, 1916, 4.
[122] Charles T. Hallinan, "The New Army Law," *The Survey*, vol. 36 (June 17, 1916), 309.

> suddenly bringing a vast army into life at the behest of the excited press. But it pumps enough downright militarism into the cherished body politic to poison us for the next ten years.

Many of those opposed to a larger military, and the public at large, tended to view the National Guard as a mostly civilian institution. They were part-time soldiers, after all, and were often much more interested in the social and political aspects of the Guard than boring weekly drills and spending their vacation in a Guard summer camp. Do not be fooled, cautioned Hallinan, for your friendly local guardsman was an...

> ...utterly uncritical adherent of the militarist point of view... and that the brains of the movement are entirely enlisted on the side of universal compulsory military service and of nearly every stupid survival of the military regime, including race prejudice, class prejudice and the bad manners of the military machine. For evidence of race prejudice see the New York papers of recent date. For evidence of class prejudice, see the two recent admirable speeches of Senator Borah of Idaho."

One Kind of Militarism

One of those speeches was undoubtedly "Modern Militarism," delivered by Borah in the Senate on May 17, 1916. He opened with some comments on the National Guard and labor. Since the Guard had been used to police and break strikes, he felt that working men would not join. This would make recruitment difficult, if not impossible.

A Senator questioned Borah as to whether the laboring classes were committed to lawful protest and Borah said he believed they were. It was the calling in of the Guard as a first resort, before any lawless conduct, that created problems. Borah believed that labor was committed to lawful exercise of their rights. He strongly objected to the recent action of the New York legislature, which opened the door to military courts-martial trials of civilians detained during labor disputes. He cited instances in British history where military courts had been reined in when they overstepped their bounds. Borah was particularly scathing about the use of military courts to punish Irish rebels after the Easter 1916 rising in Dublin. No such action should ever be permitted here:

> I do not want a tremendous organization actuated by the spirit of militarism, on the one hand, and conscious of its political power on the

> other combining both for every emergency in its own interest fastened upon the taxpayers of this country. "[123]
>
> There is now but one kind of militarism to be feared in this country. The militarism of the standing army is in my judgment not nearly so serious as the militarism in Congress through the avenue of politics and which dominates legislation through its presence here in the Capital. There can be only one kind of militarism in our Republic, and that is the militarism which arises by reason of the combination of the military power and the political power. Men who are organizing as a military force but exercise their influence under their organization as a political force constitute the greater menace to our institutions.[124]

Borah had a good illustration of the political force that could be exercised by members of the military. He related that recently he had criticized the National Guard legislation on the floor of the Senate. In the gallery he noticed a "distinguished gentleman" who was said to be a major-general in one of the state guards. He was also, according to Borah, coordinating the Guard's effort to pass the legislation. The following day he had received telegrams from officers of the Guard and business organizations in his own "far-away state" of Idaho. Since some of his criticisms of the increased funding to be provided to the Guard dealt how efficient the Guard was, he thought it relevant to enter into the record some reports of the efficiency of the major-general's home state national guard units. One such report cited "The carelessness about records, the lack of protection of property against fire and theft, the poor condition of the rifles, unsatisfactory storage of public property, shortage of equipment, and the rating in instruction, which is poor to fair, mark this organization as unworthy of further Federal recognition." There were several such reports about conditions in the Florida National Guard and many other states too, Borah claimed. He considered the situation enough to merit reconsideration of federalizing the National Guard, if not outright rejection of the idea.[125]

The Clamor of the Jingoes

Congressman Rufus Hardy of Texas was also concerned about increased expenditures for the military. In August 1916 the House was discussing military expenditures, in particular requests for authorizing the construction of new battleships. He noted that military expenditures were rising consider-

[123] Senator William E. Borah, *Modern Militarism*, Washington D.C., Government Printing office, 1916, 13.
[124] Ibid., 17.
[125] Ibid., 20.

ably every year, while Germany and England were constantly sinking each other's ships. Why our increased spending? We were friendly with all nations, so who was behind the push for a military buildup?

> The truth is that like water wearing away the stone, the agitation and clamor of the jingoes like. Roosevelt, of the militarists who believe that an occasional war is good for the world, of the big Navy people, the Navy Board, as you call it, of the Navy League, of the munition makers, of those seeking aggrandizement and preferment or profits continually, like rising storms driving the waves into a fury; all this has undermined our common sense and judgment and drives us on to gigantic and fateful military preparations. It is not the Republican Party, nor the Democratic Party, nor the administration that has made this bill. It is the hysteria whipped into fury and sustained by the propaganda of the militarists, the jingoes, and the self-interested munition makers of this country. [Applause.][126]

Expenditures such as we were now making could not be supported by taxation, Congressman Hardy continued. It would be necessary to mortgage our future through the sale of bonds "to support a system and spirit of militarism." The money thus raised would support a military class that produced nothing, paid no taxes and spent most of its time performing the "light duties of making reports and signing balance sheets." At age "62 or 64" these drones would retire, to be supported the rest of their lives by pensions provided by the taxes of working Americans "...who labored strenuously during a long life and who must still follow their trade until the working tools fall from the feeble hands of age."

And, the lives of the military elite might be comfortable, but the lives of soldiers were not. They were subject to a harsh discipline enforced by military courts. An abused employee might lose his temper and strike a boss, for which he could go to jail for 10 days. A soldier who struck a superior, on the other hand, could go to a military prison for five years, and might well not survive the harsh conditions there. In short, "There is no evading the truth that a mighty standing army, with the officials that command it, as a separate institution in this country, means the division of our citizenship into civil and military castes, just exactly what it has done in other countries. Americanism and militarism cannot walk hand in hand."[127]

Congressman Hardy wanted it known that he considered himself a pacifist but was not a peace at any price man. He did not think most pacifists were. Most pacifists were, however anti-war. They believed that while wars

[126] *Congressional Record, Proceedings and Debates of the Congress*, vol. 53, part 13, 1916, 12672.
[127] Ibid., 12673.

had always occurred in the past, they might be avoided in the future. "The pessimist, the jingo, the militarist and the war trafficker say no such means will ever be found." He saw some hope in history; practices such as slavery, polygamy and the "code duello" were dying out. Could not war, more destructive and senseless than these barbarities, also fade away? Hardy speculated that a union between the nations of Europe, similar to the United States, could be a method of ending the wars between them.[128]

Congressman Charles Kearns (R-OH,) joined Congressman Hardy in declaring his pacifism, but of a different sort. He too abhorred war, but saw it as the way of the world. There were other pacifists, not like him, who saw danger in a much larger army and navy. Most of these people, however, had seen no danger of war in Europe before August 1914 and still thought that America was not in danger. They had a poor track record, Kearns thought, but he was not willing to predict the future. Though pacifist, he was

> ...a pacifist who is unalterably in favor of a preparedness that will make the world afraid; not that we may have war, but that we may have peace. There is no danger of the development of a military spirit in America. Militarism can only live and grow and develop in a country that is overcrowded in population and poor in natural resources. Although such a nation may have wealth, yet is she impoverished. In her desire to find homes for her overcrowded population and markets for her surplus products, she must acquire other territory, and she must force her way into foreign markets.[129]

This seems to make living space a need that would justify war, but perhaps Kearns was seeking understanding of others rather than justification for aggression.

The campaign began in earnest after Labor Day. Both parties' platforms stated they were in favor of preparedness. There were differences in emphasis, but they were not major. Candidate Hughes went to bed thinking he was President-elect Hughes, but woke to find out he had lost California (then usually a Republican state) and thus the presidency. The election was close, however, and recounts were necessary in many states. It was not until December that Hughes finally conceded.

Early in 1917 things were relatively quiet internationally for the United States. Germany was holding to the Sussex Pledge and the expedition to Mexico continued to pursue Pancho Villa with no result. President Wilson had made more efforts to mediate an end to or at least a cease-fire in the war, but these had been declined by all parties unless various preconditions were

[128] Ibid.
[129] Ibid.

met. Late in January, however the Germans announced the resumption of unrestricted submarine warfare. In reply Wilson directed the breaking-off of diplomatic relations on February 7, 1917. Germany did not reconsider, as Wilson had hoped and had given them time to do. Consequently, the President asked for a declaration of war on April 2, 1917. By April 6 the declaration had passed the Senate by a vote of 82 to 6 and the House by 373 to 50. The President signed it that day.

Now that the nation was at war the armed services had to be expanded immediately. A bill to do so was reported out of a House committee on April 21. It provided for a two-step process. There would be an initial period for volunteering. Then, if enough volunteers were not enlisted to meet the Army's new requirements, a "selective draft" would come into effect and conscripts would complete and maintain the Army's expansion.[130] All of America's previous wars had been fought by volunteers. The lone exception was the Civil War. The Confederacy passed a conscription act in April 1862; the Union introduced conscription a year later.

The committee's Republican minority issued a report highly critical of the bill. The minority's spokesman, Congressman Julius Kahn of San Francisco, referred to a letter sent to him by Secretary of War Newton Baker. Baker wanted conscription to begin immediately. He thought that this was more orderly and fair. Everyone would have to register and would be told their status—if they would be inducted and when this would occur. He stated that relying on volunteers under modern conditions had been proven to be problematic. It caused divisions and resentments among the people and in the army. In the current war volunteering was not enough to sustain European nations' needs for soldiers. In all likelihood a voluntary system would fail us too, so we should begin with a draft rather than be forced into it. The Secretary wanted to make it clear that he had

> ...no alarm on the subject of militarism in America, and particularly no alarm of any such consequence from the pending measure, temporary as it is and designed for this emergency. Militarism is a philosophy; it is the designation given to a selfish or ambitious political system which uses arms as a means of accomplishing its objects. The mobilization and arming of a democracy in the defense of the principles upon which it is founded and in vindication of the common rights of men in the world is an entirely different thing..."[131]

[130] "Quotes Baker's Plea for Selective Draft," *New York Times*, April 22, 1917, 2.
[131] Ibid.

Over in the Senate, Senator Frank Kellogg (R, MN) agreed with Secretary Baker that there was no need to fear the selective draft: "I deny that this will create a large standing army or encourage militarism. Teaching young men how to defend their country does not make for militarism—it has not done so in France, Switzerland or other nations where military service is obligatory and universal." Another Senator had some statistics on volunteering for service since the declaration of war. He declared that the Army as of April 1 needed 183,898 new recruits. Since April 1 25,842 had joined. At this rate it would take five months to get the Army to full strength. The National Guard and the Army were also to be expanded by the legislation about to be enacted. Clearly, said the Senator, volunteering was not nearly enough.[132]

The Duke of Conscription

There were those in the Congress who did not agree that there was no connection between conscription and militarism. One such was Congressman Thomas (D, KY.) He stated that he believed the Army General Staff and the War College intended to get control of the country. If they did, and a military oligarchy ruled the nation, perhaps hereditary titles would be devised and conferred. Then,

> Should such new order of things obtain, the gentleman from California (Mr. Kahn) will be entitled to first honors and should be created a nobleman with the title of the Duke of Conscription. [Applause.] Without jesting, gentlemen, such a state of affairs is far from an improbable fancy. Unless the people of this country call a halt on militarism, such a state of affairs is by no means impossible. If militarism comes in full force it comes to stay. Never in the history of the world has military power once obtained been relinquished...You may say what you please about it but I know it and you know it. From militarism we may pass to food control [rationing] and next a commission may be appointed to direct just what occupation each citizen must pursue, and finally if things go on as they are now going our individual liberty may become a thing of mournful memory.[133]

Those who thought that conscription should begin after volunteering did not fill the ranks had their say, but they did not have the votes. The bill to establish a two-step process of volunteering and then conscripting went nowhere. The Selective Draft Act passed the House by 398 to 24 votes and the Senate by 81 to 8. After the conference committee finalized the Act it was sent to President Wilson who signed it on May 18, 1917.

[132] "Congress Votes on Draft Bill Today." *New York Times,* April 28, 1917, 1.
[133] *Congressional Record: proceedings and debates,* vol. 55 pt. 2, 1917, 1222.

Opportunistic Plutocrats

Some opponents of preparedness had not been pacifists, but were opposed to what they saw as unnecessary wars. Others, such as Scott Nearing (1883–1983) were opposed to all wars. Nearing, an economist and Socialist Party member published two pamphlets in 1917 outlining his analysis of why the war came about and what part militarism played in it. In *The Great Madness* he wrote that it was fear of war and invasion, stoked by the "plutocrats" of America that was behind the preparedness campaign. These plutocrats were interested in the profits to be made by war industries, not in protecting America, its citizens or its honor. The focus of the campaign was kept on military intervention in Mexico, but "...when the unwillingness of the Mexicans to fight made the manufacture of jingoistic propaganda impossible in that quarter, the advocates of 'national defense' turned to Germany as offering the greatest opportunities."[134]

Nearing explained what these opportunities were. They were not for defending democracy, as the President had claimed in his war message. Quite the opposite:

> Why did the American plutocracy desire to crush Germany? Was it to destroy despotism there? The idea is preposterous. The despotism in any bank, factory or railroad of the United States is more complete than that of the Kaiser. The American plutocracy has fattened on despotism for generations. The American plutocracy was no more interested in establishing democracy in Germany than they were in establishing democracy in the United States. They did want to see German industry crushed, however, and since the Kaiser and his group represented German business in its most highly developed form, the Kaiser was the object of their wrath.[135]

Most observers, though, believed the governing systems of Germany and America to be quite different. A thought experiment proposed by a writer for the *Independent* weekly demonstrated the difference. Suppose one read in the newspaper headlines like "Kaiser Consults Hindenburg on New Peace Offer" or "Ludendorff and von Tirpitz Demand Chancellor's Resignation." Such headlines may or may not have turned out to be true, but no one should have been startled by them. However, suppose you opened your paper one morning and saw headlines such as "Foch tells French President Not to Ask for Alsace-Lorraine," or "Pershing Insists that Wilson Dissolve Congress and Declare War on Lapland?"

---

[134] Scott Nearing, *The Great Madness*, New York, Rand School of Social Science, 1917, 8.
[135] Ibid., 36.

> Then, and only then could you say that we and the Allies had succumbed to 'Prussian Militarism.' Militarism does not mean having an army, or liking an army, or even being too fond of an army. It means being ruled by an army; that, and nothing else. ..'Militarism' isn't just a word to throw at your enemy. It means something definite. It means something that Germany has and that England, France and the United States have not.[136]

Though some pacifists and socialists continued their opposition to America's participation in the war, they were few. There was no great enthusiasm for the war, but the Wilson Administration took no chances, wielding carrots and sticks with considerable efficiency. The largest carrot was the Committee on Public Information, often known as the Creel Committee after its head, journalist George Creel (1876–1953.) It actively encouraged support of the war through newspapers, pamphlets, books, films and a 75,000-member speakers' bureau. The speakers were known as "four-minute men," being trained to give a talk of that approximate length, as to what the war was about and why it should be supported. They would then invite and answer questions. It's not recorded that they met with much, if any, hostility.

Anyone who went public with opposition to the war could come within range of one of the Wilson Administration's biggest sticks, the Espionage Act, passed in June 1917. In May 1918 the Sedition Act amendments were added, greatly broadening the areas in which dissent could be suppressed. Criticism of American participation in the war was much muted where it existed at all and was never an obstacle to a vigorous prosecution of the war.

Conscription produced an American army of 2.4 million men; about 1 million served in France.

US units did not begin major campaigning until July 1918 and suffered their heaviest casualties during the Meuse-Argonne offensive in September and October of that year. The addition of fresh American troops was a factor in ending the war in 1918. The armies of the Central Powers deteriorated rapidly in the summer of 1918 and Germany asked for an armistice on October 4. The cease-fire was negotiated and the guns fell silent on November 11, 1918.

President Wilson traveled to France after the armistice. On December 14, 1918 in Paris he commented on the end of the war and militarism. He agreed with the *Independent* that the Allies were not militarists. Militarism was indeed the curse of the German Empire and it had been defeated. But,

> It is not possible to secure the happiness and prosperity of the world, to establish an enduring peace, unless the repetition of such wrongs is rendered impossible. This has indeed been a people's war. It has been

[136] "Militarism Again," *The Independent*, vol. 95 (August 25, 1918), 3638.

> waged against absolutism and militarism, and these enemies of liberty must from this time forth, be shut out from the cruel possibility of working their cruel will upon mankind. In my judgment it is not sufficient to establish this principle. It is necessary that it should be supported by a cooperation of the nations, which shall be based on fixed and definite covenants, and which shall be made certain of effective action through the instrumentality of a League of Nations.[137]

Making Soldiers

There were celebrations in the streets in some European capitals after declarations of war in 1914. After three years of slaughter on an industrial scale the government of the United States didn't expect the declaration of war to be met with cheers and it was not. It was obvious not enough men would volunteer to build the mass army needed for modern warfare. Conscription would be essential.

The only experience that the U.S. Army had with conscription was during the Civil War and it was not a happy one. Resistance was widespread, most notably the 1863 draft riots in New York City, which required thousands of federal troops to put down. However, in the end only about ten percent of the Union Army was conscripted; the rest were volunteers. The Wilson Administration was well aware that the army they were building would not be ninety percent volunteer. In order to forestall resistance words like draft and conscription were not used in 1917; the machinery was called the Selective Service Administration. Registering for the draft was widely publicized as the duty of patriotic men, and registrants on the first day, June 5, 1917, were greeted with bands playing and the applause of officials. In the end it was a big success. By Armistice Day the Army would total almost four million men, seventy-two percent of them conscripts.[138]

Manly Fighting Strength

According to a writer for *Harper's Monthly Magazine*, it was those who were rejected by the Army who were concerned about their future, not those who were accepted. This was due to the fighting spirit of American men, which knew few bounds. Men who claimed exemptions because they were the sole support of their families often changed their minds and clamored to join. Partly, this was because women were more independent and bet-

[137] "Text of the President's Two Speeches in Paris, Stating his View of the Bases of a Lasting Peace",, *New York Times*, December 15, 1918, 1.

[138] Jennifer D. Keene, *Doughboys, the Great War, and the Remaking of America*, Baltimore, Johns Hopkins University Press, 2001, 9–10.

ter able to replace their men's earnings. Another reason why some changed their minds was the psychology applied by the draft boards. They would say about a potential draftee that he was too weak or puny to fight well, which would arouse his manly spirit and make him eager to be in the Army:

> "He could never fight, could he?" parleyed the doctors while they examined a short but stocky young man. Fight! Well, he'd show them! He puffed out his chest and stiffened his biceps until the measuring tape was taut with his manly fighting strength. And then when they put a gun in his hand he was a child again with a new toy. He thought he was Uncle Sam's best soldier, had his picture taken, and wanted to use his gun right away.[139]

Scenes like this, which the author claimed were common, showed that mericans were full to the brim with fighting spirit. There was no decrease in martial spirit once men reached training camp, according to reporter Joseph H. O'Dell. Within thirty days of arriving at camp men were transformed into an "obedient and cheerful army." Some of the men O'Dell talked to were indeed upbeat, almost maniacally so:

> At Camp Devens three men...revealed their minds to me, without reserve.
>
> "We are moving next week to one of the Southern cantonments." I congratulated them, telling them of the warm climate, the blue skies and the beautiful scenery. To my surprise, they were in a mood of resentment. "But we don't want to go. It's awfully cold here and no heat in the barracks, but we like it. We know our way around, we have lots of pals in the camp, the Y always has something good going on, the officers are white ["white" as in "that's white of you," obsolete racist slang meaning decent]. Why can't they let us stay?"

From the viewpoint of 100 years later this seems like a put-on, but perhaps the soldiers were as humorless as the reporter seems to be. O'Dell believed that among the most important reasons for this miraculous change was that the men appreciated the Army's looking out for them, trying to regularize and improve every aspect of their care. Forty percent of them, he claimed, had no one to care for them so well since they were babies. Another aspect of this care was the removal of the temptations of saloon and bordello, which was accomplished around the camps that sprung up across the country. It was not only the Army which accomplished miracles. It was due to surrounding communities which welcomed new soldiers and showed

[139] Elizabeth Miner King, "Has America the Fighting Spirit?", *Harper's Monthly Magazine*, 137:819 (Aug. 1918,) 354.

them the hospitality of their homes, social organizations, and churches. This was thought to be an antidote to militarism, which, O'Dell seemed to think, would fester in men isolated from civilian life.[140]

During the war there were differences of opinion in the Army on how to handle the masses of recruits. Older, more traditional officers wanted traditional Army forms and customs strictly followed. Younger officers, influenced by Progressive ideology, were open to using different methods of maintaining order and getting obedience to commands. Some of these officers worked in the new Morale Division of the Army's Intelligence branch. They lobbied for using new methods of management and scientific psychology in training and controlling recruits, so as to encourage the enthusiasm of draftees and recruits.[141]

Though the discipline and submersion of the individual was resented, the vast majority of American soldiers did as they were ordered and went forward to face the storm of steel in the summer and fall of 1918. Their illusions had not been rasped away by four years of suffering, enemy resistance was weakening and the end was in sight. Their views of the war as a glorious adventure and the high point of their lives are well documented in the letters and memoirs written during and after the war. Historian David Kennedy wrote that "What strikes the reader of these personal war records is their unflaggingly positive, even enthusiastic tone."[142] Disillusion would come later, and not for everyone.

Ten days after the Armistice C.W. Barron of the *Wall Street Journal* wrote about the qualities of American troops. They were "bigger, fresher, and sturdier than any troops left in the war-wearied nations...the finest troops I had ever seen. With manly step and high head they swung along and sang as they marched into that hell-gassed area of France." Barron was moved to quote from a popular song of 1918, "The Americans Come." The song was supposed to tell of a young French boy describing American troops to his blind father:

> There are men, my father, brown and strong,
> And they carry a banner of wondrous hue;
> With a mighty tread they swing along,
> Now I see white stars on a field of blue!
> And never has spring thrust such blades
> Against the light of dawn,
> As yonder waving stalks of steel

[140] Joseph H. O'Dell, "The New Spirit of the New Army, the Miracle of Democracy," *Outlook*, Jan. 23, 1918, 140.
[141] Keene, *Doughboys*, 14.
[142] Kennedy, *Over Here*, 212.

That move so shining on
And God is in his judgment seat,
And Christ is on his tree,
And Pershing's men are marching,
Marching into Picardy.

The appearance and high spirits of American troops was impressive to all, including the Germans. Beyond appearances, Barron gave his reasons why the war was won. The Germans were not, he wrote, a nation of inventors and creators—they developed the creations of others. This was true of the weapons of war; most of them (e.g. the airplane, submarine, and machine gun) were invented by Americans. The Germans perfected their war machine for more than 40 years, waiting for the right moment to use it to achieve world domination. Britain and France, however, had survived the onslaught by discovering and making use of two discoveries, one of which the Americans used to bring about the final victory. Both discoveries were about individuals. The first was that individuals, by digging trenches and resisting fiercely, could stop the powerful German war machine. The second was even more important:

> The great discovery of the war is this: we have found that we can make a citizen a soldier with thirteen weeks of training...The American Army is nowhere outranked in organization, discipline, form and military etiquette. Indeed, the British officers told me they were surprising sticklers for military red tape and prompt salutes in recognition of place and authority. Even an Alabama negro, repairing a French highway, will straighten up and give a salute that in reach, grace and precision that cannot be matched by any white soldier in Europe.[143]

The American soldier had advantages that soldiers of other nations may not have had. They were probably better-read, since the American Library Association had worked to put a book into the hands of every soldier and sailor and to establish small libraries in every camp and every ship. The educational effort extended to providing theater performances, movies, and coaches for drama and athletics—particularly boxing.

As far as the returning soldier and whether or not the war had made a militarist of him, Fiorello La Guardia was convinced it had not. La Guardia (1882–1947) was an Italian-American politician and reform leader who interrupted his service in the House of Representatives to volunteer for the army. He served as a bomber pilot on the Italian front, returned to Congress after the war and was a famously active and popular mayor of New York from

[143] C.W. Barron, "War Finance," *Wall Street Journal*, Nov. 21, 1918, 1-2.

1934 to 1945. He stated in an interview that veterans who had seen war were not anxious to repeat their experiences and further that service in the AEF should not give any man an advantage in running for political office. Americans wanted to return to peaceful pursuits: "They know that the people's army won this war. The soldiers know that no force of professional soldiers could have won it...Having won the war the thing to do is to forget military organization and return to the normal peaceful life...We do not perpetuate a military caste for political purposes." He went further by saying he had refused office in the American Legion, because he did not want to trade on his military record and had insisted that the Congressional charter of the Legion provide that it would not be involved in politics.[144]

For careers other than politics, some thought the war experience would be very valuable. The *Los Angeles Times* quoted an expert on the subject, a Major Reynolds who was in charge of helping Chicago-area veterans find jobs: "Military training has been an incalculable blessing to our men. Employers everywhere tell the same story. The man who comes from the army or navy has acquired initiative, responsibility and a sense of loyalty that are going to bear fruit in the way of business success." Reynolds told a reporter that this was especially true of ex-officers, so much so that a Washington, D.C. office had been established to help them locate jobs that would be fitted to their increased capabilities. He felt it would be unreasonable to expect men who had been "magnificently developed mentally and physically...to go back to his old job or anything like it."[145] The *New York Times* had a somewhat different view. It quoted General Anson Mills, an 85-year old retired veteran of long army service, who had good success in the army and in business, that "business opportunities tempted officers of the regular establishment to leave the service in 1865. Most of those who resigned failed to prosper in civilian pursuits...he had observed that good soldiers, as a rule, did not make good businessmen." Mills urged those who felt inclined to a career of patriotic service to put up with the frustrations of low pay and slow promotions, even though "The people forget their heroes, the army suggests militarism.[146]

Intellectual Flotsam and Jetsam

Whether a man stayed or left, there would be a period of adjustment. George Boas, himself apparently an academic, wrote about how a young professor of English, George Fort, was feeling about his return to a university in California. According to Boas, Fort was dreading it. It was variously "death...

144 William L. Chenery, "Soldier Candidates," *New York Times*, Sept. 7, 1919, 43.
145 "Military Training Adds to Efficiency," *Los Angeles Times*, June 13, 1919, 11.
146 "Staying in the Army," *New York Times*, Sept. 28, 1919, X.

the world of phantoms...a position in which he was nothing in particular...a mode of life in which the flotsam and jetsam of intellectual life alone count." The flotsam and jetsam comment is typical of the article, which seems impassioned and sincere, but at times confused. In one sentence Boas writes that Fort "still believes in the supreme importance of intellectual values;" two sentences later "He is not an intellectual and loathes those men who pretend to be." So will Fort return to academia? He might, if the university would eliminate "that which makes for the suicide of knowledge and foster that which makes for its advancement."

The crux of the matter seems to be what Boas saw as a lack of discipline and order in civilian life in general and academia in particular. He contrasts this with the Army, where a man like Fort would go from supervising the building of mess halls to being a Zone Major, to service on a Provost Court, to organizing military government in Germany. He was never asked whether he was fitted for a particular job but merely told to go do it and understood that he would be cashiered if he failed. As a sort of capper to all this, Fort was told by a brigade adjutant that he was "the most hard-boiled guy he had ever seen." It was likely true that going back to try to attract students to your freshman English courses would be very weak sauce after the experience of wartime service in France.

Still, it is hard to see exactly what Boas was trying to say. He seemed to think that discipline Army-style would cure excessive intellectualizing and the wrong kind of intellectual endeavor, whatever these may be. How an Army model would be beneficial for a university, one of whose basic principles is free inquiry, was not elaborated. In describing his own experiences, he wrote of observing American walking wounded coming back from the front. A shell landed among them and a wounded soldier was killed. His buddy stood up after having been knocked down by the explosion, shook his fist in the direction of the Germans and shouted "You bastards!" Boas thought that the "philosophy implied in that doughboy's denunciation is, I think, the philosophy of every thoughtful person who has survived the A.E.F. And when those persons happen to be well-enough read to make articulate their philosophy they will speak as George Fort has spoken and as a score of us have spoken. They will tackle everything except jobs that are too small."[147]

Besides being good preparation for civilian pursuits, the victory was seen as a triumph over militarism. Frank Cobb, editor of the New York *World*, wrote on November 12 that "The disciplined forces of militarism yield at every point to the hurriedly assembled hosts of democracy," and the Armistice was "A peace of peoples" from which "militarism is stripped bare." President

[147] George Boas, "The Professor and the Army," *New York Times*, Oct. 5, 1919, 46.

Wilson had called for the defeat of militarism, nationalism and imperialism in his Fourteen Points of January 1918, and it seemed as though it might happen.[148] This was by no means certain. General Tasker H. Bliss of the American Army, in a letter to Secretary of War Baker written shortly before November feared it would not: "Judging from the spirit which seems more and more to animate our European Allies, I am beginning to despair that the war will accomplish much more than the abolition of *German* militarism while leaving *European* militarism as rampant as ever. I am one of those who believe that the absolute destruction of all militarism under any of its evil forms is the only corner stone of any League." General Bliss thus declared himself to be an opponent of militarism, but he was not an opponent of the Army. He believed that we needed a larger army than we had before the war, but just how large were necessary and what Congress would approve—and then fund—turned out to be three different and debatable things.[149]

A Revolting Idea

Dr. Charles W. Eliot, President Emeritus of Harvard, also believed that we needed a bigger army in the future, but his analysis disparaged the need for professional soldiers like General Bliss. He wrote that Americans should not want to be paid to be soldiers, but should see military service in time of emergency as a sacred duty of citizenship: "Considering what the modern soldier has to do and bear in trench warfare, in bayonet and hand grenade assaults, and in bombing towns and cities from the air, the idea of a man doing it for pay is absolutely revolting." The high-minded citizen soldier of Dr. Eliot's imagination would have expected that the government would take care of his family while he was absent or if he was killed. They would have to step in if he was disabled while serving. But since "He imbibes while in training or in service no particle of militaristic spirit, but on the contrary learns to condemn it," he would want no pay for doing his duty.

A partial model for what Eliot had in mind was the National Army of draftees called up to fight the war. This group was both national and democratic, as the National Guard and the Regular Army were not. The Guard was more democratic than the Regular Army, but it was recruited locally, not nationally. The Regular Army was recruited nationally, but was undemocratic. It was modeled on the British Army, which was "aristocratic in structure and habits." We should have three months of military training for all young men at ages nineteen or twenty and those who proved to be the

[148] Arthur A. Ekirch, Jr., *The Civilian and the Military*, New York, Oxford University Press, 1956, 195.
[149] Ibid., 196.

most competent during this training should be the officers and non-commissioned officers of this army-in-waiting for the next emergency. Eliot believed that the war experience had shown that it did not take long for an effective force to be fielded in this manner. Somewhat paradoxically for someone who opposed any "particle of militaristic spirit," he also praised the "elements of military training and discipline [that] have had a high value for the physique and morale of those young men. These values should be obtained in permanence for the American population."

Dr. Eliot thought a further benefit could accrue from the wartime experience. He claimed that it was now understood that the "best modern soldier is the free man who has learned the value of cooperative discipline." If industrial workers would learn and apply the same brand of cooperative discipline in the factory, then there would be no need for "industrial warfare." He does not indicate who would be teaching the discipline, but it was probably not the unions.[150]

According to a correspondent of *Outlook* magazine, US Army discipline needed a complete overhaul and at least two million men (approximately the number of men who had arrived in France prior to the Armistice) would agree. The discipline administered by the officers of the Regular Army was "a barbarous system which is based upon terrorism and contains many of the features of the Prussian military system...Brutality, arrogance and snobbery should be discouraged by severe punishments and all commissions should be given only to men duly qualified who have seen service in the ranks." This last requirement was one which Dr. Eliot of Harvard approved, but he made no suggestions about forbidding arrogance and snobbery. The author of the letter to *Outlook*, a Mr. Harry W. Palmer, was an early exponent of the idea that government, including the army, should be run like a business. He gave no specifics beyond a "General Staff devoid of ornament but fully equipped with all that makes any business efficient today."[151]

Conclusions: Peace to War to Peace

It was easy in early 1916 to think of American participation in the war in Europe as some distant possibility. The position of the President was clear enough. Early on he made it clear that he was in essential agreement with those who favored universal military training. As usual with supporters of UMT he highlighted what he saw as its general benefits—it would make young men better able to contribute to the nation's economy as well as to its defense.

[150] Dr. Charles W. Eliot, "Our Future Army," *New York Times*, Jan. 5, 1919, 30.
[151] Harry W. Palmer, "Making Over the Army, a Reader's View," *Outlook*, Sept. 10, 1919, 63.

One of the reasons war seemed so far off was that no one could quite envisage how it would come about. S. Stanwood Menken of the National Security League thought our very existence was at stake but did not reveal the nature of the threat or who was making it. Not many, aside from Theodore Roosevelt, could envision our seaports being attacked and troops landed on our shores. The only point of contention for the United States with the belligerents was neutral rights, yet no one seemed to see this as the cause of war—perhaps because if it did cause war it would be a war with Germany that would require Americans to cross an ocean and land on foreign shores. In effect we would be doing the invading and attacking.

And, if war wasn't in defense of our neutral rights, then what was it defending? None other than industrialist Henry Ford claimed it would be in defense of the profits of those who benefitted from production of goods for war—especially the manufacturers of munitions. Other opponents of preparedness, such as Congressman Tavenner, spoke of the profits of the "Wall Street war trust" that they believed were a motive for support of preparedness.

Henry Ford had another reason why he thought it was unnecessary for us to prepare for war. The nations of Europe had been slaughtering each other for two years now and it seemed ludicrous to him that any one of them would be willing or able to put together a force to make war upon us. Congressman Hardy made the same point about our naval expansion plans, that both sides had suffered heavy losses and their fleets were weakened. It was difficult to imagine anyone sailing their navy against us.

Few if any commentators put "American militarism" down as a cause for entry into the conflict. "Prussian militarism" was the major cause of the war, most agreed. The Prussians had a huge army and used it to invade neighboring states. We had a small army and used it only in in self-defense—such as in Pershing's punitive expedition. We had a very large navy and plans for its expansion which would make it the equal of the Royal Navy, but again, this was for self-defense only.

The crowds drawn by speakers for the American Union against Militarism during their 1916 tour of Eastern and Midwestern cities were considerable, but were dwarfed by the numbers participating in and watching the preparedness parades of the spring and summer of 1916. True, some, perhaps many, of the participants were not eager supporters of preparedness. It still seems as though anti-militarism was a minority position and preparedness was not seriously opposed by the mostly silent majority. Democratic and Republican presidential candidates supported it and drew almost 18 million votes between them. Allan Benson, Socialist Party candidate and vocal anti-militarist, drew 590,000 votes. The issue seemed settled by the election. We would continue to prepare. With the U.S. declaration of war five months later the minority anti-militarist position would become a potentially criminal offense.

The experiences of conscription, the training camp and trench warfare would take time to evaluate. The Espionage Act called for draconian punishments for any resistance to the draft and few prosecutions were necessary. It all went smoothly. Press reports of the morale of the conscripts and of the beneficial effects of their training were quite positive in 1918 and early 1919, but anti-militarists regained their voice and began to question military values once again by the end of 1919. They were still in the minority. The facts that America was able to field a million soldiers in France in the summer of 1918 and six months later the victory was won seemed to speak highly of American patriotism and martial spirit. Now, all that would be needed for national security would be a system that would avoid the all-out emergency measures necessary for participation in the Great War. Such a system might include universal military training for young men, which would not only prepare them for active service but make them loyal and industrious citizens. A somewhat larger standing army and a strong navy would also be needed. No militarism there, according to men like Henry West. Entirely militarism and nothing but, according to those who agreed with Charles Hallinan.

Period Photographs

1. Jingo, the anti-preparedness dragon, a papier-mache statue made by the American Union against Militarism. The statue was on display during Union rallies and speaking engagements in 1916 and 1917.

2. President Wilson leading a preparedness parade in 1916. According to the picture title, with the President in the first row are William F. Gude and Randolph Kauffman. C.J. Columbus and Senator (later Senate Majority Leader) Joe Robinson is in the second row. The parade was probably in Washington D.C, in the spring.

3. Unidentified persons at the front of the bomb-damaged house of Attorney General A. Mitchell Palmer on June 2, 1919. Palmer and his wife were home at the time but were not injured. In response Palmer and his young subordinate J. Edgar Hoover ordered the arrest of hundreds of "radical agitators" and prepared to deport them.

4. General Leonard Wood around 1920. Wood had been a tireless advocate of preparedness and continued to speak out for a strong defense after the war. After the death of his close friend Theodore Roosevelt he determined to run for the Republican presidential nomination in 1920. He campaigned in uniform, the only person ever to do so. He arrived at the convention leading in delegates, but Senator Warren Harding emerged as the candidate.

5. Major Theodore Roosevelt Jr. in 1917. Ex-President Roosevelt's son served in WW I and was severely wounded. After the war he was one of the group of young officers who founded the American Legion. He returned to the US Army in WW II and led his regiment ashore on D Day. He died a month later at age 59 of a heart attack.

6. Secretary of State Charles Evans Hughes signing the Washington Arms Limitation Treaty on February 5, 1922, which specified that the US, Great Britain and Japan would limit their numbers of capital ships (battleships and aircraft carriers) to a ratio of 5:5:3. This was one of five agreements signed that day. These agreements limited the arms race and produced a relatively calm period in the Pacific Ocean area.

7. Captain, later Admiral, Dudley Knox around 1918. His 1922 book The Eclipse of American Sea Power was critical of the Washington Treaty. Knox believed that only America truly wanted peace—he believed Great Britain and japan were interested mainly in saving money. America was also at a disadvantage because its naval officers were politically constrained and not free to speak their minds.

8. This February 1924 issue of *LIFE* magazine spoofed militarism by running a contest in which readers were urged to submit their ideas for bigger and better wars.

9. September 12, 1924, in Washington D.C. A typed title for this photo reads, "The U.S. Army Band, in their new uniforms, leading the Defense Day parade down historic Pennsylvania Avenue in the National Capital."

10. President Coolidge views the Mobilization Day parade. Civilian marchers pass in review, escorted by Army officers. In the front row, left to right, Secretary of War John Weeks, President Coolidge, Mrs. Coolidge, General Pershing and an unknown Army officer.

11. Secretary of War John Weeks addressing a crowd after the parade. That evening he introduced a 90-minute radio program about national defense readiness. This was the first live nationwide broadcast, carried on radio stations from New York to California.

PHOTO CREDITS:

Image #1 of Jingo, the anti-preparedness dinosaur, is from the April 1, 1916 issue of *The Survey* magazine.

Image #8, "We Want More and Bigger Wars," was the February 21, 1924 cover of *LIFE* magazine.

All the other photos are from the Library of Congress.

3. Who Were the Militarists? 1919–1920

Anyone who thought that the end of the war meant the end of controversy over militarism and universal military training was greatly mistaken. In January 1919, two months after the Armistice, Charles Hallinan of the American Union against Militarism and Henry West of the National Security League debated the issue under the auspices of the Free Religious Society of America. West's remarks, headed "Universal Military Training," began by stating that the war had shown that good faith and righteous conduct would not protect a nation from aggression. He defined citizenship as meaning everything or nothing. Americans enjoyed all the benefits of freedom and prosperity, but they could all be lost if the nation was not strong enough to defend them. Americans must be ever ready to protect "all the privileges and honors" that we enjoyed. A powerful navy was essential, but would never be able to protect our 21,000 miles of coast by itself. This very large coastline figure may have been arrived at by measuring around bays, inlets, estuaries, etc. West did not believe the oceans to be a protection, rather they were "no longer a barrier but a highway" to attack us. Our wealth and prosperity were not advantages either, but invitations to unscrupulous and greedy nations to attack and rob. Our large population was also an advantage that was a weakness, but West did not say how this transformation had happened.[152]

Repugnant to the American Mind

Accepting that we must be ready to defend ourselves, how must we prepare? There was only one way, according to West: universal military training. This was not merely his or the League's opinion. It was "logical and in-

[152] Henry L. West and Charles T, Hallinan, *Universal Military Training*, Washington D.C., American Union against Militarism, 1919, 3.

controvertible" given two propositions. First, the navy alone could not defend us; we needed an army to defeat forces that got past the navy and landed on our shores. Second, we could not have a large, professional standing army because such an army went against national tradition and feeling: "It would represent the idea of militarism, which is repugnant to the American mind. " Given these two premises, only a citizen army provided by universal military training would protect the nation—and avoid the militarism that tends to go with a large regular army. A citizen army has the advantage that it is "purely democratic."[153] By this West meant that everyone, regardless of wealth or class, was required to serve. It would be fair to say that recruitment was intended to be democratic, but historically the wealthy and privileged were able to escape conscription and did not serve in the lower ranks unless they wished to do so. And, no matter what a draftee's background, it is one of the first tasks of a drill sergeant to explain to new soldiers that they no longer live in a democracy.

A proof of the efficacy of a system of universal military training was, once again, Switzerland. Upon the declarations of war in 1914, West noted, the Swiss mobilized 400,000 men within 48 hours as a demonstration of their determination to defend themselves. The Swiss were "...a living refutation of the charge that military training antagonizes good citizenship. The Swiss is, above all things, a free man, and there is no taint of militarism in his nation."[154] As noted earlier, however, there was no attempt to violate Swiss neutrality and no evidence that any of the combatants had any plan or desire to attack Switzerland.

As with other supporters of universal military training, West thought that its benefits went beyond national defense. It would teach young men discipline and improve their physical fitness: "If we are to continue virile as a nation we must elevate our physical standards, and if we are to be a strong-thinking, law-abiding people we must learn the value of self-restraint." It would also improve a young man's "efficiency," "economy," "teamwork," "administrative thoroughness" and "productiveness." Presumably adding all these qualities would make him a better employee. West claimed that universal military training would also be a boon for the immigrant. Like all draftees, he would be brought into a "closer relationship with his Government. "He would learn that the repressive foreign government that he was used to was not the same as the one he was now in a relationship with, a relationship in which he had some rights. With rights come obligations,

[153] Ibid., 4.
[154] Ibid., 5.

though: "divided allegiance" would not be tolerated and a "more thorough acquaintance with the English language" would be necessary.[155]

Charles Hallinan of the American Union against Militarism took the negative position on military training. His submission was entitled "Compulsory Military Training: The Negative." He naturally disagreed on all points. He was particularly scornful of West's description of citizenship as an "everything or nothing" relationship: "There is a well-defined body of thinking, known today as Prussianism, which starts out with precisely the same assumption." West listed first among the things that the government should protect "...the peaceful and orderly conduct of our business," Hallinan claimed that this meant his opponent wanted "...the armed protection and intervention of his country in whatever part of the world he *and his investments* may go."[156]

He cited four bills submitted to Congress since 1914 that dealt with universal military training. He stated that "...I cordially recommend a study of these bills to those good folks who on Sundays solemnly read Dr. Charles W. Eliot on the beauties of the Swiss system I haven't the space to describe those bills in detail, but I want briefly to discuss their major negative characteristic which is that *not one of the four bills* bears the slightest resemblance to the Swiss system."[157] In fact, Hallinan claimed, the closest system to the Swiss that existed was our own National Guard, which the "...the militarists in this country have been ceaselessly traducing for the past four years." He proceeded to outline why they are so similar, noting that the Swiss system had each canton organize and command its military, as each state did its National Guard. When a young man does his "few weeks" of military training he does it with his neighbors, who are also the officers who command their unit. The cantons were jealous of their prerogatives and did not want a "swaggering military caste" to develop. Illustrating this concern, Hallinan noted that the Swiss have a law stating that no officer can have a rank above colonel in peacetime. He further noted that the general heading the army had turned in his commission after the 1918 armistice and reverted to the rank and pay of a colonel. "Fancy General Leonard Wood doing this?"[158] Hallinan thought that the systems proposed in the bills would enact not only military training but military service for all. This was true, since every man trained would be subject to calls to duty in the event of emergencies. This and other features of the bills led him to state that there was no difference between the Prussian model and what was proposed for the United States. This does not seem to

[155] Ibid., 6.
[156] Ibid., 12,
[157] Ibid., 7.
[158] Ibid.

be accurate, but in fact a much larger standing army would be needed just to train all young men and to provide the cadres for units to be activated in time of war. It probably would not be as large as that in the pre-war "Prussian system," but would be much larger than any prior American force. And the active duty and reserves would total at least 6 million men after the system had been operating a while.

Cis-Alpine Camouflage

Hallinan admitted that the bills he was discussing did not call for two years of training, but six months to a year. He predicted, however, that the term would gradually be lengthened. But what if the "militarists" should take to heart all of the objections of American Union against Militarism and determine to really have a system based on the Swiss model? Impossible, Hallinan claimed. The Swiss system had every soldier keep his weapon and ammunition at home. He was certain that the "propertied classes" were not about to let the "working class" have loaded guns handy 24-7: "If we are to have Prussian militarism here, well and good, but let's have an end to this ridiculous cis-Alpine camouflage."[159] His final salvo against West on the topic of the Swiss model accused the National Security League Secretary of totally misrepresenting the value of Switzerland's version of military training in the World War: "No, he knows perfectly well that Switzerland's neutrality was NOT protected by the Swiss Army. He knows that Switzerland was protected from invasion by Germany because the Alps made an invasion an unpromising military undertaking and because a neutral Switzerland at her backdoor was vastly more useful to Germany...Again I say let us bury decently this overworked and specious claim."[160]

Hallinan saw another way in which he thought West's presentation resembled Prussianism. This was his assumption that wars were inevitable in international intercourse. That was the belief of General Friedrich von Bernhardi, a member of the German General Staff during World War I and author of *Germany and the Next War.* Charles Hallinan professed to believe that the negotiations underway in Paris could establish a federal mechanism for the world, through which problems between nations could be settled like problems between states (or cantons) in countries like the United States, Australia or Switzerland. "But if we should listen to our jingo press, if we should begin to mobilize our entire manpower for that "next war" that Leonard Wood harangues the Kansas Legislature about, we would breed distrust of us everywhere, we would be throwing our immense weight in the scales

[159] Ibid., 8.
[160] Ibid., 12.

on the side of the old discredited order of competing armaments, growing vaster and vaster until they toppled once again in a common ruin."[161]

Evidently this debate was conducted via the U.S. Post Office and Henry West was a traveling man. He wrote that the proofs of Charles Hallinan's rebuttal were forwarded to him in Washington, but he had to go to New York and on his arrival there he found he must take a train to Chicago. He had turned the proofs over to Lloyd Taylor, chair of the National Security League's universal military instruction and training committee, hoping that he would be able to rebut. Mr. Taylor was a man of many fewer words than either Henry West or Charles Hallinan: "It is impossible to answer Mr. Hallinan's "argument," it being based entirely on the idea that universal military training is a militaristic proposition." The League didn't think it was. Even so, they were working on a new bill that they thought would address the complaints that Hallinan had made. In the new proposed legislation all young men would be trained, but they would only be in the reserves until age twenty-six, not for twenty years. This active reserve would eventually total about three million men at any one time, but also eventually all males would have had the training. Men would be trained after they turned nineteen:

A very short period of training in the nineteenth year, with practically no thought given to militarism in the years previous to this at school, will never cultivate a militaristic idea in this country. The gathering of all classes in the camps will do much to kill sectionalism and foster Americanism. It is the essence of democracy."

Finally, the parents of millions of young men would appreciate the beneficent effects the training would have on their sons.[162]

Abating of the Militarist Mania

Some of the sons who had served did not seem to view the army as the "essence of democracy." A June 21, 1919 editorial in *The Nation* titled "American Militarism Waning" stated that "Most gratifying are the signs that come from various directions of the abating of the militarist mania in America...our troops have returned from overseas with a stomach-full of soldiering...We meet on every hand returned men who insist that no future emergency could get them into uniform again." The Nation noted an article in the *San Francisco Call* that claimed that veterans of the 77th Division "...were largely opposed to universal military service and parading...we shall not and cannot have universal discipline." From the other side of the country the *New York Tribune* had printed a letter from the publicity director of the National Security

[161] Ibid., 13.
[162] Ibid., 11.

League. In it League observed with alarm that the topic of universal military service was popular with college debaters and supporters of it were losing more than two to one. *The Nation* sarcastically noted a 'touching appeal" by the League to the editor of the *Tribune* to support military expansion. The magazine noted with considerable satisfaction that the "...the stony-hearted editor answers in the headline 'Let the League Do It.' "[163]

Oswald Garrison Villard, editor of *The Nation*, reported from London about a startling development right after the war. The city was full of soldiers who were waiting to be demobilized. These were not only English, but soldiers from units all over the Dominions and the Empire, and they were getting restive. So restive, in fact, that there were demonstrations by soldiers wanting speedy release from the armed forces. This was concerning to Villard: "Everyone who has seen these lorries full of soldiers mutinying in the friendliest and most pacifistic spirit, but still mutinying, and who remembers what troops have done elsewhere when war was ended, asks "what next?"

By "what troops have done elsewhere" Villard most likely meant soldiers' uprisings in postwar Europe, often led by communists. He did not think that the soldiers in London were going to try to overthrow the government. But "More and more evident does it every day become that if the evil of militarism is not promptly removed from the world, civilization will collapse through the spread of violent Bolshevism. It is also becoming apparent that not only militarism must go but also the preparations for militarism and war. The whole hateful business must be done away with."[164] The solution, Villard thought, was the rapid conclusion of a peace treaty based on President Wilson's Fourteen Points, which would help to eliminate war and militarism, mainly through the establishment of a League of Nations.

The conference to negotiate a peace concluding the Great War met in Paris in January 1919. President Wilson fought hardest for the establishment of a League of Nations and was successful in this, though many of the other Points were ignored or given only lip service. The treaty was signed at Versailles on June 21, 1919 and registered by the Secretariat of the League of Nations in October 1919. The U.S. Constitution required that treaties be ratified by the Senate, and the debates over the pact took place in Washington in the autumn of 1919.

Where is the Enemy?

Senator William E. Borah of Idaho was known as a staunch opponent of militarism, yet he also vigorously opposed U.S. membership in the League.

[163] "American Militarism," *The Nation*, vol. 108 (June 21, 1919), 973.
[164] "The Private and the Premier," *The Nation*, vol. 108 (February 1, 1919), 165.

Borah claimed we would have to have a huge army and navy if we were to join the League. He thought that these forces would be necessary for the United States to enforce the peace, under the collective security provisions of the League Covenant. So, League membership was tantamount to "militarism in its most pronounced form." Speaking in the Senate on January 14, 1919, Borah asked, "How are you going to raise your armies to sustain this vast military program of a league based on force? Would the citizens of the United States volunteer to enter the army for the purpose of settling difficulties in the Balkans, for instance?...In other words, we would have conscription in time of peace." That day the Senate was considering a request by the Navy for $600 million to continue its ship building program. Borah had another question to ask: "Where is the enemy?...one is bewildered and somewhat staggered at this juncture, with every enemy we have conquered and practically under our control, at being called upon to appropriate $600,000,000 to build a vast fighting machine."[165]

Borah would continue his opposition to policies that he saw as militaristic throughout his long career in the Senate, which lasted from 1907 to his death in 1940. Born in Illinois in 1865, he moved westwards as a young man, attended the University of Kansas and was admitted to the Kansas bar in 1887. In 1890 he decided to seek his fortune in California. The train trip was more expensive that he anticipated. The young lawyer heard a fellow traveler sing the praises of Boise, Idaho, as a great place for an ambitious man out to rise in the world. Borah left the train there with $16.69 in his pocket. His law practice prospered and he married in 1895. He became active in Republican politics and lost a race for a congressional seat in 1896. He first ran for the US Senate in 1902, but the Idaho legislature (Senators were selected by state legislatures until passage of the 17th amendment in 1913) selected another Republican attorney for the post. In 1907 he won the legislature's approval and went to Washington as the junior Senator. He was a progressive Republican, noted for his oratory and for his independent streak. Borah's nonconformity was well known. Knowing that he took exercise by horseback riding every morning in Washington's Rock Creek Park, President Coolidge claimed this was puzzling: "I'm amazed that he can ride at all. I had always understood that a rider had to go in the same direction as his horse."[166]

Secretary of the Navy Josephus Daniels, speaking at the National Press Club in Washington the next month, stood Borah's argument on its head. He said that if we did *not* join the League "America must build a navy incomparably greater than that of any other nation and must maintain a standing

[165] "Borah Assails League of Nations," *New York Times*, Jan. 15, 1919, 2.
[166] "The Senator who Traveled Alone, " *Milwaukee Journal*, Jan. 25, 1940, 22.

army great enough to defend everything from Tierra del Fuego to Halifax." We had an obligation to avoid that, Daniels said:

> The world looks to us. We cannot, in honor, evade our duty any more than we would have evaded our duty when, on April 6, 1917, we entered the war. We can never go back to the world we left. We are now part of all the world...We are face to face with the most serious problem and question, and that is whether this nation shall secure its own and the peace of the world, or whether we shall become a machine of militarism.[167]

Josephus Daniels and William Borah both favored progressive reforms, but from opposite sides of the aisle. Daniels (1862–1948) was born in North Carolina, where he lived all his life. He was educated at Duke and at the University of North Carolina and was admitted to the bar in 1885, though he never practiced law. He became part owner of some local newspapers and was active in Democratic politics, serving as the state printer of North Carolina 1887–1893 and in the Grover Cleveland Administration as chief clerk of the Interior Department 1893–1895. He bought the *Raleigh News and Observer* in 1894 and was a strong supporter of Woodrow Wilson in 1912. Daniels served as Secretary of the Navy throughout Wilson's presidency. His chief aide was Franklin Delano Roosevelt, who was his Assistant Secretary.

Daniels seems to have had more support for his view of the consequences of League membership than Borah did. The *Los Angeles Times* editorialized in favor of joining, stating that at a recent disarmament meeting in Geneva the discussions

> ...went awry because there was no intelligent understanding of the object of the United States in embarking on a militarist program [the Navy's large shipbuilding plan] when the nations in the League were trying to agree on a general disarmament plan. Some of the delegates to the League Assembly asserted that the United States has become, by reason of the militarist spirit it was displaying, as great a menace to the peace of the world that Germany was in 1918...Repeatedly the *Times* has asserted that this country must either become a member of the League of Nations or be prepared to expend billions of dollars on an army and navy...when one nation arms other nations will adopt the same policy as necessary for self-preservation; and their peoples will hold an undying resentment against the country whose militarist policy forces them to bear such a burden.[168]

[167] "League or Huge Navy is Daniels' View," *New York Times*, Feb. 26, 1919, 2.
[168] "Militarism in the United States," *Los Angeles Times*, Dec. 26, 1920, II4.

Senator Borah's final words in the debate about American participation in the League of Nations came on November 19, 1919. He said he believed the Treaty, with 14 reservations proposed by Senator Henry Cabot Lodge, would pass the Senate. Nevertheless, he remained firmly opposed to the Treaty's passage. Borah thought that the collective security provisions of the Treaty made force the answer to conflicts between nations:

> ...when you shall have committed this Republic to a scheme of world control based upon force, upon the combined military force of the four great nations of the world...We may become one of the four dictators of the world, but we shall no longer be master of our own spirit...we will come in time to declare with our associates that force—force, the creed of the Prussian military oligarchy—is .after all the true foundation upon which all stable governments must rest.[169]

Borah turned out to be wrong about Senate approval of the Treaty. President Wilson refused to agree to the Lodge amendments and instructed his supporters to not vote for them. Though the Treaty with the reservations had support from both sides of the aisle, it was not enough to meet the 2/3 majority for a treaty, so it failed.

A Jealous, Tribal Sensitiveness

Though the debates over the Versailles Treaty were ended, the controversy about universal military training continued. Frederick J. Libby (1874–1970) set up four benefits of universal military training and then did his best to knock them down. The good things developed by military training Libby listed were patriotism, discipline, democracy and physical fitness.

Patriotism of a sort was fostered during the war, but Libby didn't think that in peacetime young men would be so eager to serve. He also thought that wartime patriotism was of the belligerent type: "It is rather a jealous, tribal sensitiveness, an intense nationalism that verges on arrogance." Libby saw true patriotism as concerned with the general welfare of the state and all its citizens, something that citizens displayed every day at their jobs and in their communities: "A brave man will die for his country but he must have many other virtues besides bravery if he will live for it, and it is the sum of these virtues that we may call the twentieth century patriotism."[170]

[169] William E. Borah, *Closing Speech of Hon. William E. Borah on the League of Nations in the Senate of the United States, November 19, 1919*, Washington, Government Printing Office, 1919 pp. 14–15.

[170] Frederick J. Libby, "Military Training in the Making of Men," reprinted by the American Union Against Militarism from *The World Tomorrow*, date unknown, 5-7.

Discipline was taught in the army, but "...as a part of a system of blind obedience resting on brute force which free men everywhere are challenging." It was only good for forcing men to do things the military wanted but the men probably did not—like rising out a trench and churning through mud while meeting a hail of bullets and shells. If this type of obedience was so fine, asked Libby, why not live under it all the time? For the answer to that question he suggested the Belgians be consulted.

What about the fostering of democracy? Supporters of military training claimed that it brought men from all classes and walks of life and thus was a great leveler. Libby did not deny this; in fact he affirmed it, at least as far as men of many different backgrounds being brought together where they will have some interaction. However, the wealthy, educated and upper class men can become officers—those without their advantages are unlikely to do so. And in general, "Only the self-deceived and foolish would look for democracy in the most rigid type of aristocracy known to man." The commander of an army is an autocrat whose word is law and "Below him in descending scale his officer share his absolutism. What place, then, in a military machine is there for democracy?" Finally, the situation in the Army's camps leading up to and during America's entry into the war was unusual. Many volunteer efforts were made to make military training more pleasant. There was also an enthusiasm and spirit of self-sacrifice and sharing that were unlikely to persist once the war was ended.[171]

What about the claims for improving physical health? Specious, wrote Libby. Much, if not most of the physical activity was drill, learning how to march in formation and perform the manual of arms—learn, repeat, repeat and repeat again for hours every day. Very little to no value there, according to Libby and to Dr. Dudley Sargent, director of the Harvard Gymnasium. Dr. Sargent thought military training useless to improve bodies, and team sports much better to improve minds. Libby had a proposal for those who promoted military training as a health measure:

> If it is believed that this important matter of physical health cannot be left to individual initiative but must be assured by another of the rapidly increasing State regulations, would not a great industrial army digging sewers and irrigation ditches instead of trenches, building roads and bridges instead of barbed wire entanglements, and practicing forestry from the scientific rather than the military viewpoint, without the injurious and wasteful military drill, offer all the benefits accruing from army life and at the same time escape its inherent evils?[172]

[171] Ibid., 8–10.
[172] Ibid., 12–14.

A Sudden Love for Spelling

Frank Tannenbaum, who enlisted in the army in the summer of 1918, wrote an article about the effects of military training. He saw as little value in it as Libby did, but from a different viewpoint. The overall effect, as he saw it, was to turn soldiers into children. From this transformation flowed consequences, none of them good:

1. Irresponsibility. "They love to shout, to sing, to gamble, to fight, to get into escapades, to indulge in pleasantries, and take the world, so to speak, as a playhouse and life as a game where the rules are still to be made and where responsibility and laws have no existence."[173]

2. Boredom. "Monotony, constant repetition of the same fact, unending similarity and likeness in experience and labor and environment become the chief factors in the soldier's life as soon as the novelty wears off."[174]

3. Lack of self-expression. Tannenbaum thought that being ordered about and compelled to conform almost all the time made men crave activities where they had a degree of control over what was happening. If the army didn't provide "good and wholesome external influence along moral and educational lines," then soldiers would "find satisfaction in extra-military things generally frowned upon in civilian life." He acknowledged that "welfare organizations" made efforts to meet the needs of soldiers but thought they were ineffective because they failed to make "...the American war effort mean something to the world in a spiritual way. This failure to make provision for the intellectual and spiritual needs of the men left them to their own resources to find an escape from their monotonous world—and find it in some measure they did."[175]

4. Gambling. This was the favorite escape from the routine in the army, and the most popular form was "crap shooting," with poker a close second. Soldiers did not need dice or cards in order to gamble, however: "Men will gamble on who will buy a drink when in the canteen, or as to whether there will be chicken for dinner. Every dogmatic statement is met by a challenge—from the spelling of a word to the day of mustering out, or as to whether it will rain or snow in the morning." Tannenbaum had a personal experience with the pervasiveness of gambling. He was teaching an elementary English class which included spelling. There were participants and also observers in the large tent where the class was given. During an oral spelling contest participants began to bet on who could spell the next word:

[173] Frank Tannenbaum, "Life in an Army Training Camp," reprinted by the American Union against Militarism from *The Dial*, Apr. 5, 1919, 3.
[174] Ibid., 4.
[175] Ibid., 5-7.

In a little while the observers began to bet...The tent was soon filled to overflowing and the game was in full swing. Up to eleven, when taps were sounded, we had an exciting time of it. I have never witnessed so much will and enthusiasm in the learning of spelling. It was a very successful evening, also, for the schoolmaster, in spite of the fact that the rest of the schedule was crowded by this sudden love for spelling. It made the school. It gave it social standing and the teacher an unwonted popularity.

5. Sex. The men were obsessed with sex: "The lack of personal interest, the freedom from care, the absence of the restraint of family and association, the close intimacy of men to the exclusion of women, accentuates the interest of and the craving for woman...It is an expression of physical hunger desiring physical satiation." Tannenbaum wrote that efforts of local authorities to drive "the public woman" from the streets were successful, but their services were still available through the boys that loitered outside the camps. After he brushed one such off he was told, "Look a'here, soldier, I tell you it is clean, fresh and good." Venereal disease was less prevalent in the training camp than it had been in the army in the field, and even less than it was now in some American cities. But this was not due to "greater voluntary abstinence, to higher morality or even to the lack of opportunity for its spreading." It was due to the army's educational, prevention and treatment efforts, all aimed at keeping soldiers healthy and fit for duty.[176]

6. Discipline. Unquestioning obedience and conformity was "...a very great destroyer of values—values cherished in civilian life. Probably the meaning is best illustrated by a remark made by a Sergeant-Major who, upon being discharged and while saying good-bye, turned to me and said "I am very glad to be going home." "And why this great gladness?" I asked. "Well, it darn near makes a criminal of you if you stay in it long enough," was the reply."[177]

Tannenbaum disparaged the work of the "welfare organizations" attempting to attend to the moral fiber of the men in the camps, but those involved in the effort thought it was highly successful. A 1918 book, *Keeping our Fighters Fit for War and After*, introduction by President Wilson, stated that

> Our War and Navy Departments in this war have taken the position that alcohol and the prostitute must be kept absolutely away from the soldier, and where the forces that have been established to take the place of the things they are trying to eliminate do not accomplish their purpose, then the Commissions [each department had a Commission

[176] Ibid., 9–10.
[177] Ibid., 11.

> on Military Training Camp Activities] act in cooperation with various agencies to suppress these evils.[178]

A major effort was made to furnish wholesome activities on military installations. The Young Men's Christian Association (Y.M.C.A.) and to a lesser extent the Knights of Columbus were the major providers. Their volunteers organized and staffed recreation centers where the men could go when off-duty. They could smoke, read magazines and newspapers, play phonograph records or the piano, see movies and relax with friends. For the more serious readers, the American Library Association established libraries in the camps. The Commissions themselves organized athletics, which were

> Less for the purpose of recreation than for developing the fighting instinct and the technic of fighting, yet it makes for mental as well as physical fitness. Best of all, it promotes that 'everlasting teamwork' which will be so great a factor in winning the war. The Commissions have appointed sports directors, which now have military rank, and boxing instructors; and athletics is looked upon as one of the most important factors that prepare men to go into battle... Men are learning to get bumped and not mind it. The quality of persistence is being developed. High school and college men who have played upon football teams and the rest of the comparatively few among our young men who know what it is to be in personal conflict with another man are simply receiving further instruction in something which they have already experienced; but to the vast majority of the men in the army and the navy it is something brand new. To the mountaineer and the farm boy it is particularly a novelty. The contribution of athletics towards the development of an aggressive fighting spirit is tremendous, and the development of this spirit, to say nothing of the purely physical benefit that the men get from the exercise, is a real addition to the military efficiency of those soldiers.[179]

The athletics program of the army was overseen by Dr. Joseph E. Raycroft, a professor of hygiene from Princeton. Dr. Raycroft was quoted as saying

> The sports included in the camp curriculum, such as boxing, foot-ball and other personal contact games, have been selected primarily to prepare the men for the struggle to come, and the value of the training that they have received will be fully realized when they go "over the top"... Boxing has great value in developing in the individual man the sense of confidence and aggressiveness that is generally desirable in a soldier...

[178] Frank Edward Allen, *Keeping our Fighters Fit for War and After*, New York, Century Co., 1918, 15.

[179] Ibid., 42-43.

> [Athletics develop] a group spirit and solidarity in the various units, while it was recently characterized by one of the leading authorities on mental and nervous diseases as one of the most important factors in preventing the occurrence of the condition known as "shell shock." A large proportion of the casualties on the modern battlefield are classified as "shell shock," though less than half of these are due to the immediate effect of concussion from high explosives. A considerable proportion of the men suffer merely from what is called the development of the "anxiety state"— a state which we sometimes call getting stale, and which displays itself in a man in irritability and loss of appetite... They get "jumpy." They do not sleep. They do not eat. Gradually they lose their power to work and are dangerous persons to have about. It is dangerous to entrust them with any responsibilities if they are officers. It is extremely difficult for them to recover from such a state. One of the important factors in the prevention of the development of this condition is the opportunity for, and the habitual participation in, athletic activities.[180]

In the twenty-first century athletics would not be considered a prevention measure for the shell shock Dr. Raycroft described almost 100 years ago. In World War II it was called combat fatigue and now is called post-traumatic stress disorder.

Various types of unarmed combat have long been thought of as good preparation for shooting wars. Dr. Raycroft thought teaching boxing skills was excellent preparation for the battles to come:

> Boxing teaches the manly art of self-control as well as that of self-defense. It also makes better bayonet fighters. Nearly every blow and position has its counterpart in bayoneting. I have seen boxing lessons in camp given to one thousand men all at once, the class being directed by a man on a high stand...I said to an officer standing by, "How many of those men do you suppose have *struck* another man since they were boys?" "Not ten per cent," he answered, and I think he was right. The boxing which these men did in friendly bouts later taught them what personal conflict was. One of these days the quickness and aggressiveness developed in this boxing will be the means of saving their lives... The men learn to be quick on their feet, nor is this merely theoretical. The Canadian troops who have been at the front report that the agility and quickness of eye that have been gained in boxing are a valuable part of the soldier"s equipment.[181]

[180] Ibid., 50.
[181] Ibid.

A Singing Army

"Mass singing" was nearly as enthusiastically supported as boxing by the author of *Keeping our Fighters Fit for War and After*:

> The Commissions are developing mass singing in the army and the navy. It is their purpose to send men to France with the will to sing and the songs to sing. The camps are supplied with song leaders whose training and experience fit them to direct this work, and no one phase of the activities of the Commissions carries with it more inspiration, either for participants or directors.[182]
>
> A singing army is a cheerful one, and, other things being equal, a cheerful army is invincible. Therefore, as a definite part of camp drills it has a distinct military value. Authorities do not lay stress upon it in the military textbooks, but they talk a good deal about morale and esprit de corps, on both of which singing has an immense influence. A well-known officer said that, theoretically, music is a gratuity, a luxury; practically it has proven itself to be a necessity.[183]

Singing has long been recognized as an aid to efficiency, but it remained for the Commissions on Military Training Camp to Activities to develop it in an army and a navy with that end in view. A hundred years ago, when American shipping was paramount on the seven seas, the sailors before the mast sang their chanteys as they pulled on the ropes or tugged at the windlass. Chanteys were regarded as an aid to man power. They might be sentimental or dramatic or ribald—more often than not the words were as ungodly as the men who sang them—but they smacked of the salt sea, they promoted good feeling among the crew and they were an energizing influence. Those days are coming back...the United States Shipping Board Recruiting Service has appointed an Official Chantey Man for our merchant marine to help revive singing among our sailors.

'It is just as essential that the soldiers know how to sing as that they should carry rifles and learn how to shoot them,' said Major General Leonard Wood. 'Singing is one of the things they should all learn. It sounds odd to the ordinary person when you tell him every soldier should be a singer, because the layman cannot reconcile singing with killing. But when you know these boys as I know them, you will realize how much it means to them to sing. There isn't anything in the world, even letters from home that will raise a soldier's spirits like a good, catchy marching tune.'

[182] Ibid., 14.

[183] Ibid., 68.

> Another officer says, "It is the monotony that kills the men off. A man gets tired of drill, tired of doing the same thing in barracks, even tired of getting shot at. We need company leaders to teach the men new songs...Everything that can be devised by the way of wholesome amusement toward breaking up the monotony is a direct help in making better soldiers and keeping standards high."[184]

The cataclysmic nature of the war and its aftermath produced a spate of books and articles about militarism that tried to define its nature, consequences, and possible ways to eliminate it. Some even denied it was a, or the, main problem. Before the Armistice British novelist and playwright Eden Phillpotts (1862–1960) wrote that it was not militarism that had brought Germany her victories, but superior discipline. Phillpotts would have agreed with Napoleon that discipline was the soul of the army, but also saw it as the necessary unifier of the soldier and the home front. In this he thought Europeans were superior to Americans, though he might have altered his thinking when the 1917 mutinies in the French Army became known and the post-armistice revolts in the German armed forces happened. Ours should be a higher discipline than the Prussian, to be sure, but Phillpotts thought "pacifist propaganda" was destructive of the discipline needed to preserve democracy.[185]

War as a Civilizing Agent

The day before Armistice Day the *New York Times* reprinted a column from the *Rochester Post-Express*, with the startling headline "Sees More in War Than its Horrors." The columnist, who called himself Lucian, began thusly:

In the midst of a violent, and perhaps to some extent justifiable crusade against militarism, it may be well to bear in mind that something can be said for war as a civilizing agent, and as an elevating agent, in spite of its horrors. It was not war, as an English publicist has recently pointed out, that "brought death into the world and all our woe." Life kills more than war—and indeed in the end it kills us all, often with long, slow tortures, compared with which the agonies endured in even the most terrible war, are an Elysium. Humor of some kind is sorely needed to make either the pain of living or that of the battlefield even tolerable to the imagination. It is probably the lack of humor that has brutalized the German generals and soldiers.

Lucian continued for several paragraphs in this manner, giving his opinion that only civilized nations were capable of real war. He concluded that

[184] Ibid., 69-70.

[185] Eden Phillpotts, "Discipline and Democracy," *The Living Age*, 11:3861 (Jul. 6, 1918,) 51.

war was a great civilizer and destroyed outmoded practices. It was the duty of every citizen to be a soldier in defense of his country or to defend "any other country."[186]

"Lucian" of Rochester was undoubtedly imitating Lucian of Samosata (c. 120 CE-after 180,) a satirist of Rome. The English publicist would be John Dryden and the "brought death into the world and all our woe" quote is from *Paradise Lost*, so is not very "recent." Whether editors at the *Rochester Post-Express* or the *New York Times* realized the spoofing is unknowable but many more educated people had classical training one hundred years ago than now.

A religious magazine thought that postwar America was in danger: "Only too apparent is the temptation, now that we have conquered militarism, to base security on military preparation." The *Biblical World* observed that "force [is] heralded as a cure for the distemper of men's souls," as a consequence of the Allied victory. It saw dangers from both right and left. "Radicals" were calling for revolutionary change and a paradise of classless society. Conservatives wanted a harsh peace and a bigger role for the military in American society. What was really needed, however, was justice in and between nations. The pursuit of such justice should be led by churches, not armies.[187]

Justice was also on the mind of Will Durant, future author with his wife Ariel of the popular multivolume history *The Story of Civilization*. In a review of a book by a German academic who was an opponent of war and of ideas about the naturalness and inevitability of war, Durant came down on the same side as the professor. He noted that only men and ants make war, so it was hardly natural among the species of the world. A biological argument for the inescapability of war was a cover for the real basic causes, which were more related to economics than biology. Had Germany won the war it would have extended its power over all of Central Europe, irrespective of the wishes of the nations there. The Allies won, however, and now England was about to "add some unwilling colonies to her vast collection...Apparently, if the imperialistic bloc that signed the Pact of London in September 5, 1914 maintains ascendancy in Paris, the nations that have lost this war for democracy and against militarism will have won it, and the nations that have won it will have lost it. The Allies have given freedom to Germany, and seem willing to accept Prussianism in return."[188]

---

[186] Lucian, "Sees More in War Than its Horrors," *New York Times*, Nov. 10, 1918, 82.

[187] "The Moral Perils of Victory," *The Biblical World*, 52:3 (Nov. 1918,) American Periodical Series Online pg. 225.

[188] Will Durant, "The Biology of War," *The Dial*, 66:782 (Jan. 25, 1919,) American Periodical Series Online pg. 84.

Will Durant was hardly euphoric about the victory, but Dr. Alberto Martinez was. Speaking in Buenos Aires on July 4, 1919, Argentina's Director of Statistics spoke glowingly of the prospects for the postwar world, which would be led by the United States of America. He spoke at a "demonstration [that] was organized by a group of Argentineans." This was apparently not the type of demonstration that Americans are most familiar with, since Dr. Martinez heaped praise upon the United States. Without belittling what England and France had done, he stated that no victory would have been achieved had not America entered the war: "America saved Europe, but America's greatest deed is not in having lifted the yoke of militarism, but in having sown ideals of peace, justice and equality in the League of Nations, which assures happiness and welfare to all humanity." A newspaper reported that he said he approved "the American expansion policy, which he described as commercial and not political." The Monroe Doctrine was also supported and the case of American recognition of the independence of Cuba was cited. The USA had helped Cuba free itself from Spain's colonial regime, which was consistent with the Doctrine, though the Platt Amendment and frequent visits in force by US troops were seen by many Cubans as limiting their independence. Dr. Martinez asked for a comparison of American actions in Cuba to German actions under similar conditions. He did not state directly who was to be preferred, thinking it obvious.

The President of China, Hsu Chih Chang, agreed with Dr. Martinez on the importance of the League of Nations for the postwar world, but was more specific in what he wanted. He hoped that "...seeing the calamity militarism has wrought in Europe, the powers will check the inordinate ambitions of militarists in every part of the world." Getting to the heart of the matter, the President stated that China approved of the peace proposals of President Wilson, especially the League of Nations and the "cancellation of the doctrines of spheres of influence and balance of power in Europe and elsewhere." Likely President Hsu saw the collective security arrangements of the League as making the elimination of the spheres of influence and great-power competition in China possible. He also mentioned pressure from abroad to "internationalize" China's railroads and in polite diplomatic terms firmly rejected the idea. Both President Hsu and Dr. Martinez of Argentina thus counted on the League of Nations to maintain a postwar order more favorable to the less powerful; they were to be disappointed.[189]

Munroe Smith, a law professor at Columbia University, had studied in Germany and wrote about the interplay of diplomacy and militarism. His

[189] Carl A. Ackerman, "China's President for Peace League as a Safeguard of his Country," *New York Times*, Jan. 17, 1919, 1.

conclusion, based on his historical researches, was that a nation was militaristic "so far as the views and feelings natural and almost necessary in its army and navy are shared by its civilians, especially those who are able to direct national thought and to create national sentiment."[190] He wrote that it was possible for a nation to have a large army, or universal military training, or be preparing for war and still not be militaristic. The essential element was the ascendancy of military habits of thought. These habits favored attacking first in a crisis and deprived diplomacy of an important resource—time to organize and conduct negotiations.

American historian George Henry Allen admitted, in Volume I of *The Great War*, that he had a "predilection for democracy and an aversion for militarism." In defining militarism he wrote that some observers thought the term could be applied to Russia, which at the beginning of the war had the largest army among the belligerents—or to Great Britain, who spent more on its navy and army combined than Germany did. But neither the size nor cost of a military establishment infallibly indicated militarism. "Thus militarism may be defined as an arrogant, or exclusive, military spirit...There are two ways in which militarism may imperil peace. In the first place, it encourages both in individuals and states an exaggerated sensitiveness, or touchiness, and an artificial conception of honor."

Allen gave three examples of sensitivity and artificiality, two German. First there was the case of army reserve lieutenant Dr. Fritz Feldhaus. In 1905 he was dismissed from service by a military court of honor, because he had not challenged a fellow officer who had insulted him to a duel. He was dismissed even though dueling was illegal and he had already won a lawsuit against the other officer. This caused a furor that reached the Reichstag, and in reply the Prussian Minister of War indicated that he agreed with the court of honor. "It appeared from the minister's remarks that militarism has its own exclusive code of morals; and that in upholding an artificial conception of honor it disregards law and the common consciousness of right."[191]

The second example was the French Army tribunal's decision to convict Captain Alfred Dreyfus of espionage and treason, no matter what was proved or not proved at his trial. The third example was the 1913 Zabern Incident, a "flagrant exhibition of insolent militarism." Zabern, a small city in Alsace, was garrisoned by the German Army. A 20-year old second lieutenant Gunter von Forstner announced to a group of recruits that "...anybody stabbing a Wackes who insulted him would receive a present of ten marks." The term "wackes," meaning literally toad in the local dialect, is employed by the

[190] Munroe Smith. *Militarism and Statecraft*, New York, G.P. Putnam's Sons, 1918, 117.

[191] George Henry Allen, et. al., *The Great War*, Philadelphia, George Barrie Sons, 1916, 288-289.

Alsatians in addressing one another as a term of familiarity or endearment, but they resent this designation as an affront when it is applied to them by outsiders." Zabern was outraged when Lieutenant Forstner's offer became known, and an angry crowd gathered outside the barracks. The commander of the garrison overreacted by ordering the crowd dispersed, many civilians were arrested and held overnight. The arrested included the town mayor. Forstner was given only token punishment and the affair became an issue in the Reichstag. The incident demonstrated the "exaggerated, unnatural conception of military honor propagated by the militaristic tradition." Kaiser Wilhelm II illustrated such a conception when he dedicated a monument in Frankfurt in 1891. "He declared 'We would rather sacrifice our eighteen army corps and our 42,000,000 inhabitants on the field of battle than surrender a single stone of what my father and Prince Frederick Charles gained' "[192]

The above examples of an exaggerated conception of military honor were the first way in which Allen thought peace could be imperiled. The second was the professionalization of military force. It had been built into a mighty machine, and the military officers who controlled it insisted upon their prerogatives—the most important of which was speed. The insistence on speed of mobilization, and the claim that once begun it could not be stopped, lest an enemy take a crucial advantage, contributed to the likelihood of war.[193]

The Red Flower of War

J.A. Hobson, an English economist and social theorist, went deeper in his analysis. He used a botanical analogy, calling militarism a plant which had red flower of war. The flowers in turn produced seeds, the seeds of future wars.[194] Militarism itself was the expression of the will to power, which Hobson saw as a tendency in all human beings and social structures, including of course governments, which always have the option of applying force to their own citizens. The stronger states can apply force to the weaker. This will to power has its positive side, which Hobson called creative. He used the example of a parent, who uses her power over her children to nurture and educate them to be contributing members of society. Some parents, however, merely exercise their power to dominate and compel obedience.

True to his training as an economist, Hobson thought that the major influences on the will to power and militarism were economic. Capitalism provided the foundation for supplying and equipping large standing armies; without the wealth it generated such establishments would be impossible:

[192] Ibid., 290-291
[193] Ibid., 293
[194] J.A. Hobson, *Democracy after the War*, New York, Macmillan Company, 1918, 16.

> The system of capitalism, as the repository and the organ of personal and class power, in every field of human activity, is seen to be historically connected with the growth of modern militarism. There arises a presumption that capitalism needs and utilizes militarism, the particular outlet for power which militarism furnishes being connected with the broader and more various domination that capitalism represents.[195]

Another English academic, economic historian R.H. Tawney was interested in what he saw as the similarities between capitalism and militarism. He described militarism as

> ...the characteristic, not of an army, but of a society. Its essence is not any particular quality or scale of military preparation, but a state of mind, which, in its concentration on one particular element in social life, ends finally by exalting it until it becomes the arbiter of all the rest. The purpose for which military forces exist is forgotten. They are thought to stand by their own right and need no justification. Instead of being regarded as an instrument which is necessary in an imperfect world, they are elevated into an object of superstitious veneration, as though the world would be a poor insipid place without them, so that political institutions and social arrangements and intellect and morality and religion are crushed into a mold made to fit one activity, which in a sane society is a subordinate activity, like the police, or the maintenance of prisons, or the cleansing of sewers, but which in a militarist state is a kind of mystical epitome of society itself...It is the prostration of men's souls before, and the laceration of their bodies to appease, an idol. What they do not see is that their reverence for economic activity and industry and what is called business is also fetish worship and that in their devotion to that idol they torture themselves as needlessly and indulge in the same meaningless antics as the Prussians did in their worship of militarism. For what the military tradition and spirit have done for Prussia, with the result of creating militarism, the commercial tradition and spirit have done for England, with the result of creating industrialism.[196]

American sociologist Edward Alsworth Ross (1866–1950) postulated a "principle of balance" for societies in his 1920 sociology textbook. Different "elements" (classes, professions) in society competed for influence and power. Assuming that no one element was too powerful, societies would achieve a "reasonable" balance.[197] He gave some examples of unreasonable balance. One was Imperial China, which was weighted down by past and precedent.

[195] Ibid., 34.

[196] R.H. Tawney, *The Acquisitive Society*, New York, Harcourt, Brace and Howe, 1920, 10044-45.

[197] Edward Alsworth Ross, *Principles of Sociology*, New York, The Century Co., 1920, 674.

Ross termed this the rule of the dead and considered many non-western societies to be so impaired. Other examples of elements that could become too powerful were clergy and men—"clericalism" and "masculinism."

"The undue ascendancy of the religious profession gives rise to what may be termed 'clericalism.'" Ross was not an anticlerical, priests and ministers had their roles in "matters of faith and conduct," but they should not be the unchecked leaders of society. When they were, such as in "...seventeenth century Spain, Scotland and Massachusetts," the results could be dire. Even if clergy did not have complete control, they could stunt the economy if support of a bloated clergy and its bureaucracy drained a country's wealth. Ross also thought that a too-powerful clergy would concentrate on sin and its prevention and expiation, perhaps to the detriment of developing positive values. The people of a society might be helpless [198]before a dominating religious leader: "Out of their mundane experience or common sense his flock can draw nothing to oppose to his obscurantism or fanaticism. His is the one despotism without check or limit."[199]

"Masculinism" meant denying women their proper role in society and "The fighting instinct of the male sex seriously unfits it to take sole charge of society. Many wars have no other cause, and if the policies of states obeyed the wills of men *and* women rather than of men only, the world would enjoy more peace." Many other elements of society suffered from the aggressiveness of males, such as the police, courts, prisons—and business: "Yet the fighting instinct leads thoughtless men generally to look upon it [business] as a prize ring, with the implication, of course, that somebody is bound to get hurt. This is why good men long justified child labor, the wrecking of the health of working girls, the night work of women, preventable work accidents." Risky behaviors, substance abuse and suicide are more prevalent among men and negatively affect them and their wives and children.[200]

Militarism is another force that can unbalance a society. "The undue ascendancy of the military profession gives rise to *militarism*. Such ascendancy is likely to occur when army and navy officers are drawn chiefly from a hereditary upper order, so that their *professional* prestige is reinforced by *class* prestige." The affinity between a class and the military careers may be traditional, a holdover from the Middle Age or it may be the result of official or unofficial policies intended to bring the right sort of men into the officer corps. And, "The militarist bias in society is, of course, financed and promoted by concessionaires, battleship builders and armament makers."

[198] Ibid., 683.
[199] Ibid., 681.
[200] Ibid., 677.

"When the fighting caste gives public opinion its key, the pursuits of the soldier are esteemed nobler than those of the civilian." The highest purpose of the nation is to win wars and to use its military as "...the means of imposing its will on lower races..." Peace inside a nation is achievable if its military is strong enough, but peace between nations is but a dream. Wars are inevitable and those who are not willing to be ready for them will go down. International relations are a battlefield-in-waiting, where nations jockey for advantage and build their forces for the struggle to come. The struggle is evolutionary and survival goes to the fittest—who are the strongest: "Militarism strangles liberal political development and strengthens imperialistic tendencies. It is fond of dynasties and scorns democracy"[201]

Psychologist Joseph Jastrow wrote that his discipline studied how people think and he wrote about militarism and pacifism by detailing the reasons militarists and pacifists give for their respective beliefs. Most of his evidence came from statements of German leaders and thinkers. They asserted that a nation declined without competition and struggle, needed to involve the whole populace with a cause in order to progress and could not rely on the good will and forbearance of other powerful ntions in order to survive. Jastrow thought that all nations recognized the growing human and material cost of war, but that militarists would not quickly abandon the principles that underlay their thought. With the spread of democracy and Wilsonian principles, however, he thought that militarism would decline.[202]

Jastrow saw humans as very rational animals that supported their beliefs with good arguments. He wrote that Germany is the fatherland of militarism and traced uncompromising attitudes towards power and force from Hegel to Nietzsche to Treitschke to General Bernhardi. Militarism's justifications were diverse, including:

the historical—war has always been and will always be,

The political—force and the threats of force were the "backbone" of the international system.

The economic—competition for markets was vital to national survival and a nation's rights in this arena would need defending

The moral—war brought out qualities of courage and sacrifice; a permanently peaceful society would decline in moral tone.

[201] Ibid., 684.

[202] Joseph A. Jastrow, *The Psychology of Conviction, a Study of Beliefs and Attitudes*, Boston, Houghton Mifflin Company, 1918, 381.

War and Cannibalism

Havelock Ellis, the British sexologist and social reformer (1859–1939,) also thought the war would decline in frequency, though for quite different reasons than Jastrow. He believed that militarism was rooted in the passions of man, but that organized combat was a comparatively recent development. Cases of peaceful native peoples which had little or no warfare were cited, as was its absence among animals. Ellis further stated that the attitudes of the nineteenth century were greatly influenced by population growth and industrial development and competition, both of which he saw as conducive to war. Since he believed these trends were moderating, he thought there would be less war. He noted a comparison of war to cannibalism. Both were absent in the "lower savages," apparently he felt it took a certain level of development to kill or to eat fellow humans. Both became bound up with religion and morals and both were seen as a duty and at the same time were a "gratification of an appetite." Cannibalism had almost completely disappeared, though Ellis didn't cite any reasons for this beyond the advance of civilization. This advance was accompanied by a good deal of force against peoples who wanted to continue such practices as head-hunting and cannibalism. Nevertheless, Dr. Ellis thought it likely that militarism and war would decline and in the future they might well be viewed with disgust, as cannibalism was in 1919.[203]

Ramsay MacDonald, British Labor Party leader and a future prime minister, was more direct in his criticism of militarism and less optimistic than Ellis or Jastrow. He wrote that militarism had grown over the past century because it had failed to provide security. Increases in military establishments were matched or exceeded by other nations and arms races started and continued. Quite contrary to Joseph Jastrow, he did not believe that the increasing carnage of modern wars would lead to their abolition: "War belongs to emotions more primitive and elusive than those which determine bargains over a counter...I believe that as long as there are armies there will be war, because the existence of armies produces those situations under which the sacrifices of war become acceptable to the people."[204] MacDonald dated the development of militarism to the aftermath of the French revolution, when France initiated the levee en masse and a huge army in order to defend itself against the monarchies of Europe, who had united to destroy the Republic. The people, rather than small professional armies, became involved in war.

[203] "War to be Ended, Not by Love or Reason, but by Sublimation," *Current Opinion*, vol. LXVI no. 4 (Apr. 1919,) 245.

[204] J. Ramsay MacDonald, *National Defense: a Study of Militarism*, New York, Garland Publishing Inc., 1972, 14

He was deeply pessimistic about the outcome of the Great War and predicted, as did Hobson, that more wars would be the result of a conflict settled by force of mass armies:

> In its evolution militarism is grasping the whole life of the nation...The memory of pain and loss passes...But the menace and the spirit of militarism and armed force endures. The permanent memory of these years will be the need of the most thorough preparation. This war drove us pell-mell out of voluntaryism [*sic*] into compulsion, both military and industrial, and we shall begin in peace, not where we were in August 1914 but at the point to which the war brought us.[205]

Militarism exerted such a powerful influence, MacDonald believed, that it was unrealistic to think that a nation would only use its armed might in self-defense or to think that mobilization in the future could be less than total. As a remedy, MacDonald proposed public diplomacy and democracy, believing that the people of a nation, if they were in possession of the facts, would demand peaceful solutions rather than war to international problems: "There is no other guarantee of peace and national security. No army can give it; no treaty under present conditions can give it. It can only be given by the people themselves insisting upon knowing to what their rulers are committing them and what game their diplomatists are playing and upon taking responsibility upon themselves."[206]

The British League of Nations Union similarly thought that the way people looked at their militaries would have to change. The cause of war was no mystery to them: "The principal cause of war is preparation for war. The fact that this should appear to most people, even now, as a paradox rather than a truism, shows how slow the obvious is to penetrate men's minds." The Union noted Premier Clemenceau's recent discussion about maintaining the balance of power in Europe. Concern for the balance usually meant adding weight to your side of the scales. There was no such thing as a stable balance. Every increase brings a response from those seen as potential enemies, which is how arms races begin and continue. As a demonstration that arms were not necessary the Union used the favorite example if American anti-militarists, the undefended U.S. - Canadian border. The war was over and

> The militarist autocracies are smashed to pieces. The liberal democracies, by their own professions, could not contemplate making aggressive war. Therefore there is no one left to make such a war. But a defensive war is impossible if there is no offensive war. Disarm, and of necessity all disputes are settled by other means than war. Dis-

[205] Ibid., 77.
[206] Ibid., 117.

arm, and the principal difficulty in the way of a league of nations, mutual fear and suspicion, vanishes. Disarm, and permanent peace is guaranteed, as far as anything can be guaranteed in this world. Why then is disarmament, complete all-round disarmament, not the thing peoples are demanding and statesmen preparing? Simply and solely because of the inertia of bad habit. There are, no doubt, subsidiary reasons—professional militarism and navalism, armament firms, and all the interests that fatten on war, that live on human flesh and blood." But the main was ingrained habits of thought that were unlikely-if not impossible-to change. But these could not resist a real popular demand for disarmament. The demand is not there, because the knowledge and the thought are not there. Peoples say that they want permanent peace, but they will not sacrifice to it the least of their prejudices nor the thousandth part of their time and trouble. The world will therefore continue armed. And so continuing will increase a thousand fold the difficulty of preserving peace.[207]

Henry Ford an Anarchist?

Authors and politicians were not the only ones who criticized militarism. Henry Ford was an opponent of war and had financed the 1916 Peace Ship venture, which attempted to bring an end to the war. He also was against American participation in the war, which stirred some in the press to attack him. The *Chicago Tribune* went so far as to attack him as an anarchist. This was too much for Ford, who sued for libel. The 1919 trial shed light on Ford's thinking on war and government. A former employee, John R. Lee, related the circumstances of one of Ford's most famous comments, the 1915 statement that "I think the word murderer should be embroidered across the breast of every soldier." Lee said that the unqualified nature of the comment shocked him; Ford did not limit himself to professional soldiers or to Prussians. He was also certain that Ford was speaking from his own convictions; it was not "coming from Jane Addams." More was then revealed about Ford's ideas on war and militarism:

> Mr. Ford, Mr. Marshall and myself were working on the skeleton of the book [a biography of Ford] when the matter of militarism came up. Mr. Ford said the training of soldiers was wrong. He said he didn't believe in a navy...He said it was inconsistent for children to be taught that it is wrong to kill and soldiers to be taught that it is right. As to preparedness, he said he favored disarmament of all military force, the United States and all...Another of the remarks in the Marshall inter-

[207] "A British Plea for Disarmament," *The Nation*, vol. 108 (February 21, 1919), 303

view which Mr. Ford said he thought must have been suggested by Mr. Marshall was: "You don't compel a man to be a candy maker unless he wants to be a confectioner; why should you make him learn the soldier's trade if he doesn't want to be a butcher?"[208]

Conclusions: Militarism, Dead, Militarism Resurrected

The end of the prolonged and mechanized slaughter of the First World War was bound to raise questions. Prussian militarism did not satisfy everyone as an explanation and not only in Prussia. The debate in January 1919 between Charles Hallinan of the American Union against Militarism and Henry West of the National Security League demonstrated where the postwar battle lines would be drawn. To West militarism was dead with the Hohenzollern and Hapsburg monarchies, and the war had proved that nations that were weak militarily were in danger of at least domination, and at most destruction, by a foreign power. To Hallinan the supporters of a strong military for America were turning the nation towards an expensive and pointless militarism.

Soldiers returning home did not seem eager for more time in uniform. They, however, played little part in the immediate postwar struggle to define the nation's defense policy. This took the form of the efforts to ratify the Treaty of Versailles. Both supporters and opponents claimed their position was the less militaristic. Treaty supporters said that if we weren't in the League of Nations we would be on our own and would require huge military forces. Treaty opponents said if we were in the league we would have to intervene militarily all over the world at the behest of the League's collective security provisions. This meant we would need powerful military forces. In the event, the Treaty failed in the Senate. The huge army predicted as a result of failure never happened and the huge army foreseen in case of passage was always highly unlikely. There were other, stronger influences on American military policy, the major one being cost. Cutting taxes was as popular and as vote-getting then as it is now.

One militarism controversy over the size of the army declined in intensity, but another continued and would last throughout the 1920s. This was about military training, usually in the form of proposals for Universal Military Training (UMT). Supporters thought UMT made not only good soldiers but reliable workers and good citizens. Opponents would have none of this—they believed that a system based on harsh discipline and unques-

[208] "Ford Says He Kept His Son From War," *New York Times*, Jul. 24, 1919, 1.

tioning obedience was the worst possible training for living in a democracy based upon free enterprise.

Neither supporters nor opponents of UMT were willing to say that the United States was a militaristic country. Supporters, such as Professor Munroe Smith, defined militarism in ways that made it apply to Prussia and some other countries—he believed a country was militaristic if its political and cultural leaders acted and thought as did its military leaders. If this was not the case then America could have UMT and a large army and still not be militaristic. Opponents would say UMT and/or a large army would place the nation on the path to militarism.

There was also the question of inevitability. If wars were a part of human nature the antimilitarist position could be not only ill-advised, but untenable. Will Durant observed that only ants and men make war, amongst all the species, so it was a rarity in the animal kingdom. Still, humans made war throughout history, inevitabilists could claim. Those who wanted a stronger peacetime military would also say it was it was not the military training system or size of the armed forces that mattered, but things like the presence of a military caste and/or predilections towards aggressive policies-neither, of course, possessed by the United States. Let's keep it that way, antimilitarists urged, and rely upon diplomacy, international organizations and moral suasion to prevent war.

What stimulated the growth of militarism, whether or not it was human nature? Capitalism, socialists and communists claimed. The presence of a powerful hereditary upper class which prefers military careers, according to a 1920s sociology textbook. Socialist policies and the reining in of aristocratic privileges would seem to lessen the chances of war if these analyses were correct.

The more optimistic among those who considered militarism and war thought that they would decline as civilization progressed. It was not evident in 1919 that both the League of Nations and the spread of democracy would fail to prevent another world war. Pessimists like Ramsay MacDonald thought that the experience of mass armies slaughtering each other would be seen as a precedent, not a warning. Preparation for war would be seen as essential self-defense and would be difficult to oppose. The effort to limit and perhaps someday eliminate such preparation should be made, nevertheless, through open diplomacy the fostering of democracy and educating for peace.

4. Bolshevism or Rheumatism? Red Scare, 1919–1920

"Most of those arrested did not know the difference between Bolshevism and rheumatism", remark made to Congressman George Huddleston (D, AL) in April 1920

The American government was not ready for diplomacy with all nations. The State Department was wary of radicals and not sympathetic to the new Soviet government. One of the main reasons for this attitude was the Brest Litovsk peace settlement, which took Russia out of the war in March 1918. Russia was no longer fighting Germany and thus was making victory against the Central Powers more difficult. What we now call the mainstream media has never been favorable to radicals and was even less so in the aftermath of World War I. In the fall of 1918 the *Independent* editorialized about an Austrian peace proposal, observing that the emphatic rejection of it proved that the number of moral traitors in America was small. Moral traitors were people who professed loyalty but were always willing to give aid and comfort to enemies up to the point they would be subject to arrest. This type of "abnormal unfortunate" would make excuses for Germany and Austria-and Russia, such as: "Scrutinize the 'Bolshevik documents.' Some of them may be forgeries. Don't believe all the dreadful things you hear about the crimes of Trotzsky [*sic*] and Lenine [*sic*]. Remember that Bolshevism is a 'religion.' Patiently examine all the evidences, avoid 'hysteria' and await developments."[209]

The British and the American governments probably appreciated the *Independent's* sarcasm and did not await developments. They had sent military equipment to the Czarist regime and in 1918 they sent soldiers to the Arctic ports of Murmansk and Archangel, ostensibly to protect the equipment. These forces, and an even larger force sent to Siberia remained there well

[209] "Loyalty as Camouflage," *The Independent*, 96:3644, Oct. 5, 1918.

past the Armistice and were not all withdrawn until 1920. There were skirmishes between the Americans and the Red Army and it became obvious early on that relations between America and the Soviet Union were going to be difficult.

Matters were further complicated by a belief that the Soviets were "reviving militarism" while the rest of the world was disarming. An unsigned but first-person account in the *New York Times* made the revival charge in 1919. This observer claimed that the Bolshevik army now numbered 750,000 men and noted they were engaged on five different fronts. Having five fronts to fight on may have been as good an explanation for why the Red Army had 750,000 men as a revival of militarism, but the author wrote that the formation of such a large force was the one real accomplishment of the Bolshevik leaders, "Trotzky and Lenine." Though Trotsky was the visible leader of the Army, riding about Moscow in a "fantastic uniform of his own invention," the real director of military operations was an ex-Czarist colonel, General Vacetis, who was "striking-looking...clean-shaven" and very possibly disloyal to his Bolshevik masters. This was perhaps true of other senior generals in the Red Army, most of whom had served the Czar. After the Bolsheviks took Russia out of the World War in the spring of 1918 Trotsky had rounded up 1,200 Czarist officers and starved them into submission. When he gave the officers commands he warned them they would be watched closely and "pointed significantly to his Chinese bodyguard." Under these conditions the generals may not have had very warm feelings about "Trotzky and Lenine" or communists in general. The unnamed author believed this to be definitely so.[210]

The reach of radicalism was frightening to many Americans and most of the Wilson Administration, particularly in early 1920. By then the Red Army had decisively defeated one of their main adversaries in the Civil War, the army that had been led by Admiral Kolchak in Siberia. This was reported to be a direct result of a failure on the part of the Allied Powers to provision the White Army in Siberia: "...it was predicted that if the Kolchak forces lost their morale through a failure to receive supplies and military clothing" that they would be defeated by the Reds. This happened and the loss enabled Trotsky to reassign his Siberian troops to confront the White armies in European Russia. The removal of such an obstacle to the Communists was seen as allowing the Red Army to advance pretty much at will until they reached British Imperial India, where already "Red agents have been stirring up trouble among the hill tribes...holding the attention of British troops sent to deal with the uprisings." The White armies of Kolchak and Denikin were

[210] "Bolshevist Army Grows to 750,000," *New York Times*, Feb. 15, 1919, 4.

characterized as part of the "Russian nationalist movement." The American people now had

> ...come to a keener realization of the dangers confronting them as a result of the victories of Bolshevist militarism over Russian nationalism... unless the anti-Bolshevist world is ready to admit defeat by Bolshevism it must fight the Bolshevist menace to save what is worthwhile in the world from the Communist terror...allied quarters insist that their Governments must fortify themselves for a real fight against Bolshevist militarism...[211]

If the American people were becoming aware of the Bolshevist menace it was because there were powerful enemies ready to oppose it here. A corporate bulletin of the time observed that "There never seems to be a disease without an antidote...the American Legion begins a real fight on Bolshevism, IWW-ism, Anarchy and other forms of governmental and social diseases." The disease-antidote comment seems a little odd, since the antidote-less Spanish influenza had ravaged the world the previous year. The likening of disease to radicalism was however too hard to resist. The *National Association of Corporate Schools Bulletin* continued that, although diseased radicalism had spread almost without serious opposition prior to 1920, now "The American Legion, composed wholly of those who saw military service during the recent world conflict, has officially determined on a campaign against individuals or associations which seek to spread Anarchy, Bolshevism, or IWW principles. This organization is composed of a sufficient number of loyal, patriotic citizens to set at rest any fears that radicalism will become a serious menace to our civilization."[212]

Though the Whites still had armies that amounted to a force as large as the Soviets could field, western observers foresaw a Communist victory—and more. It was reported that the "Bolshevist menace is rapidly reaching the point where it may become necessary for the great powers to deal with the problem in a military way. The threat of a military invasion of Europe and the extension of Bolshevist military lines in Eastern and Southern Asia have been constantly in the mind of well-informed diplomats here [in Washington]..." The Red Army had also been making good progress on its European fronts, pushing back the most important enemy forces, led by General Denikin. Western military commentators judged that the Soviets would take their offensive into Poland and Czechoslovakia in the spring. They feared that this would "stir up the inflammable material of unrest in Germany, Austria and

[211] "Now See Red Terror as Peril to World," *New York Times*, Jan. 11, 1920, 3.

[212] "American Legion Challenges Bolshevism," *National Association of Corpoate Schools Bulletin*, vol. 7 no. 1 (Jan. 1920,) 5.

Hungary. Reactionary and militaristic influences in Germany are expected to make the most of any such situation..."[213]

There were dangerous foreign radicals much closer than Russia, in Mexico, for instance. The situation after the 1911 revolution was one of continued fighting among various factions. There had been attacks upon American citizens, some of them fatal. Ten months after the conclusion of the World War the United States had sixty thousand troops along the border and the State Department warned the Mexican government that if attacks upon US citizens continued "a radical change" in policy would be made. The nature of the policy was not specified but it would not be support of any faction, including the currently dominant Carranza government, to which the American government had been permitting arms sales.[214]

In the opinion of a Mexican newspaper, the situation was beyond repair by Mexicans: "...the physical and moral bankruptcy of the nation, the total disappearance of the cult of heroes, the lack of an eminently religious spirit, the slight confidence or lack of confidence in public servants, the absence of justice, the almost complete lack of respect for private property, and the lack of vested interests" had resulted in 80% of the population being "indifferent" to the prospect of foreign intervention. This estimate being before the time of scientific polling, it is likely to have been a very rough one and there was disagreement. A former Mexican government official wrote a friend in the American government that Mexicans were "cut to the quick" by American policy towards their country and "Americans have never been more heartily hated in Mexico than they are now..."[215]

Continuing turmoil and blood shed south of the border was investigated by Congress in early 1920, and they found what they thought was a plan to establish a "Bolshevik Republic." Not only that, there were American draft evaders in the leadership of the plot. The Carranza government was accused of "countenancing" the activities of the plotters. The "countenancing" did not include support in any form, but was more a refusal to, or lack of interest in, suppressing the Mexican Communist Party. That organization had claimed that 30,000 American draft evaders had found refuge in Mexico. "Most of them have returned to the United States, but many remain, and the names of a few have appeared in the literature of the Communist and IWW organizations as actively engaged in furthering the cause of radicalism." More specifically, several Americans were leaders of either the Mexican Communist Party or the Mexico City branch of the IWW. As far as draft evasion was concerned, there was apparently only one who might deserve

[213] "Washington Foresaw Crisis," *New York Times*, Jan. 16, 1920, 2.
[214] "Army has Sixty Thousand on Mexican Border," *New York Times*, Aug. 19, 1919, 5.
[215] Ibid.

the slacker label, Demetrie [*sic*] Nikitin. "Nikitin is a Russian, but...found refuge in Mexico when summoned by the American draft board."[216]

The *Los Angeles Times* named other, non-slacking Americans as radicals active in Mexico. They were aided by a man named Lenine, "who says he is a cousin of the Russian leader, [and] has been urging workmen to organize for the day when they will drive all foreigners across the border into the United States." And inside the United States, the radicals from Mexico wanted to send a message to African-Americans to resist efforts at conscripting them into the American Army, which might soon be used against Mexico. They urged "the negroes of the United States" to rise against the Federal Government, stating that "the American negroes, constituting the most miserable and oppressed of the American proletariat, have racial reasons, as well as economic ones, for immediate preparedness, NOT for further military service, but to prevent it. They are not aware of this." Or, perhaps they had been unaware but things changed: they had "...a sleeping sickness of many centuries, induced first by the vitiating tendencies of chattel slavery, but made even worse under the wage slavery that followed emancipation. The negro is not sleeping. He will fight no more wars for his tormentors and tyrants."[217]

Altars of Militarism and Autocracy

Communists and radicals were also dangerous at home. Vice-President Thomas Marshall, of "What this country needs is a good five-cent cigar" fame, was especially uncompromising. An account of his Jan. 26, 1919, remarks to a Presbyterian rally was headlined "Marshall Says Hang Reds." The leader misled a bit, since the report was that he had "said Bolshevism and all it represented must be suppressed and those leaders who were instrumental in trying to precipitate riot should be hanged...he hoped [sarcastically, it seems] the millennium was near and that never again would men be called upon to offer their lives on the altars of militarism and autocracy. Of an upheaval in this country, he said he had no fear." Marshall apparently wanted to remind his listeners that he considered himself a small "d" democrat, who was for equality all the way: "I want to make one political statement," he began, apparently seeing no possible disagreement with anything he had said so far. "I have always been opposed to granting special privileges to a class and for this reason I was down on a protective tariff. You must get it out of your head that you are entitled to more than your neighbor has."[218]

[216] "Slackers Mexican Reds," *Los Angeles Times*, Jan. 12, 1920, I1.
[217] Ibid.
[218] "Marshall Says Hang Reds," *New York Times*, Jan. 27, 1919, 6.

The editorialist at the *Los Angeles Times* would have agreed with the *New York Times* leader writer as to ropes for Reds, but their analysis went deeper. It was a matter of freedom—industrial freedom, which was only possible in the absence of unions.

> The world is turning from militarism to industrialism and blazing the new trails for labor and industry has begun...Industrial freedom has been maintained here in more of its pristine purity than in other big cities in this country and Canada. The result has been a prosperity so generally distributed that Los Angeles is alike the Mecca of the industrial free and the bane of union-labor despotism. Wherever the Bolshevist and IWW elements gather this sentiment is heard: We must get Los Angeles, we must unionize and dominate the industries there or they will get us.

So deep was the knowledge of the *Times* that they knew of a well-organized plan that was being put into effect even as its readers' jaws were dropping. Radical activists would work through the unions to foment "strikes and sabotage." Venal politicians would seek the union vote and be beholden to it once elected; in this way they would take over the city council and through it the police and fire departments. Next, somewhat ambiguously, these corrupt politicos would have "a chance at the flesh pots." It's not now clear what this meant. A chance to use the flesh pots? A chance to get graft from the flesh pots? Unionize them? Whatever the meaning of the fleshpots chance, the *Times* knew what was going to happen when the unholy alliance of unions and politicians was made: they would "overthrow the Federal Government by violence and establish a Bolshevik dictatorship on the ruins."

This would be no cakewalk, though: "Conditions in Los Angeles are too sanitary morally, socially and industrially, for original growth, but it is a parasite that attaches itself readily to politics and labor unionism and thrives on pink tea and parlor Socialism."

There was a current shipyard strike that could have been a source of such parasitism. The *Times* was confident that the dock workers were happy with their lot before radical "parasites" had attached themselves to the union, but now they not only demanded more money but were encouraging other unions to join in a general strike. The newspaper assured its readers that the radicals could not win, because the American people would never let themselves be led by a mob. Much damage could be done, however, if the recovery from war-time dislocations was hampered, thus adding to the "cup of human misery which the war left well-nigh overflowing." Most readers of the *Times* probably appreciated its fearless exposure of the parasitic menace and resolved to keep their subscription current.[219]

Bombs and Radial Agitators

In April 1919 about thirty bombs were mailed to public figures, including several U.S. Senators. One innocent person was maimed but none of the targets were harmed. This was followed by a June 2, 1919 bomb attack on the Washington home of A. Mitchell Palmer, the U.S. Attorney General. Palmer was home at the time but was uninjured.[220] No evidence was found to prosecute perpetrators of these and other attacks, but many politicians and journalists demanded action. Palmer and his young subordinate J. Edgar Hoover devised a plan to round up and deport those they considered to be dangerous radicals, and obtained six hundred warrants to be served in cities across the nation. The first wave of arrests came on Nov. 7, 1919, when 200 aliens were taken into custody, all members of the Union of Russian Workers, which was said to have 7,000 members in the U.S. The Union had called for a social revolution and the overthrow of capitalism at its summer 1919 convention. Excerpts of statements from the convention and from Union literature were printed by the *New York Times*, which characterized the arrestees as "alien radial [*sic*] agitators...plotters worse than Bolshevik." The *Times* also quoted the US Justice Department to the effect that "More than 200 Russian Reds were taken into custody last night in raids that covered fifteen of the largest industrial centers of the country...all the leaders of the union were now in custody." The arrests were made in Eastern and Midwestern cities and revealed, in two separate places, bomb-making equipment and a currency counterfeiting plant.[221] On Dec. 21, 1919, 249 aliens were put aboard a troopship headed for Europe, dubbed by the newspapers the "Soviet Ark."[222] This type of action received support from the courts. In 1919 the Supreme Court upheld wartime convictions under the Espionage and Sedition Acts, in the Schenk and Abrams cases. The Court held that "any action constituting a "clear and present danger" to the social order did not enjoy the protection of the First Amendment."[223]

This was very small potatoes compared to the next raids on Jan. 2, 1920, which netted about 10,000 suspects from which 3,500 deportable aliens

[219] "Will They Get Us?," *Los Angeles Times*, May 31, 1919, II4.

[220] Ted Morgan, *Reds: McCarthyism in Twentieth-Century America*. New York, Random House, 2003, 70.

[221] "Will Deport Reds as Alien Plotters," *New York Times*, Nov. 9, 1919, 3.

[222] Morgan, *Reds*, 76.

[223] Ellis W. Hawley, *The Great War and the Search for a Modern Order*, New York, St. Martin's Press, 1979, 51.

were detained.[224] This time, however, opposition to the tactics of Palmer and Hoover developed. Hearings were held in Washington in April, and one congressman stated he had been told that "most of those arrested did not know the difference between Bolshevism and rheumatism."[225]

Put Down the Red Flag

Republicans had been optimistic about their chances in 1920. Theodore Roosevelt was considered a leading candidate for the Republican nomination. His death on January 5, 1919 made the race much more open. Soon after the death of Roosevelt, General Leonard Wood decided to run for the Republican nomination.

In the aftermath of war there had been labor unrest and strikes in America. In September 1919 Wood commanded troops which were sent to restore order in Omaha, Nebraska after a race riot. The following month a steel strike in Gary, Indiana and unrest in the coalfields .of West Virginia required his attention. He completed these assignments with his usual dispatch and with no casualties, and also found his campaign issue—law and order. As a career military man he could hardly be expected to sympathize with those who challenged the establishment. His recent experiences with politicians convinced him that he knew better than they what was wrong with the country and how to fix it.

In May 1919 the General discussed his prospects with former Secretary of War Henry Stimson, who advised him to take a low key approach. There were two reasons for this advice. One was that the American people did not want someone who appeared too ambitious to be president. The other was they did not want anyone who seemed militaristic. This would mean that Wood should avoid talking about war and preparedness, both of which he had been commenting upon vigorously, and for a time he did stop talking a lot about military matters.[226]

There was another subject, though, that Wood discussed more and more, and that was radicalism. He saw radicals and especially Communists as enemies of the nation and himself as someone who was well qualified to deal with this dangerous element. Wood believed that the 100% Americanism favored by the American Legion was an effective counter to Bolshevism. What was most definitely not a good weapon against enemies of America was pacifism. He called noted antiwar activists David Starr Jordan and William Jen-

[224] Ibid.

[225] Ibid., 82.

[226] Jack C. Lane, *Armed Progressive, General Leonard Wood*, San Rafael, Presidio Press, 1978, 232.

nings Bryan a "vaporing fool" and a "white rabbit," respectively. On June 9, 1919, Wood addressed the graduating class at Union College in Schenectady, New York. He told his listeners that there could only be one flag for America and urged them to "Put down the red flag...It is against everything that we have struggled for. It is against the integrity of the family, the State, the nation." He also spoke of preparedness and deplored the fact that "the draft has shown the existence of physical conditions which are alarming—conditions which incapacitated half of our men of military age for hard military service. This is serious from a military standpoint, but it is infinitely more serious from the standpoint of industrial efficiency."[227]

A Lack of Militarism

As the 1920 primary season approached Leonard Wood was the front runner. He had support from many adherents of Theodore Roosevelt, from people who feared postwar disorder, and from those who felt he had been unfairly treated by the leaders of the Wilson Administration and the Army during the war, when he had been denied the service in France that he so ardently desired. Wood was still on active duty and campaigned in uniform, the only presidential candidate ever to do so. He was also accompanied by uniformed junior officers who assisted with campaign details and his campaign manager was another active duty officer, Colonel William Cooper Proctor. In February 1920 supporters were already explaining why a vote for General Wood had nothing to do with militarism. Professor Herbert S. Hadley, ex-Governor of Missouri, stated that "General Wood is a soldier, but he hasn't a military mind." Maude Wetmore, a member of the National Women's Campaign committee of the Republican Party, had a similar thought: "Though a military man, General Wood's lack of militarism should appeal to the women of the country."[228]

On April 23, 1920, Wood addressed the subject of militarism and whether his election would be a triumph for it. He gave his own definition of the term: "Militarism is a huge military establishment...in which the military class demand and receive social and official precedence and in which this class exerts a most powerful influence in the affairs of the nation concerned. Nothing of that kind is possible in the United States...the cry of militarism is a bugaboo...It is an entirely contemptible attack..." The General stated his opinion that most of those making the charge were "...persons who in the hour of trouble never found the opportunity to don the uniform of their country." In sum, militarism in the USA was impossible and those who said

[227] "Put Down the Red Flag, Gen. Wood's Appeal," *New York times*, June 10, 1919, 7.
[228] "Gen'l Wood to Fight 'Artificial' Booms," *New York Times*, Feb. 3, 1920.

it were likely unpatriotic, cowardly, or both. Wood stated further that he advocated only preparedness and if the nation had been "moderately" prepared "...there would have been no world war. I believe this is as true as there is a God in heaven." His rock-solid belief notwithstanding, it is hard to envisage what effect "moderate" preparation an ocean away would have had on Imperial Germany in 1914.[229]

As befits a military man, the Wood campaign was efficiently run. In May 1920 a reporter for the *New York Times* marveled at the qualifying experiences of the candidate, as described by a campaign staffer. It was not only that the General had been Governor of the province of Santiago in Cuba, then of the entire island of Cuba and then of the Philippine province of Mindanao: "As an administrator, he was in his island work Secretary of State, Secretary of Agriculture, Secretary of the Interior, Secretary of Commerce, Secretary of Labor, Postmaster General, Commissioner of Education, Commissioner of Health, of Highways, of Construction, of Harbors, and in addition he was engineer, accountant, and real estate adjuster." In 1920 the US President's cabinet had all of the above Secretaries and the Postmaster General. In addition there were the Secretaries of War, the Navy, the Treasury and the Attorney General, but six out of ten was evidently enough to keep the General busy. The reporter characterized this as a "dizzying analysis."[230]

From newspaper accounts of the time it seems that Wood's campaign was most interested in refuting charges of militarism and highlighting his experiences as a military governor in Cuba and the Philippines. In Indiana in May Wood addressed himself again to the charge of militarism, emphasizing that he was the farthest thing from a militarist. He favored an Army of around 200,000. The Wilson Administration was recommending an army of 576,000 and a Republican Senate Committee had suggested 300,000. Obviously, there was little or no militarism in Leonard Wood.

The General entered the convention with the most delegates followed closely by Governor Frank Lowden of Illinois. Among the minor candidates was Senator Warren Harding of Ohio. The convention deadlocked through 9 ballots. On the ninth a trend developed towards Harding which became a stampede and he was nominated on the tenth ballot. Republican insiders/kingmakers had met at 2am that morning; this was the famous "smoke-filled room" in which it was decided there had been enough voting and Senator Warren Harding should be the nominee.

Wood was and always had been a political general, in the sense that he understood the value of friends in high civilian places. He had friends in the

[229] "Gen'l Wood Urges Sane Preparedness," *New York Times*, Apr. 24, 1920.

[230] William Chenery, "Storm Center of the National Political Campaigns," *New York Times*, May 2, 1920, XI.

Republican Party, beginning with Theodore Roosevelt. He won some primaries, but in 1920 the primaries did not decide the nomination as they do now. The first presidential primaries were held in 1912 and by 1920 twenty states had them. Most, however, were non-binding. This meant that the convention decided who would be the nominee. The last convention in which there was more than one ballot was the 1952 Democratic convention. Party bosses remained interested in confining voting to the fall elections—the number of primaries declined from twenty in 1920 to twelve in 1948.

It's difficult to assess the impact of the militarism issue in 1920. Issues polling, or any other public opinion polling on a systematic basis, lay in the future. It does not seem as if the charge of militarism was directly connected with Wood, in the form of "General Wood is a militarist." His primary opponents spoke of militarism as a danger to the country, leaving their audiences to decide which candidate was the militarist. As noted above, Wood's reply to those who thought that he might be, was to state he wanted a smaller army than other candidates.

The fall was a Republican triumph; likely it would have been no matter who was the nominee. If the choice had been Wood, no doubt he would have been persuaded to downplay both preparedness and the Red Menace and adopt a more positive attitude. He could never have been more positive than Warren Harding, who was noted for his sunny disposition. He could have supported normalcy, as Harding did, but it could never have been a Presidential theme for this driven and high achieving man.

War Plans White

General Wood was not the only Army officer who thought himself qualified in political matters. There were quite a few in the Army's Military Intelligence Division (MID.) At the time of the Armistice their officers were in Europe gathering information on radical groups that they saw as hindering the war effort. At home, the MID had been working with the civilian volunteers of the American Protective League (APL) to keep tabs on groups opposed to the war. Both the APL and the MID wanted to continue their operations at the same level to curtail the new menace of Bolshevism, but the APL was officially disbanded in February 1919. The MID testified before Congress that its wartime scrutiny of German-Americans had kept them from obstructing the war effort, in an attempt to justify further activities. To bolster their case the MID historian, P.M. Buck, began to collect reports from MID field offices. Reports from the Southern Department showed increased I.W.W. action in Mexico and Arizona. "Word came from Los Angeles that pacifist groups were attempting to revive propaganda to unite radical and pacifist groups to bring about universal peace and to prevent the formation of armies and navies. On 1 May, when socialist parades took place throughout the country, soldiers and radicals had clashed in the streets."[231]

The MID officer in charge of counterespionage, one Wrisley Brown, was certain that the danger from radicals and others that he considered unpatriotic would not abate. In order to combat this menace he recommended extensive investigation and recordkeeping by the MID of organizations and individuals that had radical or even internationalist tendencies, since both would be harmful to any future war effort. At the time that Brown was making his recommendations, June 1919, Attorney General Palmer was asking Congress for $500,000 to investigate radical involvement in recent bombings in the capital. This inspired the MID chief, General Churchill, to request the same amount for the MID to continue its operations. Exactly what those operations were to be was disputed. Newspaper accounts of Churchill's testimony before Congress clearly indicated that the MID intended to keep tabs on those that it thought capable of disloyalty, but in response General Churchill stated that these accounts were incorrect—the MID only wanted funds to continue investigatory activities abroad and would only investigate wartime contracting fraud at home. Domestically its officers would also read radical publications and attend open meetings, just to keep their hand in. Their appeal was successful; they were granted $400,000 to continue investigating and reading.[232]

Events in the spring of 1919 convinced the MID that radicalism was on the march, including racial unrest and race riots in Washington D.C. and elsewhere. There had been trouble between black and white war veterans and this escalated into a full-blown riot in the District of Colombia in the summer of 1919, leaving ten whites and five blacks dead. The Army assigned two black officers to investigate; they reported that black soldiers believed that their wartime service would lead to better treatment at home and they were resentful that such treatment was not forthcoming. The officers' report stated that they deemed the resentment justifiable and recommended some modest improvements in service to black veterans.[233]

The officers acknowledged that radical propaganda had some effect, but mainly because the black veterans' grievances were real. Others saw a more central role for radical influence. These included a Congressional committee and the soon-to-be-appointed head of the Bureau of Investigation's Radical

[231] Joan M. Jensen, *Army Surveillance in America, 1775–1980*, New Haven, Yale University Press, 1991, 182-3.

[232] Ibid., 184.

[233] Ibid., 185.

Division, J. Edgar Hoover. Congress decided that the major cause of the riot was agitation by Bolsheviks and the I.W.W. and the Justice Department directed agents to report on activities in black communities. Actions like these indicated that official Washington thought all would be well if radical agitators would stay away from segregated African-American neighborhoods. These troublemakers were also thought to be a, if not the, cause of white labor unrest surfacing in actions like the Boston police strike and the Gary, Indiana steel strike.

In the fall of 1919 a conference was held at the Army War College. Part of the work there was developing what would later be called intelligence estimates for some of the major players on the world stage. Three committees were assembled to review the world situation for Great Britain, Japan, and the United States. The one studying the US decided that the most important thing to consider was the tendency towards "socialism and Bolshevism." It characterized America as an Anglo-Saxon country ruled by native sons of native parents. Immigrants and African-Americans were susceptible to subversion and thus were less reliable than white natives—and made poorer soldiers. Although African-Americans still lived mostly in the South and the immigrants clustered in Eastern and Midwestern cities, they were to be found everywhere and thus every section of the country was at risk if a class-racial war was brewing—and the committee believed that it was. The fact that most radical leaders were native-born whites only showed their natural, if in this case perverted, superiority.[234] The combination of riots, strikes, a serious recession and Communist success in Europe (Russia, Hungary, and Bavaria) made many Americans fearful that the center would not hold.

War Plans White (each war plan was given a color code, e.g. Plan Orange was for a possible war with Japan) was the response of the War Plans Division of the Army. It was designed to combat an uprising led by radicals. Reports by the MID convinced General Haan of the Division that "a well-organized movement for the overthrow of the government did exist, that personnel available for an overthrow amounted to more than 600,000 and that nearly 1,500,000 could be mobilized in thirty days. Though not a military organization, the movement was under "marked control," its aim being to seize transportation lines to keep food from industrial centers and thus force the public to seize the food supplies. An organized force would then step in, take over the food depots and distribute food, thus gaining control of local government and the support of the people. This, said General Haan, was the

[234] Ibid., 188.

same method the Reds used in Russia, Hungary, and the Ukraine in taking control. Class war would begin within two or three years.[235]

It was obvious to General Haan and those who agreed with him that the danger was real, immediate and must be opposed. Though the Red Scare continued into 1920 opposition was developing, particularly to the use of the Army to investigate American citizens. In order to continue what they saw as vital work, the Army used civilian volunteers to spy on individuals and groups they believed must be watched. These volunteers included ex-members of the disbanded American Protective League, adherents of new groups like the United Americans (New York) and the National Constitutional League (Denver) and, especially, the American Legion. Across the nation Legionnaires from many posts, often but not always in cooperation with local police, took it upon themselves to attack meetings, burn literature and assault Socialists, Communists, Wobblies and others it deemed un-American and/or subversive. The MID came to view the Legion as a reliable ally, whose members could serve as a force to maintain law and order when the expected radical uprising took place. There were many expressions by legionnaires of their readiness to do just that. War Plans White was general and particularly vague on just how force would be used against civilians. An MID officer once noted however, the effectiveness of German methods. He observed that they had had great success using tanks and strafing aircraft against radical insurgents and suggested similar heavy weapons would be effective here.[236]

Although the Red Scare petered out by the end of 1920, the MID managed to maintain some surveillance of radical groups. The Corps of Intelligence Police was established and tasked with monitoring revolutionary activity along the US-Mexico border and attempts to subvert military personnel both within the national borders and in the Philippines, Hawaii and the Panama Canal Zone. This Corps was available to MID officers for use as agents, but they had to be careful not to arouse public suspicions about Army spies. They thus continued to use volunteers like ex-APL men and Legion members. Congress declared the war officially over in July 1921 and the new Army Chief of Staff, General Pershing, took command in that month. His staff was not enamored of the MID and its activities; they soon renamed it G-2 and by early 1922 ordered it to end all domestic investigations.

The impulse to snoop, however, was still strong. There were incidents of G-2-inspired surveillance of civilians in 1922 and 1923 which became public, much to the annoyance of Army Secretary John Weeks. The 1923 contretemps involved a chart devised by the Army's Chemical Warfare Service, "a

---

235 Ibid., 190.

236 Ibid., 194.

spider web chart that linked major national women's organizations as part of an international Bolshevik plot to disarm America." By this time the Army was viewing peace and pacifist organizations as a definite obstacle to the national defense, but Secretary Weeks disowned the chart and had all copies destroyed when women's organizations objected to it. His successor, Dwight F. Davis, was not always so opposed to G-2 domestic involvement. In 1925 the head of G-2, Colonel James H. Reeves, asked Davis for authority to investigate the growing opposition to the ROTC, led by the Committee on Militarism in Education established that same year. This time the G-2 instigated active countermeasures. They used their civilian contacts to publicize criticism and opposition to the Committee. They also directed the army officers supervising Army ROTC cadets to organize the cadets and other students to oppose ROTC critics in print and by way of demonstrations. Such activities were not widespread, however, and G-2 generally maintained a "low profile" during the later 1920s.[237]

When the war was over a more dispassionate view of Communism and Bolshevism was possible. Journalist Clara Savage reported in 1919 on the short-lived Communist regime in Hungary, led by Bela Kun. Ms. Savage and unnamed companions were conducted to Budapest by armed Red Guards, whose solicitous regard for their charges was frankly admitted to be based on the fact that they were Americans. Her evaluation of the basic nature of the regime was that it was following the dictum of from each according to their abilities, to each according to their needs. As she put it, they take Jesus' story about how it is impossible for a rich man to get to heaven literally and "begin to take away his riches from the poor rich man!"[238]

Savage was impressed with her observations of the operation of the Communist justice system. She reported on a trial of a military officer whose defense was that he was only following orders. He was acquitted. She was given a tour of a prison where political prisoners were kept; it seemed almost idyllic except for the fact no one could leave the idyll. The reporter interviewed people on both sides and found many opponents of the regime willing to express dissent privately. Aristocrats and the wealthy feared they would have no place in the new order, but the regime was inclusive and seemed willing to accept all who could support its policies, no matter what their background.[239]

Her final evaluation of the Bela Kun government was favorable as to the social services it was providing, especially to children. He himself was "an absolute dictator" and Savage thought the regime was imposed and probably

[237] Ibid., 201.
[238] Clara Savage, "Adventures in Bolshevism," *Atlantic* vol. 34 (Dec. 1919,) 840.
[239] Ibid., 843.

not favored by the majority of Hungarians. It was also over-organized and the newspapers "printed every day long columns of rules to govern your daily life." Kun personally was absolutely dedicated to his cause, in daily telephone contact with Lenin, and "an ugly little man."[240]

As far as American Communists were concerned, few found much good to say about them. An observer of the "Socialist assemblies held in Chicago during the first week of September, 1919," Gordon S. Watkins, discerned three factions: "...the Socialist Party on the Extreme Right, the Communist Labor Party in the Centre and the Communist Party on the Extreme Left." The model for all three now was Russian Communism. Taking them in turn, the Socialist Party still condemned capitalism and its oppression of the proletariat, but was optimistic about developments in Europe, less so about the situation in the United States. The Party approved of the accomplishments of the Bolsheviks and stated that their violent methods were necessary. Their support of the Soviet regime, however, did not extend to an endorsement of the Third International. In the US the strategy was to regain the civil liberties lost during the war and use these rights to proceed in an evolutionary rather than revolutionary way.[241]

The Communist Labor Party, one of whose founders was John Reed of *Ten Days that Shook the World* fame, was not in favor of the evolutionary strategy of the Socialists, but wanted direct action by the masses to overthrow capitalism. Whatever violence accompanied the overthrow was acceptable to the Party. While the Socialists ran for elections and served in legislative bodies, hoping to effect change, the Communist Labor members thought the only reason to be in a Parliament or Congress was to make propaganda. This being said, Watkins characterized the Communist Labor Party as "a vacillating group of Centre-Left Socialists who are too radical to feel comfortable in the Socialist Party and not sufficiently communistic and revolutionary to gain admission to the Communist Party."[242]

To the Communist Party, the Socialists were counter-revolutionaries and the Communist Labor Party was "betrayers of the class struggle and the Third International." The Communist Party was under the domination of the Russian-language federations and Bolsheviks. They aimed for a one-class state which was to complete the suppression of the bourgeoisie and lead to a classless society. [243]

---

[240] Ibid., 845.

[241] Gordon S. Watkins, "The Present Status of Socialism in the United States," *Atlantic Monthly*, vol. 34 (Dec. 1919,) 826-827.

[242] Ibid., 828.

[243] Ibid., 829.

Watkins finally characterized American Socialism as dividing into moderate Socialist and revolutionary Communist parties. His final sentence reads "There is an unmistakable tendency towards revolutionary doctrines and Bolshevistic philosophy and the ready capitalization of this tendency by Leninists in America contains ominous signs of a concentrated, revolutionary attack upon the economic and political foundations of the present order of society"[244]

Gordon Watkins waited until his last sentence to sound the alarm, but John Spargo's second sentence in his article was "Revolutionary Communism is a menace to civilization." Spargo, a "leading spokesman" of the orthodox Socialists of America continued "Bolshevism is wrong because it is anti-social, because its ideals and its methods are as selfish and tyrannical as those of unrestrained capitalism, or even those of Czarism itself. It emulates the worst and most oppressive policies of past oppression to bring about future freedom."[245]

Spargo had several lines of attack against the Bolsheviks. First, he asserted that their reliance upon the revolt of a downtrodden proletariat was out-of-date and had been so for a long time. Marx had theorized that the condition of the working class would continue to decline and make them little better than impoverished slaves, but this had not happened. Trade unionism, the extension of suffrage, and social legislation had improved their lot and they were not and would not be the oppressed mass that would rise up and destroy capitalism. Second, Marx himself thought of the social revolution that he desired to be a long and gradual process, not to be hurried by a coup d'état. And thirdly, Bolshevik leaders mistakenly held up the Paris Commune of 1871 as an example of revolutionary action. According to Spargo this was insisted upon by Trotsky, Lenin and American Communist leaders. He relates that Marx himself came to reject the Commune tactics and regretted the adoption of them. To unthinkingly use methods developed in an entirely different and much smaller situation almost fifty years ago was a "ghastly experiment" that amounted to "vivisection of the writhing and bleeding body of Russia."[246]

Conclusions: Militarism and Radicalism

Among the offenses ascribed to the new regime in Russia was militarism. They did indeed have a large army, employed in battling supporters of the

[244] Ibid., 830.
[245] John Spargo, "Bolshevism, a Caricature of Marx's Theories," 28.
[246] Ibid., 32.

old regime in several parts of the country. The Communists in power had abandoned the fight against the Central Powers, allowing them to concentrate on American and Allied forces in the climactic battles of 1918. The new leaders of Russia had made no secret of their desire for revolutions like theirs to spread into Europe and then the rest of the world. In that year the allied powers had landed troops in various parts of Russia, ostensibly to prevent supplies of munitions given to the former Czarist government from falling into the hands of the Germans. Some of these troops stayed long after the war ended and skirmished occasionally with units of the Red armies. These events made clear the hostility of the American and Allied powers to the new regime in Russia.

Russia was far away, but there were communists, radicals and supporters of the Bolsheviki much closer. The continuing revolutionary unrest in Mexico had its radical elements and they were well-armed. Radicalism was present in America as well. Newspapers large and small sounded the alarm that there was an enemy within, which would have to be vigorously opposed, with armed force if necessary. The "Red Scare" that developed in 1919 came to a head after a series of bombings in the fall of 1919 when the government rounded up thousands of radicals and deported several hundred to the Soviet Union. General Leonard Wood was one of those who made dangerous radicalism an issue in the election year of 1920.

Advised by former Secretary of State Stimson to avoid much talk of preparedness, so as to avoid charges of militarism, for a while Wood did so. Later, however, he thought it better to deal with the issue head on. He deflected accusations of militarism by observing that he favored a smaller standing army than some of the other candidates. In the end he was not nominated. The reason for his campaign's failure was not, however, that he was thought to be a dangerous Prussianizer, but that party leaders thought Warren Harding was a better candidate.

Though the Red Scare died down in 1920, officers of the Army's Military Intelligence Division thought that their activities investigating dangerous radicalism should not be shut down, but continued and even expanded. They believed that along with war plans for possible conflict with Japan or Great Britain, a plan was needed to combat a radical uprising at home. War Plans White was the result. It was general in nature and contained very few details, more of a placeholder or perhaps budget justification than anything else.

Although there was consideration of the threat of Soviet militarism in the aftermath of the war, particularly when the Red Army invaded Poland in 1920, it does not seem that it was ever taken too seriously. Probably the major reason was that the Soviets did not have a large modern navy capable of battling the US Navy and sending troopships to invade our shores. There was a War Plans Red—but the enemy it envisaged was Great Britain. No plan was made for war with the Soviet Union.

5. Neither Masses nor Classes: American Legion, 1919–1924

"...to combat the autocracy of both classes and masses..."[247] Preamble to the Constitution of the American Legion, approved May 1919.

Veterans' organizations have formed after every war America has fought. Sometimes, as with the Grand Army of the Republic, established by Union veterans after the Civil War, these organizations become quite powerful and exercise a strong influence on postwar government and society.

The promoters of the Army and Navy had allies after the war, first and foremost the new and energetic American Legion. An official history of the American Legion relates that a group of four officers discussed, in January 1919, the formation of a veteran's organization. Theodore Roosevelt, Jr. was one of the four, as was William Donovan, the "Wild Bill" Donovan of the World War II Office of Strategic Services (O.S.S.) fame. The Civil War had produced the Grand Army of the Republic (G.A.R.) and United Soldiers of the Confederacy, the Spanish-American War the United Spanish War Veterans and the Veterans of Foreign Wars (V.F.W.) and now it was time for World War veterans to come together.

The earliest book about the Legion was published in the year of its founding, 1919. The author calls it a "consensus" among men who had served. At first it was a consensus among four officers aboard a troopship in September, 1918. One of the groups says that "there's some saving to do for the United States when this European mess is over. Us fellows won't ever get out of Uncle Sam's service."[248]

---

[247] Preamble to the Constitution of the American Legion.

[248] George Seay Wheat, *The Story of the American Legion*, New York, G.P. Putnam & Sons, 1919, iv.

There were some special circumstances surrounding establishing a veterans' organization in 1919. One was that although the enemy Central Powers had been decisively defeated, there was a new enemy—Bolshevism. The separate peace with Germany signed by the Soviet government in March 1918 released German troops to fight against the Americans for the remaining 8 months of the war. After November 11 American soldiers were kept busy with what they saw as busy work, while they "read of the Bolsheviks who were said to be at work in America in the mill and factory towns and big city industries, creating disturbances and causing other problems."[249] And, "Even the restless lack of discipline in the A.E.F. itself was vaguely attributed by some to Soviet ideas. A safe and sound organization of veterans might be the best insurance against their spread."[250]

Roosevelt was the main mover. He was as forceful as his father and as eager for service in wartime. Severely wounded in France in 1918, he would lead a regiment onto Utah Beach in 1944 at age 60, a cane in one hand and his forty-five in the other, and win a Medal of Honor for his actions. Hearing that the morale of the American Expeditionary Force (A.E.F.) was a serious concern to General Pershing, Roosevelt managed to arrange a meeting with the flinty A.E.F. Commander. Pershing authorized him to call a "morale conference" and approved the names of twenty officers from the list of fifty that Roosevelt brought with him. The conference took place February 15–17, 1919, in Paris. At a dinner on the evening of the 15th Roosevelt suggested the formation of a "G.A.R. for the World War." By the time the conference adjourned it had been decided to call for a general caucus of the A.E.F. to meet in Paris on March 15, hopefully to establish the organization.[251]

Founded 1919—or 1915?

Was the Legion the brainchild of Theodore Roosevelt, Jr.? One contemporary account describes a moment of enlightenment for Colonel Roosevelt. While recuperating from his wound in a hospital in France, he encountered a sergeant and asked him what he will do when his wounds are healed. The man replies he will return to the front and finish the job of defeating the Germans. What then, Roosevelt asked? "Go home and start a veterans association for the good of the country," he answered. Though he had thought about the idea himself, this was the first time that he heard about it from some-

[249] Thomas A. Rumer, *The American Legion, an Official History 1919–1989*, M. Evans and Company, Inc., 1990, 9.

[250] Richard Seelye Jones, *A History of the American Legion*, Indianapolis, Bobbs-Merrill Co., 1946.

[251] Rumer, *The American Legion*, 13.

one else. Roosevelt talked to other patients at the hospital and discovered that particularly those who had been badly wounded and could not return to duty wanted to have a veterans' organization. They saw this as a way of continuing their service.[252]

It's possible that Roosevelt had some glimmerings of an idea before serving in France. In 1948 a World War II veteran and former American Legion employee named Justin Gray published The Inside Story of the Legion, which was critical of the organization. Gray wrote that Roosevelt and Donovan were among the listed founders of a "membership organization bearing the name American Legion, Inc., [according to a motion] filed with the County Clerk of New York County"[253] in 1915. Four other attendees of the 1919 Paris meeting were also involved with what Gray called "American Legion I." The purpose of this 1915 group was stated to be the organizing of former military men so as to be ready to serve their country when needed. Gray wrote that finding about Legion I was disillusioning to him. Though he could not be certain exactly what the original purpose was, whether to push for entry into the World War, form a Rough Riders-like organization for T.R. Jr., or to serve as a campaign committee in the 1916 election, Gray felt that the idea of forming a strong veterans' association did not arise as official histories said it did. It was not spontaneous combustion but a well-laid fire.

Gray also revealed what seems to have been reluctance on the part of the Legion to discuss their initial funding. It was well known that the Legion had received a loan of $300,000 to cover startup expenses. During Gray's employment by the Legion, after World War II, he was told that "friends of the Legion" had made the loan and that it had been paid back with interest after the 1919 Minneapolis Convention. Gray's research revealed that Senator Borah had introduced a petition in the Senate to revoke the recently granted Legion charter, on the grounds that the leadership of the Legion "...organized it with tainted money, for the purpose of giving the men who placed themselves in control an opportunity of misrepresenting the wishes and desires of former servicemen wherever such wishes and desires clashed with those of the unknown men who had furnished the money, and who are now the real power behind the Legion." The names of the contributors were never released, though at one point the Legion stated that their identities were "common knowledge." Gray considered that the same reason explained Legion reticence about the 1915 incorporation and the names of the men who lent money to establish the organization. In both cases the men involved were wealthy members of the elite, of "Wall Street," as Gray put it: "I think

[252] Wheat, *Story*, 3.

[253] Justin Gray, *The Inside Story of the Legion*, New York, Boni & Gaer, 1948, 44.

they realized that if they hadn't tried to put over the idea that the legion was a grass roots organization representing *everybody's* interests, they wouldn't have had any Legion."[254]

Caucusing in Paris and St. Louis

The large meeting proposed by Roosevelt took place in Paris March 15–17, 1919. The group met in a spacious hall, the Cirque de Paris. There were representatives from all the divisions of the A.E.F. Photographs of the caucus show placards on poles with the names of divisions, making the whole look very much like a political convention. Several hundred men, mostly officers, attended. Some observers felt that considerations of rank went out the window: "Then generals forgot their rank, corporals engaged in hot debates with colonels, sergeants argued with majors, and everybody talked with everybody else in a most boy like spirit of fraternity and equality."[255] This group decided, on a temporary basis, that the new organization should be called the American Legion, that it should have several leadership posts and standing committees and that it should be organized by state. The caucus confirmed that a similar meeting should be held in the United States in a few months. Theodore Roosevelt, Jr., had already arrived in the United States and had established temporary offices for the Legion. He was busy traveling the country to spread the Legion idea and contact interested veterans to serve as state chairmen and delegates to a national caucus.[256] It was decided that the U.S. Caucus would be held in St. Louis in May.

After an organizational meeting on May 8, 1919, a full caucus of the attendees was held. Two other conventions were being held in St. Louis when the Legion met, but George Seay Wheat was well able to tell who was a Legionnaire. They would be like his old college friend Bill, whom he met in St. Louis after not seeing him since well before the war:

> The little, quiet, timid youth of the past was now a big, burly, strong-bodied, clear-minded man. As we entered the taxi he was telling me that he "intended to raise hell if they didn't take some action against this blank Bolshevism, and furthermore that this new Legion was going to be the most tremendous organization that the U.S.A. had ever seen." If he had told me that Swinburne's *Faustine* was written in iambic hexameter it would have sounded more like old times. But here was a new man, strong and virile, intensely interested in the future of

[254] Ibid.,69.
[255] Wheat, *Story*, 15.
[256] Marcus Duffield, *King Legion*, New York, Jonathan Cape and Harrison Smith, 1931, 7.

> the nation. What had happened to Bill? Eighteen months in the army was the answer.[257]

Just as "Bill" wanted, the convention dealt with radicalism. Considerable time was spent on deciding what to do about the Soldiers and Sailors Council of Seattle, Washington. That group had a representative at the caucus and evidently had some members who were also in the Industrial Workers of the World (I.W.W. or "Wobblies"). The I.W.W., founded in 1905, was a radical union that tried to organize workers as a class, as opposed to the craft union approach of the American Federation of Labor (A.F.L.). The union was on the record as believing that workers and employers had nothing in common and that employers were going to resist their efforts with all means at their disposal, up to and including violence.

The caucus objected to even hearing Sergeant Sherman Curtin from the Seattle Council, but finally he was allowed to speak. He stated that all of the leadership except one wanted to "throw out those I.W.W.'s" and that the Council wanted to rewrite its constitution and merge with the Legion. A sticking point emerged. Sergeant Curtin was questioned on whether or not former officers could be members of the Council and his answer was rather evasive, claiming that a prohibition on officer membership was the letter of the Council's law but not its spirit. His response was met with non-evasive boos and catcalls. Another attendee rose to defend Curtin, stating that he knew him well and that during a recent demonstration "for Bolshevism in Seattle... [He] had commanded a machine company on the side of right and law and order." That got Curtin some cheers but then Captain C.B. McDonald, formerly of the "Intelligence Department" at Fort Lewis, Washington, was called upon to speak. He denounced the Council, and demanded that if Curtin wanted to join the Legion he should do so and quit the Seattle group. This seemed like the right solution to the caucus, which voted

"Aye" to reject participation by the Seattle Soldiers and Sailors Council. George Seay White commented "That aye answered the question of what the American soldier thinks of Bolshevism or anything tainted with it. That aye answered the lying statement that our troops abroad had been inoculated with the germ of the world's greatest mental madness"[258]

Wheat wrote that the raison d'être for the Legion was that the United States was now the most powerful country in the world. Our first line of defense against the "wolf" of Bolshevism was veterans:

> Our men of the army, navy and marine corps got schooling in Americanism which our military establishment naturally teaches. Those

[257] Ibid.

[258] Wheat, *Story*, 89.

> who were aliens by birth and those native sons with inadequate educational advantages learned a great deal by association with men of better types and by travel. These men can and will stem the insidious guile of the wolf, and to aid them in so doing the Legion has an active speakers' bureau under Captain Osborn teaching Americanism in every section of the country.[259]

The St. Louis caucus made many decisions, but they were to be subject to approval by the Legion's first convention, which was scheduled for Minneapolis in November. Legionnaires from all 48 states, thousands of them, converged on that city for their November 10–12 meeting. They were welcomed by Minnesota Governor Burnquist, who stated that when "the fundamental principles of the American republic are being attacked; you advocate the upholding and the defending of the U.S. Constitution."

An important report was made by the Committee on Military Policy. Its view was that "National safety with freedom from militarism is best assured by a national citizens' army based on the democratic and American principles of the equality of obligation and opportunity for all." The Committee favored universal training "not under military control" and was opposed to a peacetime draft. They also wanted the Regular Army to be kept small, a citizen's army which could be quickly expanded in case of war, and an "immediate revision of our military system and a thorough housecleaning of the inefficient officers and methods of our entire military establishment."[260]

The next day the delegates heard some shocking news. In Centralia Washington on the previous day (November 11) there had been an armed confrontation between Legionnaires marching through the town and a meeting of some I.W.W. members. Four Legionnaires had been shot dead and one Wobbly had been lynched by angry veterans. The incident remains controversial as to who was the instigator, but there had been non-lethal attacks on the Wobblies by Legion men before the "Centralia Massacre," and it is likely that both sides were expecting trouble.[261]

Raymond Moley, Jr., writing in 1966, described the event in *The American Legion Story*. An I.W.W. organizer had been "escorted" out of town by Legionnaires in early 1919. Several months later, in the fall, a group of I.W.W. men "dropped from a freight train," rented a hall in town, and set about organizing. On Armistice Day, the Legion marched in Centralia and a halt was called in front of the "silent, red-draped hall," in order to close up the parade. In the pre-parade briefing there had been no mention of the I.W.W. or its

259 Ibid., 184.
260 Ibid., 91-92.
261 Rumer, *The American Legion*, 93.

hall. After the men had stopped shots rang out from the hall and other buildings in the town. During the gunfire three marchers were killed. The hall being the closest cover, Legionnaires broke into it and captured several armed men. Some armed men escaped, including a man named Wesley Everest, who ran away firing a revolver at his pursuers. An armed Legionnaire caught up with Everest and ordered him to surrender. Everest shot and killed this man, but was captured by other Legion men. Though a mob "intent on invoking lynch law" formed, local law enforcement and the Legion protected the imprisoned I.W.W. men.

> But the angry mob had purpose and methods other than singling out and beating a few defenders. It seized the municipal electric plant, turned out every light in town, rushed the jail and abducted one prisoner-Everest. In the morning his body was found swinging from a bridge over the Skookumchuck. This mob vengeance, deplorable from the standpoint of law and order, removed a desperate ringleader from the subsequent trial and provided radicals with a heavy propaganda weapon.[262]

Ten I.W.W. men and their "legal advisor," who was accused of helping plan the attack, were put on trial. The Wobblies testified that they had been told that the Legion was going to attack their hall on Armistice Day. The I.W.W. men had planned their defense several weeks before November 11, one of them stating "We expected to be killed and we done this with the intention of protecting our hall." Seven of the ten were convicted of second-degree murder and sentenced to 25 to 40 years imprisonment.[263]

Moley believed that had the Legion in Centralia acted differently there would have been serious damage to its image. He quoted from the *American Legion Weekly*:

> Thrown into the limelight where the slightest faltering or misstep would have reflected nationally against the American Legion the men of Grant Hodge Post no. 17 acted with a firm, just hand...had it not been for the spirit of the men of the Legion in the early hours the jail would have been emptied and a score of bodies would have dangled from Centralia's telephone poles...If there have been incidents when veterans, impatient over official disinterest, have in the name of Americanism, taken the law into their own hands, it must be recalled these are the isolated actions of individuals.[264]

[262] Raymond Moley Jr., *The American Legion Story*, New York, Duell, Sloan, and Pearce, 1966, 98-99.
[263] Ibid., 100.
[264] Ibid., 101.

There ensued a debate at the convention about what sort of help the Legion should provide to the forces of law and order. The Committee on un-American Propaganda suggested that Legion Posts should make plans to assist law enforcement in the event of riot or disturbances by "anarchists and traitors." Many, including William Donovan, thought this was going too far and the more aggressive plans were shelved.[265]

The convention made a strong impression on Americans. One report gave prominence to the Americanization platform of the Legion, of which it approved strongly. The Legion's intent to conduct a "continuous and constructive patriotic educational campaign throughout the land" was applauded, as was the hit list of those to be punished and/or deported for their disloyalty during the war. The list included aliens who had renounced citizenship or the intention to become a citizen, draft dodgers, those convicted of offenses against the prosecution of the war, conscientious objectors, "officials of the War Department responsible for the tender treatment of conscientious objectors," and Victor L. Berger, the socialist congressman from Milwaukee. The Legion also had some recommendations vis-à-vis our relations with Japan, which were not as popular. It wanted abrogation of the Gentleman's Agreement and an end to Japanese immigration, the Constitution "amended to the effect that no child born in the United States of foreign parentage shall be eligible for citizenship unless both parents are eligible. This would prevent the naturalization of any child born of a union between an American citizen and an excluded Oriental" and "that Congress send a committee to the Pacific Coast, Hawaii and the Philippine Islands to study alien colonization conditions." Some abstruse logic was applied to deal with the convention's calls for universal military training and no compulsory military service in peacetime, since if all young men were to have military training some compulsion would be necessary.[266]

Finesse was applied to the no-compulsory/universal conundrum at the 1920 convention in Cleveland. The Legion called for compulsory military training for all young men, but:

A. the purpose was not to "develop soldiers, but to make true Americans, physically, mentally and patriotically" and

B. though this was "training for military service," those who were trained were not to be used as soldiers in peacetime.

There was some other fancy footwork at Cleveland, having to do with organized labor. The Legion had made statements of neutrality regarding disputes between capital and labor. A minority report on the issue confirmed

[265] Rumer, *The American Legion*, 95.

[266] "The American Legion: Its Convention and Its New Commander," *Outlook*, Nov. 26, 1919, 348.

that, but added "The American Legion is not opposed to organized labor when it conducts itself, as we believe it customarily does, in conformity with law and order. Heated discussions followed and the minority report was finally amended so that the last sentence was eliminated." Debate, however, continued. Finally, the California delegation came up with a solution which the convention adopted—a substitute for the minority report. It simply endorsed, without quoting, an earlier statement of strict neutrality vis-à-vis capital and labor by the Legion's national commander. This avoided having anything read into the record on the issue, which according to a newspaper account, was the "bone of contention."[267]

In 1919 the Legion was granted a charter by Congress, the first veteran's organization to be so recognized. There was discussion in congress as to why the step was necessary. Supporters of the Legion stated that it wanted to be a national corporation to do business in any state, own property, sue, etc., and also wanted the honor of having its purposes recognized by the national government. A few congressmen asked why this was necessary since Civil War and Spanish-American War veteran groups seemed to do fine without it. Representative Volstead replied it would help the Legion hold itself together, and that was enough for the charter to be granted.[268]

Legion posts proliferated throughout the country. Each post elected its commander and officers and answered to its state commander as far as Legion policy was concerned. Much of the work on the national level was done by committees, which gave reports on their areas of responsibility at the annual convention. At the outset the Legion had pressing concerns about demobilization and reintegrating veterans into American society, which diverted their attention from military policy. By the time of the debate over what was to become the National Defense Act of 1920, though, the Legion was fully involved. It denied any interest in "...bringing about a military autocracy. The world has had enough of Prussianism." It did advocate a small Regular Army, with a citizen army which could be expanded quickly to meet developing threats. Some form of universal military training would provide the manpower for this citizen army, avoiding the need for a large standing army which the Legion considered to be undemocratic and against American traditions. They wanted the citizen army to be under civilian control, not the commanded by the Regular Army.[269]

Some in the Legion found it hard to calm the passions of war. One Legionnaire, Albion R. King, thought he understood. He was a past commander

[267] "Neutral to Labor, Legion Declares," *New York Times*, Sept. 29, 1920, 32.

[268] Duffield, *King Legion*, 13–14.

[269] Roscoe Baker, *The American Legion and American Foreign Policy*, New York, Bookman Associates, 1954, 115.

of his post but had become disillusioned with the attitudes and politics of most Legionnaires. He thought this was because the war stirred up strong emotions of fear and hate. The fear of the German, Austrian and later the Bolshevik enemy was turned into hatred by military training camps. The stimulation of these emotions was easily turned on but not so easily stopped. Veterans whose minds were still influenced by their experiences could not, in King's view, be expected to react rationally when presented with the controversies of the day. This was why, he wrote, there was the "the growing concern of many loyal Legionnaires about the undeniable facts which cause writers in the public press to put the Legion in the same category as the Ku Klux Klan."

Many Legionnaires, King thought, believed that their war experiences made them better equipped to deal with problems of national policy. He believed quite the opposite.[270]

For several years after the war Legionnaires freely expressed their detestation of Germans. In the fall of 1919, the Austrian violinist and conductor Fritz Kreisler, who had been an officer in the Austro-Hungarian Army, toured American cities giving performances. Local posts protested and urged that Kriesler's concerts be cancelled, successfully in a few cases. When he played at Ithaca, New York, at Cornell University, Ithaca Mayor Frank B. Davis urged the public not to attend. After Kreisler's arrival police intervened to prevent Legionnaires from storming the hall. Some members of the crowd then managed to cut off the electricity to the building, so that Kreisler concluded his program in the dark. Those inside the hall cheered to drown out the Legion protesters chanting "Hun! Hun!" outside.[271]

Even more than Germans, many Legionnaires detested "slackers," those whom the Legion thought could have served in the war but did not. This would include conscientious objectors and others who felt the war was unjust or immoral. The Legion was strongly opposed to any amnesty or reduction in sentence for those imprisoned for anti-war activities. This included most notably the Socialist leader Eugene Debs, who remained in prison, convicted for opposing conscription, until December 1921. They also detested "alien slackers." These were aliens living in the United States who had begun the process of becoming citizens when the war came in April 1917. About two thousand of these then did not continue the process, since becoming citizens would have made them subject to conscription.

The slacker who outraged the Legion the most was Grover Cleveland Alexander Bergdoll. Though an American citizen by birth, he evidently felt

[270] Ibid., 156–157.
[271] "Crowd Hoots Kreisler and Cuts off Lights," *New York Times*, Dec. 11, 1919, 3.

Germany was his true home. He attempted to join the German air force before America became a belligerent and when drafted tried to evade service. Bergdoll was sentenced to five years hard labor for this and confined to a military prison on Governor's Island. He was granted permission to visit his mother's home in Philadelphia, accompanied by two armed guards, and arrived in that city on May 20, 1920. At 2:55 pm the following day the telephone rang in the bathroom on the second floor. Bergdoll, who had been sitting in a second floor room with the guards, went to answer it. When the telephone rang again a few minutes later the guards became suspicious and went to look for their prisoner. He was nowhere to be found. It was soon revealed that there was a door in a side of the bathroom that led to another room, which in turn led to the hall and stairs to the first floor. Upon leaving the house Bergdoll "jumped into his own high-powered automobile and accompanied by his chauffeur Isaac Stecker, fled. D. Clarence Gibboney, counsel for Mrs. Emma Bergdoll, the slacker's mother, said that he had probably gone towards Baltimore."[272]

For a time the military authorities did not seem to know why Bergdoll had been allowed to leave his New York prison. Their first statements were about a "secret mission that it would not be in the interests of the military service to disclose...Philadelphia was not his objective, but he had to stop there to sign certain confidential instructions..." According to "one story that reached agents of the Department of Justice," however, Bergdoll was going to retrieve $125,000 that he had buried in Maryland while he was a fugitive from justice.

Grover Cleveland Bergdoll was the son of a wealthy German brewer, who had left his family a considerable fortune. He was reputed to be one of the best automobile racing drivers in the country, along with his brother Erwin. He had been in trouble with the law, having been convicted of reckless driving and sentenced to four months in jail. This did not interrupt his preparations to attend Pennsylvania State University; tutors that were helping him study for the entrance examinations worked with him in his cell. His later brushes with the law included citations for driving without a license and flying an airplane too low over the City of Brotherly Love.

When the war began in 1914 the Bergdolls sided with Germany. Grover wrote letters to the .newspapers predicting a German victory. One such he signed Llodgreb Revorg, thus cleverly disguising his name. When the U.S. entered the war he and brother Erwin registered for the draft but were no-shows for their induction physicals. They took it on the lam, Grover writing "derisive postcards" to the Philadelphia Draft Board from all over the United

[272] "Bergdoll Escapes from his Guards in Philadelphia," *New York Times*, May 22, 1920, 1.

States. After the Armistice Bergdoll returned to the Philadelphia home of his mother. If he thought the end of the war meant all was forgiven he was mistaken; agents of the Department of Justice surrounded the house and attempted to enter. They were met by

> ...Mrs. Bergdoll, who flourished a pistol and a blackjack. With reinforcements the police stormed the house, disarmed the mother, and dragged Grover Bergdoll, partially dressed, from under a window seat...Mrs. Bergdoll spent money freely, engaging lawyers and detectives to fight the case. Two former Burns agents in her employ [were] charged with an attempt to corrupt Government witnesses...Harry Weinberger, defender of [famous radicals] Emma Goldman and Alexander Berkman, was engaged as chief counsel.[273]

Legion leadership was furious and provided a group of lawyers to help the government prosecute the hapless guards. Investigations and various proceedings against the guards and Army officers responsible for various lapses did not lead anywhere in particular; neither did efforts to locate the money Bergdoll claimed to have buried. Bergdoll left America and became a German citizen. He could not be extradited, but this did not stop the Legion. A $500 reward was offered to anyone who would kidnap him and return him to the United States and the Legion would then provide guards to make sure he didn't escape again. There was an attempt made in January 1921 to abduct Bergdoll and his chauffeur from Eberbach in Germany. Two American detectives and four German aides were arrested after a struggle with Bergdoll supporters. The Baden provincial government issued a statement claiming that "The Eberbach affair shows the world Germany's impotence and what foreign governments dare to do to the German people without Germany having a chance to obtain reparation."

There was another attempt to kidnap Bergdoll in 1923. One of those arrested in the attempt was US Army Lieutenant Hooven Griffis, who was being driven in an official car. The Army said he was touring German cemeteries looking for graves of American war dead. Besides Griffis and his driver there was another American who had been wounded named Roger Sperber (a Carl Schmidt had been killed) and a Russian named Prince Gagarin. Sperber soon confessed; according to the German authorities they found a letter from the commander of an American Legion post in Columbus Ohio to Griffis, wishing him good luck in his mission. They took the mission to be the kidnapping of Bergdoll and may have believed that Griffis' army specialty, intelligence, was also damning. Bergdoll himself "repeatedly states his belief

[273] Ibid., 2.

that the American Legion plotted to have him abducted, and he names the Paris post of that organization as specifically responsible."[274]

The actions and positions of the Legion were not supported by all legionnaires. The Willard Straight Post #842 of New York City was a center of dissension. They first appear in the *New York Times* in 1921, in an editorial about moves by the New York County Legion leadership to revoke Willard Straight's charter. They wanted to do this because of the Post's opposition to a proposed amendment to the New York State constitution, which would have given veterans an absolute preference in hiring and in promotion examinations. They based their action on the fact that that the New York County Legion Convention, which delegates from Willard Straight had attended, voted unanimously to support the amendment. They were also unhappy that Willard Straight had made statements such as the amendment was "...a dishonest attempt on the part of the Legion to obtain something for nothing." The *Times* was absolutely opposed to it, stating that "It would destroy every reason on the part of the civil servant to work hard and so get ahead. It would establish a military caste of officeholders. Inevitably it would make the civil service cost a great deal more and be worth a great deal less. It should be beaten, if for no other reason than it denies the democratic principles on which the war was fought."[275]

Willard Straight Post survived the animus of the County Committee and lived to fight another year. In 1922 they publicly opposed Legion efforts to have the Federal government pay a bonus to all who served in the armed forces during the war:

> This bill makes an unjust and unpatriotic demand for compensation in exchange for duty patriotically performed. It discriminates in favor of a special class and is thus undemocratic and unsound economically and socially. The amount of compensation that might be provided by any bill of this nature cannot materially improve the economic status of the ex-service man or woman. It conflicts with the nation's paramount duty to expend its supreme effort for the benefit of the disabled. It would establish an open precedent for similar demands upon the state by special groups, thus heralding the breakdown of the fundamental principle that the individual and class must voluntarily sacrifice their special interests for the sake of the nation as a whole.[276]

The fight over the bonus continued in 1923 and 1924, apparently with no expulsion of the Willard Straight Post. This was possibly because they

[274] "Eberbach, Aug. 15, Associated Press," *New York Times*, Aug. 16, 1923, 8.
[275] "To Smash the Merit System," *New York Times*, Oct. 29, 1921, 11.
[276] "Legion Post Scores MacNider," *New York Times*, Feb. 25, 1922, 2.

were joined by some other Legion posts in opposing the bonus, mostly in New York.

Conclusions: Avoiding the Danger of Militarism

The first national convention of the Legion called for universal military training to provide a capability to organize a large citizen army in time of need. Such a system would, in the opinion of a Legion committee, avoid any danger of militarism. A large regular army was not favored. Unions were not favored either, though not disfavored—the Legion considered itself neutral in differences between capital and labor.

President Coolidge keynoted the Legion Convention in Omaha on October 6, 1925. His speech called for less reliance on military force and more effort to live our ideals and give a moral example of free and peaceful progress to the world. He supported some budget cutting in all federal departments, but the generals and admirals who followed him on the speaker's rostrum were carefully non-committal, and the Legion went on record as opposed to reductions.

The Legion did more in the policy area than support one side or the other in budget battles. It devised its own plan for mobilization the nation's resources in time of war, the Universal Draft Plan. This called for drafting both labor and capital, that is, extending government controls over the economy as well as individuals. This idea was pursued by the Legion for a while but finally went nowhere, probably because it lacked support from either labor or capital.

The Legion was firm in opposition to individuals and groups it considered to be disloyal or un-American. Bolsheviks and similar radicals were considered to be both the above. Its opposition to a larger regular army and to military control of universal military training made for less criticism by anti-militarists. This was balanced by their support of more ships for the navy and for naval parity with Great Britain.

The Legion's individual posts could dissent from positions taken by national and state leadership or by other posts. This could even extend to questions of foreign policy as when one post supported the US sending marines to intervene in Nicaragua and another opposed it. It was not monolithic, but since its lobbying in Washington was well organized and extensive, it was heard much more clearly than associations like the American Union against Militarism and the Committee on Militarism in Education.

6. Soldiers and Ships, 1920–1922

Though anti-militarists opposed more than minimal armies and navies, most of them did not call for their complete abolition. Thus the controversies in the 1920s were about how large the armed forces should be, not whether or not we should have them. Oswald Garrison Villard was a prominent opponent of militarism and universal military training (UMT). As owner of the *New York Evening Post* and *The Nation* magazine he had his own bully pulpit and he made use of it to publish his views on UMT. The American Union against Militarism published a pamphlet written by him in 1918, titled *Universal Military Training: Our Latest Cure-All.* He ridiculed the idea that military training would make better citizens: "Is our democracy halting? It is the tonic of a democratic army that we need in which all men shall pay for the privileges of citizenship by a year of preparation for poison gas and of learning how to destroy other human beings. Our melting pot is a failure? Then let us pour into it the iron of militarism and it will fuse every element at once."[277] In fact, Villard wrote, armies and army training are the enemies of democracy, especially large armies. He quoted James Madison: "large armies and heavy taxes are the best-known instruments for bringing the many under the domination of the few."[278]

Supporters of UMT often used the example of Switzerland, which had UMT and was democratic. Villard thought that the comparison between a small mountainous country and the continent-spanning United States was useless. He also thought that the availability of so many soldiers would be a temptation to imperial adventures, but there would be even more serious

[277] Oswald Garrison Villard, *Universal Military Training: Our Latest Cure-All*, Washington, D.C., American Union Against Militarism, 1918, 1.
[278] Ibid., 2.

consequences for the very nature of Americans. Our traditions of independence and liberty would be endangered if we became a nation in arms, inured to unquestioning obedience and deference to authority.

In the summer of 1919 the Army General Staff proposed that a standing force of 510,000 be maintained and that all young men be given three months of intensive military training at the age of 19. The number of men to be trained annually was estimated to be 600,000. To those who thought this was not enough, a *New York Times* editorial writer reminded readers that the 4 million men trained by the Army during the war would be available to plug any gaps, at least for another two or three years, in the event of a "sudden war." The editorialist allowed that the removal of 600,000 young men from employment or education for three months should not cause much of a problem, but cited General Wood and others as calling for a longer course of training, perhaps six months: "But no one wants anything approaching militarism in this country; a short period of intensive training is all that can be expected...We should have a force exceeding a million soldiers ready for a call to the colors in a great emergency."[279]

Major Richard Stockton Jr. agreed that the ready force should be around a million men; this was much more achievable now, since the onset of a great war had shown up the follies of "peace fanatics" and "ultra-pacifists." There would be more war, with or without a League of Nations. The main problem was how to get the most military efficiency out of a relatively small standing army, since a large standing army went against the American grain. The only way to do this was to have a Regular Army capable of rapidly adding already-trained citizen soldiers. Stockton thought the scheme of training 19 year-olds was a step in the right direction, but could not be the only training the young men got. They must have more and regularly scheduled training and be assigned to the units which they would join upon mobilization. Obviously, Universal Military Training was required.[280]

It was required also by the plan preferred by Major General John O'Ryan. He was the commander of the National Guard of New York, and, unsurprisingly, thought that the Guard, rather than the Regular Army, should be the structure that that young men would join after their three months training. He testified before a Senate Committee on Sept. 3, 1919, that he was opposed to the bill proposed by the Army and the War Department. He believed that the Regular Army of 500,000 was too big, too expensive, and useless:

[279] "The American Army," *New York Times*, Aug. 6, 1919, 8.

[280] Major Richard Stockton, Jr., "The Army We Need," *North American Review*, vol. 210 (Jul.-Dec. 1919,) 655.

> The maintenance of a large regular army is objectionable because such an army can have no peacetime functions. We have no boundaries to protect from invasion. Mexico has not the power to invade. An invasion from Canada is unthinkable. Regular Army garrisons in the Philippines and other possessions would seem to be unnecessary and even unwise. The defense of the possessions is a naval problem. If the navy maintains control of the sea, defensive action by garrison troops will be unnecessary. All the leaders in the movement for real preparedness have urged the organization of an Army like Switzerland or Australia and one of the strongest arguments used was that the possession of such an army would avoid the maintenance of a large, costly and ineffective regular army.[281]

Representative Julius Kahn of California had heard that some people were saying advocates of UMT wanted to "Prussianize" America. A letter from him to the American Defense League asserted "There is not a particle of foundation for such a statement." Kahn wrote that the German system was indeed universal training and universal service and this would definitely not happen here. He offered proof that such training would not encourage militarism. We had given military training to more than 4 million men in 1917–1918 and most of these men were now civilians again. Just ask them "whether they have been converted to militarism. Their answer invariably will be, "No." The positive side greatly impressed Kahn. He wrote that men gained weight and strength and he believed military training made for a more patriotic and "efficient" citizenry: "If anything, I believe that such training will crush any desire for militarism in this country. I believe it will make for a sturdier manhood of the country, that it will give us a much more virile and rugged population."[282]

Senator Borah thought that schools should be giving more attention to physical training and didn't think military training was a good path to a more fit population:

> Universal military training will add an additional charge to the taxpayer of the country from $700,000,000 to $1,000,000,000 a year. Only the most immediate necessity would justify adding this additional expense. That necessity does not, it seems to me, exist. But aside from the question of taxes I have come to the conclusion that we do not want and do not need universal military training in this country. Militarism is just the same in a republic as it is anywhere else, as we have found out. Universal military training and conscription in time of peace are the taproots of militarism. I do not want to see the young men of

[281] "O'Ryan Advocates Big Citizen Army," *New York Times*, Sept. 3, 1919, 12.
[282] "Sees No Dangers In Army Training," *New York Times*, Sept. 19, 1919, 14.

> this country put into military camps under the harsh and sometimes brutal dominance which characterizes militarism. There isn't in this war anything more cruel or intolerable than the treatment which the court-martial proceedings demonstrated in our Army.[283]

All Army officers and the War Department had drawn the lessons of the war regarding mobilization of the economy. General Peyton C. March, the Army Chief of Staff, stated in his 1919 annual report that "The national mobilization of resources, including the complete and successful diversion to essential war work of practically every industry and activity of the country... rendered the participation of this country a decisive factor in the winning of the war for civilization and constitutes a national achievement of which we may well be proud." He warned, however, that the circumstances of a future war may not allow the same amount of time to prepare.[284]

March also believed that we needed a larger army of five corps, "skeletonized" at fifty percent of its strength, so that it could be rapidly expanded in time of war. This would be a volunteer army. He also recommended universal military training, which would make the expansion of the Army much easier. The General thought that the four million men trained during the war would ensure that no country could possibly attack us during the next five years. If we established a peacetime force of the size and type he envisioned and had universal military training, March was confident Germany would not have dared to declare the unrestricted submarine warfare which brought us into the war. He was also sure that such preparations would protect us for the foreseeable future.[285]

The Army's efforts to educate its soldiers in job skills did not end with the Armistice, in fact it accelerated. Five months after the end of the fighting William H. Crawford of the Y.M.C.A. outlined the plans for a comprehensive educational program for American soldiers in France. It would require the services of over 3,000 teachers and administrators. An Army general was in overall charge and he was to detail "such military officers as are necessary to enforce discipline and to connect the schools as an integral part of the army and subject to its regulations. He is also furnishing the Y with such details of teachers as are needed."

The academic portion covered everyone from illiterates to preparation for entering college and even college itself. Crawford wrote that 40,000 plus American soldiers were attending universities in France and England on detached duty from the Army. The main focus, however, was on vocational

[283] "Assails Training Bill," *New York Times*, Feb. 2, 1920, 28.
[284] Walter Millis, *American Military Thought*, Indianapolis, Bobbs-Merrill Company, 1962, 357.
[285] Ibid., 361.

training. Each army division was to establish 40 schools, in the Y.M.C.A. "huts" if that would accommodate all the students and in army barracks and mess halls if more space was needed. The vocational training was to include everything from clerical to industrial to farming work. The U.S. Department of Agriculture was to bring forty tons of exhibits to show to students the right and wrong way to farm, "with concrete examples of the results of both methods." There was even a sort of forerunner of the New Deal Works Progress Administration:

> Nor have the arts been neglected. Eminent men in painting and sculpture have been engaged to direct the art schools at Chaumont. The struggling young artists who gave up their art in America will be better prepared to do good work in the future because their souls have been enlarged and their views broadened by the struggle which they have just been through and their technique improved under the skillful direction of these famous men.[286]

There were several reasons for this emphasis on education for the peacetime A.E.F. One was to keep the troops busy. Another, related reason was concern about morale. Worry about the state of mind of the troops was said to be one of the reasons why General Pershing supported the formation of a veteran's organization, which became the American Legion. Both the Army's educational effort and the Legion were thought to be effective prophylaxis against Communist propaganda. There was also the idea that a larger peacetime Army was needed and one of its main responsibilities would be education in literacy, in trades, and in patriotism.

U.S. Secretary of War Newton Baker gave his enthusiastic endorsement to all three. He invited particular attention to the Recruit Education Center at Fort Dix, New Jersey, one of six at Army posts in the United States. At Ft. Dix the Center had a "student body" of 1800 men and there were 48 nationalities represented. The job of the Center was to take illiterate and non-English-speaking recruits and make them into "intelligent, patriotic and disciplined soldiers and citizens." Baker wrote that 25% of inductees during the war were found to be unable to read a newspaper or write a letter in English. While some of these had gone overseas and had performed bravely in combat, unnecessary casualties had been suffered because of communication problems. Because of this the War Department instituted "development battalions" for the illiterate and non-English-speaking, where they would receive intensive training in Basic English along with their military training.

[286] William H. Crawford, "Schools for Army Occupying France," *New York Times*, Mar. 2, 1919, 49.

It was decided to continue this practice after the war, after eliminating the prewar requirement of being able to read and speak English. Those men who needed the services of the Recruit Education Center would be enlisted for three years and given thorough training in English. They would be more valuable to the Army and to society after their military service as a result of this education. A major task of the War Department in peacetime was to solve problems revealed by the war. Should another war come, the Army would be ready to deal with the 25% deficient in English language skills; this "would further real preparedness." The educational mission of the Army was "rapidly forming the Army on a new basis; one that makes the Army a most valuable asset in time of peace without destroying its function as an insurance against war...this is the kind of an army the people want, the kind of an army the Congress will support and the only kind of an army we will be able to maintain in time of peace"[287]

The educational aspect of the Army was stressed by General March in his fall 1920 report. He stated it would be wrong for the Army to use three years of a man's life and send him back to civil society without the means to make a living. The *New York Times* noted that the "military life is no longer popular...Recruiting is now so great a problem that more than good pay habitable quarters and diversified recreation must be offered." Good vocational training would be another inducement. The inducements however were expensive and the Army was "more expensive per man than that of any other country, save, perhaps, Cuba, and the taxpayer does not want to support a single superfluous battalion."[288]When March issued his report the Army totaled 210,000 officers and men. His view was that if we were to be at least minimally prepared there could be no further reductions. The *Times* agreed and observed that "A leading world Power like the United States, as a matter of fact the foremost power, can no longer function with a small peace army." Even though it was smaller than it should be, we were in no immediate danger. In an emergency the ranks could quickly be filled with veterans of the 4,000,000-man Army of 1918. There were also enough supplies and munitions left over to provision a greatly expanded force. All in all, if current Army standards could be maintained, especially as regards vocational education, the U.S. should "'have the most intelligent and contented army in the world...today it can so be described."

[287] Newton D. Baker, "The Army's Work as Americanizer," *New York Times*, Nov. 21, 1920, 47.
[288] "The New Army," *New York Times*, Nov. 21, 1920, 26.

A Stiff Sort of Snob

Everyone agreed that more training was needed, but Kansas Governor Henry J. Allen thought that the war had revealed serious deficiencies in the training of Army officers. He was very dissatisfied with the way West Point trained officers, which he believed was responsible for breakdowns in the provision of critically needed weapons and other supplies for the troops. Many Regular Army officers were fond of red tape and unable to respond to the new demands that were made upon them. It was a problem of attitude: "the system of military caste was...a "Prussian" military attitude. When I talked to reserve officers their reflections were unanimous to the effect that the system of West Point has produced rigidity, narrowness and a cheap aristocracy in officers. It created out of a democratic American lad a stiff sort of snob who lost his initiative."[289] Allen's suggestions for improvement included having West Point cadets take part of their education in civilian universities, requiring all prospective cadets to have served a few years in the ranks before the Point, detailing officers to the business world to learn management skills and admitting National Guard and Reserve officers to Army postgraduate training such as the Command and Staff College and the War College. Measures like these would prevent the repetition of the "stupid failure of a usually keen nation to make any preliminary preparation for a crisis."[290]

Dr. Charles W. Eliot, President Emeritus of Harvard, also wanted no aristocracy of officers. He believed that the postwar Army should be national (completely Federalized, rather than a collection of state National Guards) and democratic. In order for it to be democratic its officers could not be like the officers of the Regular Army. The Regular Army's "organization and its manners and customs were originally adapted from those of the British Regular Army, which has always been aristocratic in structure and habits." The Regular Army, both officers and enlisted men, was also a professional army and inevitably separated from civilians and civilian life. If the postwar army was to be democratic it would have to consist of non-professional, part-time officers and men. This type of army would "not breed a military class." A soldier was "not meaning to be a soldier for life. Far from it. In the training camp or in actual war service he is wishing to get home as soon as possible and to return to civil life. He imbibes while in training or while in service no particle of a militaristic spirit."[291] Eliot wanted universal military training

[289] Henry J. Allen, "Wanted-Army Reorganization," *North American Review*, 210, (1919: Jul.-Dec.,) 43.
[290] Ibid., 47.
[291] Eliot, "Our Future Army," 30.

and assumed that the soldiers in this new army would all abhor war, though he gave no real basis for assuming this.

Author and biographer Henry Wysham Lanier also favored UMT. He wrote a four-part series of articles for *World's Work* magazine in 1919, supporting it. Lanier wrote that he interviewed many senior officers immediately after the armistice and all told him many American casualties were due to the lack of training of American troops. One general estimated half, another said half was possible, others said they couldn't give a number but were sure it was substantial. Lanier wrote that the six major wars before 1917 cost the nation about 250,000 battle deaths, not including death from disease, and more than about 100,000 of these, or 40%, were due to lack of training. He gave no basis for this estimate, but rested his case for the "necessity of training our citizens on those hundred thousand of our own men sacrificed to—every student sorrowfully admits—a nation's prejudice, vanity and inertia. The bloody offerings to grim Huitzilopochtli upon the Aztec *teocalli*, at which we shudder, were surely more capable of justification."[292]

That was the bad news from wars of the past and the most recent war. The good news from 1917–18 was that even if the military training didn't necessarily make competent soldiers it did improve citizenship, "it demonstrated that the men who went through our army camps came out so much better citizens in body, mind, and morale, that the training would be well worth while for that end alone...We did, then, pull ourselves up by the bootstraps in health, efficiency, self-discipline, cooperative effort among classes, education, economy, and Americanization." Lanier offered examples large and small. One that he thought might be large enough to justify the program by itself had to do with food economy. The Army was wasting about four pounds of food per man per day. A group of men trained in food service operations was sent to the large army training center near Spartanburg, South Carolina. As a result of their efforts the wastage was reduced to a fraction of a pound. Lanier boggled at prospect of such savings nationwide. Lanier noted a more pedestrian result of army service by a man who claimed that his feet were "several sizes larger, but this is offset by the disappearance of several corns."[293]

[292] Henry Wysham Lanier. "Lest We Forget: The Price We Paid for Being Unprepared." *World's Work*, Dec. 1919, 201.

[293] Henry Wysham Lanier, "Lest We Forget: The Price We Paid for Being Unprepared," *World's Work*, Jan., 1920, 279.

That Bogey

In the concluding article in his series Lanier made his case for UMT, beginning by explaining to his readers what UMT was not. It was not Universal Military Service, only training for service in time of a national emergency. It was not a course of instruction suited for public secondary schools and this was the opinion of "more intelligent sponsors of the movement," including him. It was not a cure for all social ills. It did "*not* mean "militarism" in any possible expression of that bogey, as implying a large standing army. "The American Federation of Labor is very fearful of this peril."[294]

Among those who were not frightened of militarism Lanier cited the American Legion, General Bullard, General Wood, the Universal Military Training League, and the Military Training Camps Association. They, and he, believed that it was essential in view of "radical agitation for one big union as a class weapon." In order to resist such agitation, young men should be educated in some facts of American life, most importantly that the Constitution made us "One Big Union of all classes"—no radical agitation needed here. Working from the fact that nearly one quarter of the young men who volunteered or were drafted in 1917–18 were illiterate or did not speak English, Lanier wrote that "the more fortunate of us, the people with incomes and property, are personally and acutely concerned in the intelligent outlook of these millions." Even a selfish individualist might well be concerned about "Red activities and propaganda, strikes and social unrest."[295]

Without the physical training that UMT provides Lanier saw a grim prospect. According to his research the large majority of deficiencies in fitness were correctible by the right regimen. He shuddered to think of the "army of bodily defectives" that would arrive at induction centers in the next emergency, without proper planning. What a difference, though, if all young men received the right training in physical fitness. This was no time for false economies. While the lack of enough physically fir young men had cost us 7–9 months and some billions of dollars in 1917–1918, such un-preparedness in a future war could cost us "*everything*."[296]

An editorial in *World's Work*, the magazine where Lanier's articles appeared, favored UMT quite as much as he did. The editorialist wrote that opposition came from two groups—those who thought it would cost too much and those who believed it would foster the growth of militarism. Militarism

---

294 Henry Wysham Lanier, "Lest We Forget: The Price We Paid for Being Unprepared," *World's Work*, Feb. 1920, 381.

295 William Chenery, "Storm Center of the National Political Campaigns," *New York Times*, May 2, 1920, XI.

296 Ibid., 384.

produced by UMT had serious consequences. It would provoke other nations to prepare for war and thus make war more likely. It would cost too much money. It would produce an undemocratic officer class. But the real question was whether we could survive if we assumed "that if we do not have an army we will not need one." Who was making this unusual assumption was not specified; presumably the *World's Work* thought it was opponents of UMT. A bit later the editorial divined the thinking of those opponents on the subject of preparedness: "Yes, we shall have wars, but it is better to have them at enemy instigation once in a while and conduct them with a maximum of waste and suffering and deaths than to be open to the suspicion of having increased the number of wars by preparedness." Put that way it just didn't seem reasonable to *World's Work*. And like Lanier, they thought preparedness would turn out in long term to be less costly than unpreparedness.

As far as the danger of a large officer class to democracy, that too was a straw man. It was true in Germany, but that country was ruled by the Kaiser and we were ruled by Congress, so our people controlled the army. "A country which in which the people have no control over its army may justly be accused of militarism," but the United States is not such a country. If in this country "a dangerous or undemocratic officer class can grow up our democracy has lost most of its rugged characteristics." This was of course hardly likely, and besides it hadn't happened in Switzerland.[297]

A Preposterous Scheme

The Army's proposal for its postwar force was called the Baker-March proposal and it called for an army of 500,000 men, organized into five corps containing twenty divisions of infantry and one of cavalry. An air service of approximately 1,700 aircraft comprising eighty-six squadrons would make up a fourth branch of the Army, joining infantry, artillery and cavalry.[298] This plan was savagely attacked by Senator George E. Chamberlain of Oregon as an outcome of "a militaristic despotism in the general staff...its usurpation of power was responsible for the total unpreparedness of the country for the recent war." Chamberlain thought the proposal so dangerous that it required immediate legislative action at a minimum and impeachment of Secretary of War Baker if such action could not be taken. Since it did call for a much larger army more officers for the general staff would be needed, but Chamberlain

[297] "ABC of Universal Training," *World's Work*, 39:537-8, Apr. 1920.
[298] "Recruiting the Peacetime Army," *Independent*, 98, 3670 (Apr. 12, 1919,) 54.

thought the increases were outrageously excessive. He also considered that the powers of the chief of the general staff were expanded beyond all reason: "this preposterous scheme spells one-man dominance, staff despotism, and militarism to a degree never surpassed in the palmiest days of the Great General Staff of the German Army." Another provision limited the authority of Congress to allocate appropriations; according to Chamberlain

> ...if Congress should accept this invitation to tie its own hands in the matter of making appropriations in support of the Army...it would create a situation remarkable for its simplicity and entirely in accordance with the militaristic aspirations of those who have the hardihood—perhaps effrontery is the better word—to prepare and lay before Congress the astounding proposals embodied in Section 38 of this altogether militaristic bill.[299]

A supporter of the bill, Edmund Francis Hackett, Captain of Infantry, USA, gingerly characterized Senator Chamberlain as a supporter of a small army and unaware of the great success that Army recruiters had recently been having. Due to this success, the Captain claimed, it was evident that recruiting a half-million man army would be no problem. This was because Americans now understood that things had changed in major ways. The Army was now a vocational training center that would give enlistees an invaluable leg up in the civilian job market once the service was complete—free of charge. It was no longer a menace to "...those who fear militaristic tendencies or who believe that our peace-time army is merely a parasitical institution, in which officers loaf and look pretty while enlisted unfortunates black their boots and mow their lawns. " Presumably most soldiers would be too busy learning trades for such activities.[300]

An editorialist for *The Dial* magazine saw the proposed legislation as "a complete betrayal of liberalism at a time when scarcely another important government in the world dares take up the issue of conscription. Its real objective is not military training but a military establishment." Secretary of War

Baker was quoted as admitting that the three months training for all 19 year olds specified in the bill was not enough to do more than take stock of the physical condition of the young men. In *The Dial*'s opinion this was just bringing them under military control and the fact that the bill had been "stripped of all vocational or other educational features clinches the fact of its militaristic intentions. The bill even subsidizes the exemption and ap-

[299] "Senator Declares Army Bill Sets Up Staff Despotism," *New York Times*, Sept. 14, 1919, 1.

[300] Edmund Francis Hackett, "Can the United States Get 500,000 Volunteers?" *New York Times*, Jul 6, 1919, 62.

peal boards with a provision of ten dollars pay daily so that we may enjoy the European blessing of a professional sub-army of procurers. And finally, by way of imperialist overtone, it extends its benefits to Porto Ricans and Hawaiians!"[301]

In the event the provisions of the bill did not become law. By the fall of 1919 there were proposals passed by the House and by the Senate awaiting a conference committee. The Senate proposal called for universal military training and an army of 280,000. A reserve army was also provided for, but no compulsory military service. The House proposal contained neither universal military training nor compulsory service and called for an army of 318,000.[302]

Opposition to universal military training grew in the Senate. There was little direction from the White House and many Democrats were opposed. Most of the Republicans supported the provision. Senator Wadsworth of New York, in presenting the bill, said it was essential, mainly because in all the nation's wars most of the fighting was done by citizen soldiers, not by the small regular army. In the future, he claimed, seven-eighths of the fighting would have to be borne by the citizenry at large. In order to give this seven-eighths a "decent chance for their lives," they must have some training. Wadsworth noted that the Regular Army was to be reduced gradually to 210,000 men from 280,000, as universal training built up the organized reserves to strength of 3,000,000. He was challenged to say why the Army could not be reduced to 210,000 right away, since we had millions of men already trained from the war. He replied that such a reduction would not be prudent in view of unsettled world conditions, and the millions of men already trained had done their bit—it was time for other citizens to do theirs. He did note that the planned gradual reduction would almost exactly offset the cost of universal training.[303]

Militarism Run Mad

Of those Senators who were opposed to universal military training, none could have been more passionate that Senator McKellar, Democrat of Tennessee. He denounced the bill containing the provision as "militarism run mad, a militarism of the ultra-German type, a militarism never dreamed of by our forefathers, a militarism that is wholly unnecessary, a militarism that cannot be defended, a militarism that is wholly unjustifiable when we look at our history and at our future." It was also too expensive. McKellar be-

[301] "The Old Order and the New," *The Dial*, vol. LXVII, no. 797 (Aug. 23, 1919,) 157.
[302] "American Aftermath of the War," *Current History* 11:2:2 (Feb.1920), 215.
[303] "Senate Takes up New Army Measure," *New York Times*, Apr. 6, 1920, 15.

lieved that the total cost would be 1.3 billion annually, as opposed to the 600 million that the War Department estimated.[304]

Few supporters of universal military training were as inventive as one Benjamin De Casseres. In his *New York Times* opinion piece he lumped together pacifists and prohibitionists, seeing both as opposed to natural instincts of men. It was the most natural thing in the world for a man to defend himself and what is his. More than this, our problem was that we were not militaristic enough. If we would train everyone to fight no one would dare to attack us. Such preparedness was highly unlikely, though, because the "Hindenburgs and Ludendorffs of prohibition and pacifism are in the saddle." A cartoon accompanying the article pictured an alert, lean prohibitionist and a fat, sleepy pacifist with halos wired to their top hats, mounted and gazing off into the distance, possibly scanning for drunkards and soldiers. Prohibitionists and pacifists (and suffragists) were linked, in Mr. de Casseres' mind:

> Some of our women suffragists have resurrected the grand old American battle hymn, "I'll Never Raise My Boy to Be a Soldier." Raise him to be a prohibitionist instead. Teach him how to be knocked down. Teach him that nothing is of any human moment that doesn't bring home the bacon...Every human being ought to be taught not to fight but how to fight. Universal boxing and military training would reduce black eyes and wars to a minimum.

There was also the matter of cost. Americans had been told that a law requiring universal military training was too expensive and infringed upon their freedoms, but Prohibition was going to limit their freedom and require an "army of spies" for its enforcement.[305] As it happened, Americans got Prohibition, but hardly anyone ever had trouble getting a drink or suffered from being spied upon while drinking. They did not get universal military training, but there was still a lot of fighting, particularly in speakeasies.

Both the House and the Senate worked on the legislation through the spring of 1920. The major issue was the universal training provision of the Senate version. On April 9, 1920, the Senate voted to amend the bill so as to make military training for civilians voluntary, thus no longer universal. The tally was 46 in favor and 9 opposed and was not along party lines. Some of the opponents had wanted an up or down vote on military training and some had wanted no military training at all. Senator Chamberlain voted for it, though he preferred true universal training. He characterized some of

[304] "Militarism run Mad if Army Bill Passes," *Los Angeles Times*, Feb. 1, 1920, I11.

[305] Benjamin De Casseres. "Has Pacifism Come Back?" *New York Times*, Mar. 21, 1920, XXX5.

those who voted against as pacifists who had opposed the wartime draft law, which opposition could have led to America's defeat.[306]

The 1916 National Defense Act was extensively amended by act of Congress as of June 4, 1920. The amended act provided that "the organized peace establishment...shall include all those divisions and other military organizations necessary to the basis for a complete and immediate mobilization for the national defense in the event of a national emergency declared by Congress." The "peace establishment" or peacetime military organization was to include a Regular Army with a maximum authorized strength of 17,500 officers and 280,000 enlisted men. An expanded National Guard was envisioned to total 425,000 by 1924. There was also provision for Organized Reserves of indeterminate strength, whose personnel would come from R.O.T.C., the Citizens Military Training Camps, and officer and enlisted veterans.[307] The Army was empowered to establish R.O.T.C. wherever it could get the support of school administration. It lobbied continually throughout the 1920s and beyond to make it compulsory once established. The act also strengthened the generals' hand vis-à-vis the Secretary of War, since it authorized high-ranking officers to communicate directly with congressional committees, without going through the Secretary as had been the practice and the requirement.

Most Army officers were pleased with the 1920 legislation. Major Robert C. Cotton wrote that "Many things have transpired to induce a general military spirit throughout the country." One of these, evidently, was support from unnamed "influential and far-seeing citizens of the city and vicinity." Not only the elite were called upon, however, and no one was expected to serve for free. Major Cotton devoted four lengthy paragraphs to quoting the Act's detailed provisions for paying the National Guard. He saw a benefit for the citizenry at large if enlistments in the National Guard were sufficient. His reasoning was that if the National Guard could not be brought up to strength then a larger Regular Army would be needed. This larger force would have to be paid for by taxes; thus a weak National Guard equaled heavier tax burden. However, the Major saw a way to maintain a well-manned National Guard; it would only require an attitude change: "If public opinion would brand as a slacker the young man who deliberately avoids military service in peacetime, we would have...a better citizenship."[308]

Major General W.G. Haan explained the War Department's *modus operandi* in devising the legislation. They had surveyed the world scene and con-

[306] "Senate Adopts Voluntary Drill," *New York Times*, Apr. 10, 1920, 17.
[307] Major General W.G. Haan, "Our New Army," *Forum*, Mar. 1921, 291.
[308] Robert C. Cotton, "Assurance of Safety in Strong Military Program Here," *Los Angeles Times*, .Feb. 20, 1921, II3.

sidered what nation or group of nations might want to make war upon us and how we would need to respond. A manpower curve was devised that showed how the expansion would proceed by successive periods after the declaration of an emergency. The War Department decided that it was necessary to have all the officers who would be required to command the mobilized force trained beforehand, and based on the provisions of the National Defense Act and their manpower curve they thought 150,000 officers would be necessary. This figure was composed of the 17,500 Regular Army officers, 28,500 National Guard officers, and 104,000 officers from the Organized Reserves. These officers would be sufficient to command an army of 54 divisions organized into 19 corps and 6 field armies, a force of more than one million men.[309]

General Haan naturally did not reveal what country or countries the War Department considered as potential enemies. There was not much doubt in the press, however. Japan, and to a much lesser extent Great Britain, were the usual suspects. The spread of "Bolshevik militarism...toward Japan, China, India, Persia and Western Europe" and the withdrawal of American troops from Siberia had changed the situation. Japan was now alone as an occupying power in Siberia and did not seem inclined to leave. Some thought she possessed the greatest military advantages in the world. Foremost among these was that with the disappearance of the military forces of the Central Powers, Japan alone had a large army which could be used without restraint by a Parliament or a Congress. The Pacific islands mandated to her by the League of Nations, when combined with her other possessions, gave her a perimeter that was well defensible, particularly by a submarine capability that she was working hard to develop. As far as a threat from the Asian landmass, there was none, except for the "menace contained in the eastward advance of the Bolshevik forces through Siberia." There was a White leader Semenoff, who from Mongolia was attempting to block the Bolshevik march, and Semenoff was "now under the domination of the Japanese militarists, and it is fully realized that with the control of Mongolia, Japan would be in a position to dominate the pagan world from China to India." Non-Christian equaled pagan to Robert B. Armstrong of the *Los Angeles Times*, who indicated further complications from the ambitions of Turkey in Central Asia.[310]

The *Times* was willing to be fair. In an article headlined "Jap Ambassador Says Militarism a Myth," they quoted Ambassador Shidehara as saying that "One of the most mischievous stories in circulation is that Japan is under the influence of militarism. The accusation is wholly unjustified." Shidehara

[309] Haan, "Our New Army," 295.

[310] Robert B. Armstrong, "Japan Now Has the World's Greatest Mobile Army," *Los Angeles Times*, Jan. 22, 1920, I1.

added that all political parties would oppose any change in the current policy, which was one of maintaining national security.[311]

It was one thing to set an authorized strength level for the Army but quite another thing to reach and maintain it—especially if legislators were in a budget-cutting mode. Although the 1920 Act authorized an Army of 280,000, Congress had passed a resolution instructing the Army to recruit only to a limit of 175,000. President Wilson had vetoed this measure, stating that the unsettled condition of the world and an effective defense of the nation required a bigger army. In his view, such a limit would result in an army that would be overstaffed and not have enough combat soldiers to be effective. He further noted that the developments during the war, such as the emergence of chemical warfare and air power, called for more men. There was also the intent of the legislation, as he saw it, to provide a large enough nucleus of trained men so that, in the event of an emergency, the nucleus could be quickly expanded to produce an army of up to two million men. The Congressional limitation would make this very difficult if not impossible. The House was not persuaded and overrode the veto by a vote of 271 to 16. Republican Congressman Julius Kahn was pleased and could not resist a final dig at the lame duck President:

> I have always been for preparedness and believe that the condition of affairs in this country warrants a cut of the enlisted force of the army to 175,000 men. If anything untoward should happen the patriotism of this country would immediately bring to the colors of the United States a force that could handle the situation...I am for relieving the taxpayers of my country and for that reason I am proud of the action of the House. President Wilson before the war was a pacifist, now he is for preparedness.[312]

The President was not the only one who warned of the potential of new means of warfare. General William Mitchell testified to a House committee about the state of Army aviation. He told the representatives that the aircraft still in the inventory were outmoded and becoming dangerous to fly. An account of his testimony noted that he told his listeners that the French had a force of 3,000 planes ready and the British were also keeping a strong force. Great Britain was developing "ocean aircraft carriers and machines to fight above the water." The committee heard this with "wonder or incredulity... more than one Representative seemed to hear it for the first time."[313]

---

[311] "Jap Ambassador Says militarism a Myth," *Los Angeles Times*, Mar. 5, 1920, I1.
[312] "House, 271 to 16, Overrides Veto of 175,000 Man Army," *New York Times*, Feb. 6, 1921.
[313] "Preparedness in the Air," *New York Times*, jan.31, 1921, 8.

Plans of Great Magnitude

The administration of the new President Warren G. Harding was determined to present a resolute face to the world. The new Secretary of War was former Congressman and Senator from Massachusetts John W. Weeks (1866–1925,) who called for the highest degree of readiness no matter who the future enemy might be:

In the event of another war I want it to be possible to issue an order that will put the Army on the move on an hour's notice. Thus spoke Secretary of War Weeks in announcing today the decision of President Harding to place General Pershing in charge of plans of great magnitude for the war organization of the Army. Gen. Pershing will be appointed head of a skeletonized general headquarters of the army, which will have supervision of all organization of the land forces and national resources to achieve complete preparedness for war...the Army is to be made ready to act instantly and effectively in time of war.

The example of the pre-war organization of French armed forces was given, noting that Marshall Joffre was designated as overall commander in the event of war and had a command staff designated well before August 1914. Harding further believed that we had learned nothing from the Great War if we did not take active steps to prepare for any future conflict.[314]

Secretary Weeks did not accuse any nation of militarism or name potential enemies while addressing the New York University graduating class in June 1921, though he did say that there were "active and feverish military preparations among those with whom we might possibly come in contact... [I don't] give a moment's consideration to the possibility of war with Great Britain." He also wanted to make it clear that he believed that he and all reasonable citizens detested war and wished to avoid it in all cases save where the alternative was a "...dishonorable peace. Then every patriotic citizen wants war." In the world of 1921 there were nations with expanding populations which may want more territory and more resources and it could not be guaranteed that such nations would not want to take what America had. Weeks regretted the absence of universal military training, though he understood that the mood of the country did not favor it. Voluntary military training was better than none, though, and it would aid the War Department in providing for the nation's defense.[315] Representative Kahn was on board, supporting Weeks and telling his colleagues in the House that at an Army strength of 175,000 the U.S. had a an army proportionate to its population among the smallest—in fact, only Paraguay and Colombia had smaller

[314] Arthur Sears Henning, "Great War Plans Laid," *Los Angeles Times*, Apr. 22, 1921, I1.
[315] "Folly to Disarm Now, Says Weeks," *New York Times*, June 9, 1921, 13.

among the nations of the world. Perhaps feeling that arithmetic was a powerful convincer, he reminded his listeners that America had spent 24 billion during its participation in the war. If we were to spend 50 million annually on preparedness starting in 1921, it would take us 480 years to reach 24 billion. This made spending more on preparedness now a good deal to Kahn.[316] Not everyone agreed. Senator King of Utah, using a different set of numbers, claimed that with the Army at 150,000 men and a Navy that continued the wartime building plan, we would be spending more per capita than any other nation on our defense establishment. A *New York Times* editorial of January 1922 admitted that this was so, but was opposed to Senator King's suggestion that the Army be reduced to 75,000 men and the Navy to 50,000. The reduction in naval personnel would have the effect of ending the ship-building program. The *Times* suggested that the Senator be encouraged to save money, but "beware how he meddles with the security of the country." Since any cuts would be probably be seen by Representative Kahn and those who stood with him as endangering the Republic, the *Times*' position works out to little, or more likely no, cuts.[317]

The Spirit of Militarism

Congress continued to reduce appropriations for the Army, but in January 1922 Weeks pronounced himself satisfied that a basic structure was in place for mobilization in time of emergency. The core was the Regular Army, which then had a totaled 165,000 officers and men, considerably below the 297,500 officers and enlisted maximum that the 1920 legislation allowed. Weeks indicated he thought it should be larger, by noting that we had overseas possessions that required military bases and that a modern army required much more knowledge and training, particularly of officers, to remain an effective fighting force. However, a small regular army was, he acknowledged, traditionally American. In order to avoid "any basis for the fear of militarism—in such a manner as to indeed lessen the danger of militaristic influences," the Regular Army would remain relatively small and the National Guard and Organized Reserves would be increased and training improved.[318]

The three groups would be known as the Army of the United States. The National Guard was presently had 126,000, but plans "contemplated" its expansion to a maximum of 425,000. The Guard was to remain primarily

[316] "Kahn wants Army Raised to 175,000," *New York Times*, Apr. 30, 1921.

[317] "War not yet Abolished," *New York Times*, Jan. 26, 1922, 14.

[318] John W. Weeks, "Keeping Our Army Ready for Defense," *Current History*, 15:4 (Jan. 1922,) 591.

a state force, for use by state governors in "casual" emergencies, but when expansion was complete would comprise eighteen infantry divisions. As far as possible the names and numbers of the National Guard divisions which had served in the war would be retained. This would preserve the A.E.F. "traditions, memories, and experience...the traditions not those in any respect of a military class, but rather those of the historic Army of the United States, composed mainly of the citizen soldiery."[319]

Decentralization was part of the plan. The country was to be divided into nine corps areas, each having one Regular Army division, two National Guard divisions, and three "skeletonized" Organized Reserves divisions. The corps, and indeed the War Department were to have representation by officers from the National Guard and the Organized Reserves, who would participate in decision making. This participation and geographical decentralization would help prevent militarism, because "Toward centralization and concentration the spirit of militarism trends."[320]

Weeks wrote that this was similar to the Swiss system, but without their universal military training requirement. However, our voluntary training through ROTC and CMTC should enable us to provide at least the officers that would be required for a rapid mobilization. He was optimistic about this, for "The World War demonstrated how our young men at need will make sacrifices to defend our country. Our young men, in greater proportion, perhaps, than those of any other major power, love the out-of-doors and appreciate the benefits of moderate training along military lines. Hence we have every reason for believing that we can maintain an efficient overhead organization for mobilizing an army of 2,000,000 men in case of war."[321] Weeks observed that 64,000 men had enrolled as officers in the Organized Reserves, most of them veterans of the World War. He expected more would join and that with 91,000 in ROTC and 11,000 attending Citizens Military Training Camps (CMTC, 1921 figures) future replacements should become available.[322]

Decentralization would make mobilization easier. Assembling mobilized units could be done closer to home and supervised by local officers. It would take thorough preparation beforehand, but under the general oversight by the Regular Army and participation at all levels by National Guard and Reserve officers, militarism would be avoided:

[319] Ibid., 592.
[320] Ibid., 593.
[321] Ibid., 594.
[322] Ibid., 595.

> ...all civilian service will be voluntary and as the civilian forces will be distributed more or less evenly as to population, the very soul of the system will be democratic. Such an army by its very nature cannot be militaristic in the aggressive sense, in the sense of pursuing the science of war as an end sufficient unto itself, in the sense that contradicts democratic institutions and the peaceful instincts of our people. The plan is economical, democratic—and safe.[323]

Weeks was much concerned with safety from militarism. Others, including a *New York Times* editorialist, thought his concern was misplaced, because our Army was so small. The Secretary had to defend the Army from budget-cutters, who thought 150,000 men too many and preferred 116,000: "All the oratory in the world cannot create an issue out of such a difference: there is no question of militarism *versus* pacifism, no question of a large *versus* a small establishment. Both figures represent a small establishment." The *Times* thought US policies were neither imperialist nor pacifist and definitely did not demonstrate a "militarist attitude." The size of the army was a matter for experts to decide and should not be taken, in our case, to indicate either militarism or a withdrawal from world affairs.[324]

A wholly different attitude towards the danger of militarism was taken in the pages of *Current Opinion.* Wars come and go, but preparation for war is constant. The constant preparation is the true militarism: "When a nation has gotten along about so far in the work of preparedness, war breaks out as a matter of course...We are now engaged in piling up fagots for the next bonfire." This editorial noted that the United States was making no effort to promote collective security (the League of Nations had been rejected the previous year.) It proposed that the nation work on the two root causes of war: "1. Heated national vanities and hates and 2. Great armaments." The editorialist was not optimistic, noting that military expenditures consumed 74% of tax revenues and "Thus militarism goes merrily along."[325]

The Victory at Sea

Just as the 1916 National Defense Act and the war experience formed the generals' thinking about the postwar army, so the 1916 Naval Expansion Act and the battle against German submarines greatly influenced the admirals. But the American Navy had something the Army did not—the hugely influential Captain Alfred Thayer Mahan, whose books on naval history and strategy were carefully studied by officers of every navy in the world.

[323] Ibid., 596.

[324] "Our Little Army," *Independent and Weekly Review*, 108, 3811 (Apr. 1, 1922,) 324.

[325] "Militarism Goes On," *Current Opinion*, vol. LXX no. 4 (Apr. 21, 1921,) 456.

Captain Alfred Thayer Mahan, USN, was a powerful influence on the thinking of governments and navies during the first half of the twentieth century. His influence upon historians was almost as great and his views on the necessity of strong navies, as expressed in *The Influence of Sea Power upon History*, were known worldwide. He wrote that there were two conditions under which a strong navy was necessary; they were times of peace and times of war. In peace time a nation with coasts must promote the "natural growth of a people's industries and its tendencies to seek adventure and gain by way of the sea." When Mahan discussed sea power, it is important to note, he meant both merchant and naval fleets and believed it was hardly conceivable that one would not require the other in order to exist. When peace turned into war the size of the navy was not as important as "its institutions, favoring a healthful spirit and activity and providing for rapid development in time of war;" in other words, quality was more important than quantity. Times of war also brought out the necessity of naval bases abroad, which were most easily provided by colonies.[326]

Mahan thought that isolation was harmful to powerful nations. His view of history and warfare led him to believe that no matter how strong a nation's economy and armies, if she was deficient in sea power her external and internal commerce would suffer greatly in wartime and likely lead to her defeat by a stronger sea power. He also believed power abhorred a vacuum, writing that the situation in Central America, once the Panama Canal was completed, would likely become perilous:

> The geographical position of those [Central American] States, the climatic conditions, make it plain at once that sea power will there, even more than in the case of Turkey, determine what foreign State shall predominate, if not by actual possession then by influence over native governments. The geographical position of the United States and her intrinsic power give her an undeniable advantage; but that advantage will not avail if there is a great inferiority of organized brute-force, which still remains the last argument of republics as of kings.[327]

It was not enough, however, to have a preponderance of sea power—it must be properly used. Mahan's reading of history convinced him that commerce-raiding, favored by many in the American Navy, was not the best use of naval force. The direct defeat of the enemy's strongest fleet was the object to be sought.

---

[326] Alfred Thayer Mahan, *The Influence of Sea Power Upon History, 1660–1783*, 15th ed. Boston, Little, Brown & Co., 1898.
[327] Ibid., 226.

By 1916 the Wilson Administration realized that the United States might be drawn into the fighting and so it supported legislation to increase and improve the armed forces. And, even if the nation was not involved in the conflict, it would be involved in the aftermath. The victors would be dictating the peace and determining the shape of the postwar world. America would need a strong voice at the peace conferences, one backed up by naval power. The Naval Expansion Act of 1916 was intended to provide a navy of the first rank, one with enough battleships to win a fleet action against any other navy in the world. This was in complete harmony with the theorizing of Captain Mahan, but would be no use against German submarines. For that, the Navy would require much smaller vessels, patrol craft and especially destroyers—lots of them.

No Spirit of Militarism

There was vigorous debate in Congress about providing a larger navy and some charges of militarism were made. Representative Carl Vinson (1883–1981) of Georgia replied that the bill "is not open to criticism hurled at it by some that it seeks to saddle on the people of this republic a form of military despotism. If for a single moment I thought that this policy of preparedness for defense in any of its forms provided for in the various bills in this House would give birth to a spirit of militarism in this free country I would oppose it to the utmost of my ability."[328]

It was submarine warfare against commerce that brought the United States into the war, however, and defending against German submarines would be the navy's main task. Construction of battleships was slowed down and construction of antisubmarine and merchant vessels was speeded up. The Navy was outstandingly successful in defending the troopships carrying American soldiers to France; not a single troopship was lost. Some American merchant vessels were sunk, but not enough to give the Germans any respite.

The US Navy's Admiral William Sowden Sims went to England in the summer of 1917 to command operations there. Admiral Sims (1858–1936) was well known as outspoken and as capable of taking direct and unorthodox action when he thought it necessary. In 1902, as a relatively low-ranking officer, he had become disturbed at the poor state of gunnery in the Navy. Unable to convince his superiors of the problem he wrote a letter to President Roosevelt. TR investigated and becoming convinced that Sims was correct, he appointed him to a new office, Inspector of Target Practice. With the

[328] Joseph Kirschbaum, *The Naval Expansion Act of 1916: Planning for a Navy Second to None*, Dissertation UMI #3311364, George Washington University, 2008.

President's support, Sims was able to champion higher standards of accurate gunnery throughout the Navy.[329]

In London Sims had thought that since the British Navy had completely neutralized the German Navy, and since the British public was being told that German submarines were not having much of an effect, that the war was almost won. He discussed the situation at length with First Sea Lord Admiral Jellicoe, Prime Minister David Lloyd George and King George V and was told that in fact the war would be lost if the U-boats could not be defeated. His conclusion was that American destroyers and patrol craft must immediately be placed under command of the British, for these vessels, not the much larger battleships and cruisers, were the force that could defeat the submarines.[330]

Sims was not the first choice of Secretary of the Navy Josephus Daniels, but once he was selected, Daniels had him in to his office to discuss the mission. Prior to the US entry into the war Sims had made a speech in London and stated that "If the time ever comes when the British Empire is seriously menaced by an external enemy, it is my opinion that you may count upon every man, every dollar, every drop of blood of your kindred across the sea." Seemingly quoting from Abraham Lincoln's letter to an obstreperous General Joseph Hooker, Daniels told Sims that it was not because of this statement but in spite of it that he had been selected for the mission to England. Prior to his departure there were remarks made by Admiral Benson to Sims about trusting the British Admiralty, which were to be made public and be controversial after the war.[331]

Sims was Canadian by birth and was suspected by President Wilson and Navy Secretary Josephus Daniels of being pro-British. This suspicion extended to the point of not allowing Sims to attend the British Admiralty planning meetings to which he had been invited. By the fall of 1917, however, 375 American naval vessels manned by 75,000 officers and men were based in European waters. Sims put his point of view directly and clearly in his post-war book: "I decided that our forces should become, for the purpose of this war, virtually a part of the allied navies; to place at the disposal of the allies our ships to reinforce the weak part of their lines; to ignore such secondary conditions as national pride, naval prestige, and national ambitions; and to subordinate every other consideration to the defeat of the Hun."[332] When that defeat was accomplished, Sims wrote that "the transportation of these American troops brought the great struggle to an end. On the battlefield they

[329] "William Sims," http://en.wikipedia.org/wiki/William_Sowden_Sims, 11/15/2009.
[330] William Sowden Sims, *The Victory at Sea*, New York, Doubleday Page and Co., 1921, 15.
[331] Josephus Daniels, *Our Navy at War*, New York, George H. Doran Company, 1922, 39.
[332] Sims, *The Victory*., 246.

acquitted themselves in a way that aroused the admiration of their brothers in the naval service."[333]

Working with the British, however, did not mean that Admiral Sims and the Wilson Administration were in agreement. Sims continued to press for more destroyers to be sent and Secretary Daniels didn't agree. He also began to lobby Congress for a three-year postwar building program that would bring the US Navy close to the British in power. His (and President Wilson's) motive here was to strengthen the US hand at the peace conference which would make the postwar settlement. If the US navy could become the equal of the British, then they and the other allies would have to respect Wilson's ideas for collective security through a league of nations and national self-determination [334]

As mentioned before, the Navy was outstandingly successful in convoying American troops to France. The Germans had a little more success against empty transports returning to the United States. Five of these vessels were torpedoed and three of the five were sunk and an escorting cruiser, the *San Diego*, struck a German mine and sank. In December, 1918, Navy Commander Charles Gill was at pains to praise all involved in the effort, but also to correct some misapprehensions. One such was a press report that seven British passenger liners had carried 80% of the American soldiers to France. This was wrong, Gill wrote. The liners had actually carried 10%. Gill also wanted to credit the officers and men of the US merchant marine who had volunteered for service with the Navy: "These have rendered splendid service and the interests of the United States for the future require that the cordial relations of cooperation established between the merchant marine and the navy be maintained." The Army was not the only service that could be expanded rapidly in case of war.[335]

Just how expandable was described by Secretary Daniels in a January 1919 article. In July 1916 naval personnel totaled 58,527, 4,293 officers and 54,234 enlisted men. In July 1917 the number had increased to 179,171, 8,038 officers and 171,133 enlisted. On Armistice Day the totals stood at 529,504, 32,474 officers and 497,030 men. The number of naval vessels when war was declared was 197; by November 1918 there were 2,003. Most of the increase was transport and other ships volunteered or taken into naval service, but there were also considerable new vessels added, among them 2 battleships, 36 destroyers, and 355 submarine chasers, which were quickly built, 110-foot

[333] Ibid., 366.

[334] Paolo E. Coletta, *The American Naval heritage in Brief*, Washington D.C., University Press of America, Inc., 1980, 273.

[335] Charles C. Gill, "Overseas Transportation of U.S. Troops," *Current History*, Vol. 9:1:3 (Dec. 1918,) 412.

wooden vessels. Construction of almost all battleships and cruisers was suspended, so that the shipyards could concentrate on building destroyers to combat the submarine menace.[336]

When the 1916 naval building program continued after the war it caused some questions to be asked in England. A US Naval Reserve officer tried to allay fears of a growing dominance of the world's oceans by America. Captain Thomas G. Frothingham's 1920 *Current History* article may not have been completely reassuring. He did state at the outset that the US was merely continuing to build warships only for defense; it had no aggressive designs on anyone. However, much of the article was devoted to a discussion of why American battleships were better the British. It was basically because the British had favored the building of battle cruisers, which were faster than battleships. In order to be faster they had to have less armor, a definite disadvantage in Frothingham's eyes. The naval gun comparison was also unfavorable to the Royal Navy. The Americans had 16 inch guns while the newest British guns were 15 inch. Not only that, for guns of equal bore, such as the 14 inch guns that both navies had on some vessels, the American shells were more powerful. Highlighting facts such as these probably did little to soothe those British who were concerned about US naval policy.[337]

Building Like Mad

Britain was not the only competition for the American Navy. There was also Japan, whose navy was large, modern—and growing. Press reports claimed, on the basis of "secret intelligence" collected by the Navy and sent to the President every week that Japan was building ships at a rapid pace. She would increase her navy 50% by 1924 and more than 100% by 1927, while our navy will have increased by 19%. Our navy would still be 2/3 larger than Japan's, but nevertheless

> ...the carefully guarded opinion in the inner circle of government is that the Japanese are forging a weapon to use against this country...with undeniable information that Japan is building like mad it is the settled purpose of President Harding to complete the great American naval building program of 1916...even partial disarmament is a long way off... under the guidance of President Harding the Navy will be no. 1 in the world's list of naval strength.[338]

[336] Josephus Daniels, "The United States Navy in the War," *Current History* 9:2:1, (Jan. 1918,) 112–113.
[337] Thomas G. Frothingham, "Increased Strength of the United States on the Sea, *Current History*, 12:6 (Sept. 1920,) 950.
[338] "Japan Builds Secretly to Double her Navy," *Los Angeles Times*, Apr. 21, 1921, I1.

The President had been informed that the doubling of Japanese naval strength by 1927 was a minimum estimate. The Navy's "secret intelligence agents" believed that the true figure was closer to 125%. Harding was "known to favor deep-reaching economies in the Army," but this did not mean he was for disarmament; in fact he had "politely squelched disarmament proposals." His cabinet secretaries were firmly behind him; Secretary of the Navy Denby was a "big navy" man and Secretary of War Weeks wanted to continue and expand training reserve officers and military training in general.[339]

Japanese government leaders, politicians and military men responded to such press reports that Japan was only building in response to the American construction program. T. Okamoto wrote that when he arrived in London he was asked at every turn whether Japan was going to go to war with America. This was unexpected, since he knew that almost no one in Japan said or even thought that such a war might be coming. The exceptions were those who might be influenced by "a few novels and magazines, whose object is to please the young generation with thrilling stories of adventure, or some yellow journals which are quite chauvinistic in their purposes." Okamoto defended every Japanese military action for the last nineteen hundred years as self-defense, with the exception of an unsuccessful sixteenth-century invasion of Korea. As far as more recent history, he conceded that "Foreign critics point, by way of proving Japanese militarism, to the two wars of 1894-5 and 1904-5 in which Japan was successful, and expanded her territory. It must, however, be remembered that these wars were forced on Japan and we only fought for our very existence." Okamoto fleshed out the logic of the 1894-5 war with China by writing that the Chinese had claimed authority over Korea. Since:

A. Korea really belonged to Japan, and

B. the weak Chinese were incapable of defending Korea from imperialistic Westerners, Japan had no choice but war with China. He did admit that the "militarists" have a great deal of influence over Japanese foreign policy, but was confident that their influence will diminish in the future.[340]

Admiral Bradley Fiske's 1920 book *The Art of Fighting* was probably not very reassuring to either the British or the Japanese. Fiske considered the prewar United States to be more under the influence of pacifism than any other country. This was due to the influence of the doctrines of Thomas Jefferson (who avoided war with Britain during his terms of office and believed peace to be the natural state of persons and nations) and the preoccupation with making money. Consequently the United States was more unpre-

[339] Ibid., 12.

[340] T. Okamoto, "American-Japanese Issues and the Anglo-Japanese Alliance," *Contemporary Review*, 355.

pared than any other nation when war broke out. The German mistake was to bring the US into the war: "The German statesmen seem to have been convinced that the people of the United States were so wholly engrossed in money-making and so under the influence of the doctrines of Jefferson that they would endure any insults and continue blind to any national danger from Germany."[341] The situation after the First World War was in strategic terms no different than before it:

> ...great nations have, both as a cause and an effect, developed highly complicated armies and highly complicated navies. We do not know why it should be, but it seems to be a fact that no nation has ever been able to attain a high level of civilization, or to maintain it afterward, without developing a highly complicated army and navy. A nation seems to have natural enemies, as a man does, these enemies being both external and internal. In the case of a nation, the enemies are foreign nations and barbarians outside and unruly elements, now comprised under the general name of bolsheviki, inside. In the case of a man his enemies are other men outside and noxious bacilli inside. *In all cases strength is needed to overcome the enemies outside and inside and live in health.*[342]

Since there always had been war, it was idle to try and make it go away. Fiske believed that all of recorded history demonstrated how nations that become wealthy and enjoy (or suffer?) long periods of peace become victims of other nations. If we did not stay prepared militarily, "...the barbarians (or Bolsheviks or anarchists) may triumph over us—and probably will." The competition between the civilized (such as the USA) and the barbarian (undemocratic) nations was not, however to be feared, because it brought progress as well as misery and bloodshed. History did provide a cautionary lesson about "excessive militarism," which existed when the Roman Praetorian Guard had become so powerful that it could depose and install emperors. The problem, though, was not the praetorians but the Roman people, their "abominably corruption, profligacy and effeminacy" which allowed the Praetorian Guard to change emperors whenever it so desired.[343]

Fiske was a convinced and determined disciple of Mahan, who believed that America must have "invulnerable strength" at sea. He was forward-looking, telling the *Los Angeles Times* that the day of the battleship as the decisive weapon was over. In a very few years it would be aircraft carriers that would rule the seas. The British already had several carriers and we were working on one that would, however, be smaller and slower than the British models.

[341] Bradley A. Fiske, *The Art of Fighting*, New York, Century Company, 1920, 315.
[342] Ibid., 325.
[343] Ibid., 377.

He was credited by the newspaper as being the inventor of a system for the launch of torpedoes by aircraft and was almost lyrical about the possibilities of such attacks: "A torpedo plane can attack without notice until it is too high. High up, it is invisible and inaudible. It can descend so swiftly that it cannot be hit even if seen. It can come within close range of the battleship, launch its torpedo and swoop upward again so swiftly that it is practically safe. Even if it is not safe, what is one man, one inexpensive plane, against the loss of a giant ship?"[344]

Sucking the Hind Teat

He was not alone in his view of the future. Admiral Sims agreed wholeheartedly in a story appearing in the *New York Times* the following week. Sims told reporters that an aircraft carrier was like a battle ship that could fire at targets one hundred miles away. It could carry up to eighty aircraft and launch planes that could fly at 90 to 150 miles an hour to attack slower battleships. He theorized about a future battle between a fleet of 16 battleships and 4 carriers and another consisting of 20 carriers, both fleets having the same complement of auxiliary ships. The fleet with the 20 carriers would sweep the air clear of the outnumbered aircraft of the opposing fleet. It would then have the battleships at the mercy of its bombers and torpedo planes. Antiaircraft guns would be of very little effect and the battleships would be doomed. Sims was not optimistic about the what the building program for the navy would turn out to be; he told the Chairman of the House Naval Affairs Committee that the Committee should "accept the preponderance of the evidence; that they would probably decide wrong; and that, as usual, the United States would continue to suck the hind teat in naval construction."[345]

From the Armistice to the Washington Conference on Limiting Armaments there was a running battle between Admiral Sims and Secretary Daniels, which continued after the Harding Administration took over in 1921. Immediately after the war Secretary Daniels traveled to Europe to consult with the Allies and evaluate the peacetime needs. Upon his return in May 1919 he told the press that the US was still committed to the 1916 building program and would remain so unless the League of Nations imposed an effective disarmament. Daniels also expressed commitment to maintaining the large merchant marine that had been developed during the war. He commented upon the former enemy navy, saying that the desire by some that the German Navy had come out to fight so that the superiority of the British Grand Fleet could be unequivocally established was understandable. The

[344] "Fiske Sees War in Air," *Los Angeles Times*, Feb. 13, 1921, I1.
[345] "Battleship Doomed, Says Admiral Sims," *New York Times*, Feb. 21, 1921, 19.

"tame and inglorious" surrender without a fight, however, could be as damaging to morale as a defeat. "A navy depends not alone on men and ships; it must rely on noble traditions that must be its inspiration if it attracts valiant men.[346]

Differences about how the Navy's valiant men were to be recognized caused the tensions between Admiral Sims and Secretary Daniels to become public. All naval commanders had submitted their recommendations for the award of medals recognizing wartime service. The recommendations went to a board of retired naval and marine officers chaired by retired Admiral Austin M. Knight. The Secretary of the Navy had the final authority, and Daniels had indeed changed some of the recommendations to a lower award, denied some and added some. Admiral Sims wrote a letter to the Secretary, declining the medal that had been offered to him and several other admirals did the same. Others sent letters objecting to the award assigned or to the outright rejection of recommendations. Daniels made all correspondence about these matters public and the Republican Congress returned by the 1918 elections decided to appoint a joint committee to investigate.[347]

Daniels changed the decisions of the Board to give more medals to enlisted men, which caused Admirals Sims and Mayo to decline their decorations. This led to an investigation by the Naval Affairs Committee, chaired by Maine Republican Senator Frederick Hale (1874–1941.) In his testimony Daniels claimed that Sims was ambitious to a fault and deferred to the British too much. In January, 1919, Sims replied in a letter to Daniels, giving his opinion that in 1917 the Navy had been unprepared and too slow in taking up its wartime duties. Some of the specifics he mentioned were that there was not a single submarine ready for action when war was declared, the fleet was unbalanced because it lacked cruisers, and scouting and screening ships were scattered around the world rather than concentrated with the fleet. His startling conclusion was the deficiencies in the Navy (and its civilian leadership) delayed the end of the war by four months and caused the loss of 2.5 million tons of shipping and 500,000 lives.[348]

Militarism the Spirit of our Fleet?

Whether or not the US Navy was powerful enough for the missions it was assigned was debated in America—and also in Europe. In the fall of 1921 a Current Opinion editorial claimed that "...militarism seems to the press abroad to be the spirit of our fleet and of our army. Never, it thinks, has the

[346] "Daniels Returns Firm on Navy Plan," *New York Times*, May 18, 1919, 25.

[347] "Daniels Gives out Protests," *New York Times*, Dec. 28, 1919, 1.

[348] Coletta., *American Naval Heritage*, 276.

American Government been is such a great bustle over guns, battleships and artillery." Though the Washington Naval Conference was scheduled to begin soon, the press in Europe was observing what they thought was an increase in preparation and readiness. The "easygoing" Secretary Daniels was gone and his "vigorous" replacement was making sure that the navy was combat-ready. In order to do this it was divided into Pacific and Atlantic fleets. Several reasons were given for this. One was the greater efficiency of stationing coal-fired vessels in the Atlantic and oil-fired ships in the Pacific fleets. Coal-fired ships needed more frequent refueling and thus were better suited to the smaller expanse of the Atlantic Ocean.

But "The reasons given in Washington for all this energy in dealing with our fleet are pooh-poohed in Europe." Europeans believed we were more concerned about a Japanese squadron visiting South American ports. Some congressmen and diplomats professed to believe that Japan and England were scheming to entice some South American power (likely Peru or Chile) into providing a base of operations on the Pacific Coast of South America. Japan denied it and the British called it nonsense, but some in Washington were still wary of Japanese intentions. They were even more wary of the "affair of the Dutch oil wells." This came about when a British oil company made a sudden deal with the Netherlands to obtain oil from the Dutch East Indies (Indonesia). This was an exclusive deal. Washington was unappreciative and told the Dutch so. This affair, the South American base business and other recent events were making the United States uneasy. This unease was the real motive behind the call for the Washington Conference to limit naval arms.[349]

Conclusions: What was Settled before the Washington Conference

The traditional prejudice against a large standing army was still alive in the aftermath of the World War. Even some National Guard officers made use of the prejudice to call for expansion of the Guard. These officers were not opposed to UMT—so long as the graduates of military training camps went into the Guard. A supporter of a more powerful army like Congressman Julius Kahn continued to see the benefits of military service as Theodore Roosevelt had seen them—the army not only made soldiers but responsible and manly citizens. Anti-militarists thought quite the opposite. Having all men trained in the arts of killing would tend to brutalize them. And, rigid obedience to orders was not best characteristic for a citizen of a democracy—they should rather be encouraged to think, debate and question.

[349] "Europe Thinks We Grow Militaristic," *Current Opinion*, vol. lxxi (October, 1921), 424.

Again and again the military system in Switzerland was admired and recommended by those who advocated for UMT. Anti-militarists could point out that a citizen's militia like the Swiss Army was hardly the model that was being proposed by the US Army. Both sides picked and chose the features of the Swiss system that best fit their pro-or-con positions on UMT.

The Army made extensive efforts to position itself as necessary in peace as it was essential in war. One of these efforts was its educational program. Some of the men drafted were immigrants who needed to learn English and skills necessary for employment in industrial America. The schooling was broad in subject, ranging from basic instruction in English and arithmetic to painting and sculpture to the latest agricultural techniques. Surely such training would be a huge contribution to the national welfare, supporters of the military claimed. A huge waste of money, according to anti-militarists.

In September 1919 The Senate took up the proposal of the Army for its peacetime structure. It called for a volunteer army of 500,000 men and for three months' military training for all 19-year olds. This got little support, and two alternative bills were proposed for the postwar army, one with UMT and one without. In June 1920 Congress passed the amended National Defense Act, which called for a volunteer army with a maximum strength of 280,000 enlisted men. Expansion of the National Guard, Organized Reserves, R.O.T.C. and Citizens Military Training Camps were also authorized. Later in 1920 the ceiling was lowered from 280,000 to 175,000.

The Harding Administration realized that what the Army wanted was not attainable, most especially the size of the Regular Army. They would have to increase readiness by improving and expanding in other areas. With more local involvement through decentralization readiness for war could be "economical, democratic—and safe" [from militarism.] Making the best of it, Army generals fell into line and praised the new arrangements. The peacetime US Army would be small and remain small until the eve of the Second World War. Strong tradition and strong motivation to keep taxes low after the Great War were enough to accomplish this, with assists from organizations like the American Union against Militarism and individuals like Senator William Borah.

The navy, however, was a different matter and there were fewer arguments about the size of the navy. It was still seen as primarily defensive and not as a means of projecting power as it is currently. The Navy continued to build ships so as to increase its power to equal that of Britain and surpass that of Japan. It was easy to see an opponent for the U.S. Navy, difficult to see a large and hostile adversary of the U.S. Army. Consequently, and because of the large economic impact of naval construction, the Navy continued to expand after the Armistice, though at a reduced rate. The expansion would continue until a halt was called for the US, Great Britain and Japan by the Washington Naval Treaty of 1922.

7. A Navy Second to None, 1921–1922

> "If militarism is an enemy of mankind and should be wiped out, does not the same rule apply to the Navalism practiced by England? We want a Navy second to none, for trade and protection."
>
> O.H.E. Kramer, 1919.

A Commercial War of the Severest Sort

If most Americans came to agree that a small US Army was acceptable, the same could not be said for their view of the US Navy. Many legislators saw a need for a powerful navy and some for a powerful two-ocean navy. Woodrow Wilson and his admirals were agreed that the end of the war did not automatically mean the end of strengthening the Navy. Quite the contrary, for as Admiral William

Benson put it, America was "on the threshold of the keenest and most active commercial competition that the world has ever seen," what Secretary of War Newton Baker called the "fierce and final competition." Both men were mindful that that Germany had been Britain's rival not only in naval but also in merchant fleet terms. Woodrow Wilson agreed with Benson and Baker in the most emphatic language: "It is evident to me that we are on the eve of a commercial war of the severest sort, and I am afraid that Great Britain will prove capable of as great commercial savagery as Germany has displayed for so many years in her competitive methods."[350]

---

[350] George Baer, *One Hundred Years of Sea Power: the U.S. Navy, 1890–1990*, Stanford, Stanford University Press, 1994, 85.

The power of the Royal Navy was an important consideration to the American delegation to the Paris Peace Conference. Great Britain was aligned by treaty with France, Italy, and Japan, while the United States was an Associated Power. This status was the American government's desire, so that it could maintain its freedom of action. Secretary of the Navy Daniels had maps made which showed the trade routes most important to the United States and those most important to Britain. The routes would require defending and that meant navies of about equal strength—since the routes were roughly of the same total length. The maps showed U.S. routes that included almost the entire coasts of North and South America. This was evidence of a primary goal of the Americans, recognition of the Monroe Doctrine by the rest of the world, by its recognition in the League of Nations Covenant. To British Prime Minister David Lloyd George, this was "preposterous...You are a self-contained republic with no large empire...Do you mean to say that your country dominates Mexico, Central America, and all South America?" Daniels replied in the negative, but his maps said yes. The Versailles treaty did recognize the Monroe Doctrine, but discussions about naval parity and how to temper the rivalry had no result.

In spite of the wrangling with the British, the US Navy was coming to see Japan as the main problem. In 1919 Secretary Daniels decided to divide the Navy into Atlantic and Pacific forces. This went against what had been the tradition of a single fleet which would engage the enemy in a decisive battle. He reasoned that the mandate of German islands in the Pacific to Japan gave the Japanese bases that could threaten American lifelines to the Philippines and Guam. There was also concern about Japan's intentions toward China. There was division in the Navy about the change. Admiral Sims, for one, thought the single large fleet would appear more formidable to the Japanese.

Along with the division of the fleet the Navy wanted to fortify bases in the Pacific so that if the Japanese should aggress eastwards, their supply lines could be attacked. Plans to spend more money on the Navy, though, were having a very hard time in Congress. The argument that we needed a powerful navy because we had failed to join the League of Nations and thus could not avail ourselves of its peacemaking machinery was not persuasive to the politicians. The postwar economic decline added to their reluctance about the bases and about continuing to build more battleships.

Americans were not the only ones worried about militarism in the United States. Some Japanese were. A 1921 book of essays by Japanese observers of events in both countries had a chapter titled "Militarism and Navalism in America." Its editor, Henry Satoh, noted that the authorized strength of the American Army and National Guard was about 480,000, though their actual strength was about 260,000. He did not compare this with Japan, but did compare naval strength and plans for expansion, which showed the American Navy to be much larger. Satoh wrote that there were 570 American institutions for training army officers, that secondary school military training was widespread, and "Very strong efforts are being made all over the United States for training men for military service."[351] Under a heading of "Encouragement of Warlike Spirit," Satoh disapprovingly noted that there had been an essay contest on "Benefits and advantages of being enlisted in the American colors," that ten million students had been eligible to compete, and that the Secretary of War and General Pershing had been the judges. To make matters worse, the winners and their parents received an all-expenses paid trip to Washington for the awards ceremony. This was not the only way a warlike spirit was encouraged. Satoh cited a speech by University of California Chancellor Dr. David P. Barrows, in which he told freshmen that every man must assume personal responsibility for the defense of the nation, and "he condemned evasion of such responsibility as the greatest shame."[352]

The Danger of Arrogant Militarism

Another essay, by Professor Rikitaro Fujisawa, examined American foreign policy, focusing on the Monroe Doctrine. The Professor believed that future calamities, which he was certain would occur, would not be like past disasters: "In the dizzy eyes of the too-ardent advocates of any peace movement, the danger of arrogant militarism outshines all other sources of danger, which are, in reality, equally appalling..." Perhaps the new "isms" would be on the Bolshevik model, or even by an altered, "Ultrabolshevism." He also thought "Capitalistic Imperialism" might cause wars, apparently referring to the European colonial powers. There were other possibilities, including "Dictatorism." Since his essay was written before 1921, he was not referring to mass-movement leaders like Mussolini and Hitler, but to those powers who sought to "dictate" a world order. Professor Fujisawa did not care to name names, but there was a "great nation" that was

...monopolizing the privilege of interpreting fineries such as rights, justice freedom, and so forth in a manner that suits its own convenience and in a way conforming to its exalted and advantageous position among the comity of nations...and unconsciously but aggressively setting itself up as the dictatorial arbiter of all disputes among nations...Viewed from the historical standpoint it is the eighteenth century spirit of 'enlightened despotism'

[351] K.K. Kawakami, *what Japan Thinks*, New York, Macmillan Company, 1921, 109.
[352] Ibid., 110.

clothed in the garment of the twentieth century fashion of 'safe for democracy.'

The reference to Woodrow Wilson's famous statement of the American goal of "making the world safe for democracy" must have informed attentive readers that Fujisawa was talking about none other than the United States of America.[353]

Another essayist in *What Japan Thinks*, Professor Sakuzo Yoshino, wrote about liberalism in Japan. He had an explanation for the origin of Japanese militarism, having to do with Japan's history of isolation from other nations. When Japan did come into contact with China she was very impressed with Chinese literature and institutions. These were imitated. Coming into contact with Western nations "...it was the power of militarism which impressed her most forcibly. " All the ships that came to visit were warships and "The idea that the Japanese got was that militarism was the only thing worthwhile." In order to resist western encroachments Japan would have to have a powerful military. According to Yoshino the "bureaucratic class" in control of the government was convinced that the West intended to dominate Japan. They controlled the educational system and saw to it that children were educated to believe that might is right. However, among the people there was a reaction against the bureaucratic class and "Then, gradually, and perhaps unconsciously, this changed to a reaction against militarism. The reaction, which first appeared as a reaction against despotism, has gradually changed until today we can recognize it as a reaction against militarism that is, speaking of the people at large." Yoshino believed that "ninety out of one-hundred Students" wanted a more democratic Japan that depended less on a strong military. For this reason he believed that a freer Japan was coming, one with a bright and peaceful future.[354]

Militarism and Navalism

Vice Admiral Tetsutaro Sato, president of the Naval College in Tokyo, saw Japan's position in the world differently. Before the war, he wrote, Germany was "...held up to the odium of the world as the champion of militarism, a dangerous principle jeopardizing the peace of the world." Some nations during the war argued that Japan was militaristic too, and would have to be dealt with postwar. And, those hostile to Japan now accused her of "navalism," of attempting to dominate the world with her navy as the Germans had done with their army.

[353] Ibid., 22-23.
[354] Ibid., 82-84.

Admiral Sato did not see much difference between militarism and navalism and saw nothing wrong with having either a powerful navy or army—or both. He saw both as reflecting strong defenses and not a problem for any nation. Problems arose when these strong armies and navies were "...prostituted to a base purpose. For instance, when Germany tried to dominate the world with her militarism and provoked the enmity of the world, she was abusing her militarism. Indeed militarism has degenerated into a doctrine of conquest in the hands of Germany."[355]

Could Japan's navy sail the world as a prostitute? The Admiral did not think so. Japan's forces were meant for self-defense and in the case of the navy, defense of its seaborne trade. Japan's population was increasing rapidly, as were the demands upon its merchant shipping. Besides protecting the home islands, its navy must protect the nation's trade with the world. Further, the US and Britain had powerful navies, active in the Pacific. All was calm now, but what if difficulties should develop between them? If Japan had a strong navy, her services as a mediator might be very welcome. But with a weak navy, she would probably have little influence: "Should Japan be disqualified to maintain the peace between the two great nations of England and America on account of her weak navy, she should be held responsible for her failure to safeguard peace, at least in the Pacific."[356]

The Admiral expanded on his views in a 1920 article in the Japanese press. A translated copy of his article was sent to the New York Times (and, presumably other newspapers) by the Japanese Embassy. The Embassy's transmittal note stated that the Admiral was a noted authority on naval matters and a "keen observer of the international situation." It was of course not the Japanese government speaking, nor the Embassy, but as believers in the value of free speech the diplomats thought it worth sharing. The Admiral thought Japan was being unfairly singled out:

> If militarism and navalism are to be criticized at all, then the expansion of the army as planned by Italy and France or the expansion of the navy as purposed by England and America is to be equally denounced. It must be remembered that Japan is not the only nation constructing warships. England and America, too, are building warships in spite of the fact they have far stronger navies than Japan. Therefore, if any nation in the world is guilty of navalism it is England or America, not Japan"

However, Sato believed that the western powers did not intend to conquer other nations. Their big navies were meant only to defend themselves.

[355] Ibid., 93-94.
[356] Ibid., 102–103.

The situation was the same for Japan—everything for defense, nothing for aggression. "In other words, the Japanese mean to enjoy a happy life as well as their traditional nationality, in their own country by making adequate armaments to defend it."

The Admiral had a three-part theory of national security. He claimed there were three bases of national security. These are justice, wealth and military power. Nations that had all three should be assured of a peaceful and prosperous state of affairs. Sometimes just two of the three might suffice. America had great wealth but for long periods of time her military forces were negligible. However, Sato promptly provided a counter-example—Belgium, wealthy, just and attacked, occupied and sacked by the Germans. So, military power was in most cases the most important factor. A country would need wealth to provide the resources that make up military power. Finally, it would be well if a nation would treat its own citizens and the other nations of the world with fairness and respect.

So, if Japan did not intend to act aggressively, what would its military forces be doing? Sato's answer was protecting its international commerce. Japan had not the resources of a continental nation like the United States or a colonial power like Great Britain. She had to import and export to survive and must have a strong navy to protect that commerce. He asserted that "Commerce, not backed by naval force, is always destined to dwindle. However flourishing a nation's trade may be it will be stopped in an emergency unless it has naval strength to fall back upon." Oceanic commerce was Japan's life line and lifeblood and it must be protected/

> If critics of Japan denounce her naval program as navalism, what shall they say about the programs of England and America? If Japan be guilty of navalism, does not America stand convicted of still greater navalism? Creatures, like States, should have those weapons to defend themselves which are in keeping with their nature, and Japan's nature requires a navy—a navy solely for defense. Those who condemn this as navalism must do so from interested motives.[357]

The Champions of Economy

In the United States there had been a short recession in 1919, but the recession that started in early 1920 was much more serious. During it the United States had its highest rate of deflation recorded before or since and suffered a precipitous decline in business activity. Unemployment, which

[357] Vice-Admiral Tetsutaro Sato, "Japan's 'Navalism' Explained," *New York Times*, May 30, 1920, 2.

had gone up sharply in 1919, continued to rise, leading to the first-ever White House Conference on Unemployment in September 1921. The economic wisdom of the time decreed that government expenditures should be cut during downturns, to free up money for expanding the civilian economy. Thus, "the government must either find new revenues or reduce expenditures...no considerable reduction in expenditure can be made until the appropriations for the army and navy can be reduced. It is this rather than abstract pacifist sentiment which led Congress to halt recruiting for the Army and is now inspiring investigations as to the real needs of the Navy. The champions of economy are making a particular attack on the big battleship because it is the most costly military instrument known. The cost of a single modern battleship would keep a nation in aircraft or submarines..."[358]

Even generals deplored the costs of preparing for war. Major General Tasker Bliss, the Army's Chief of Staff in 1917–1918, testified before Congress in January 1921. He stated that

> ...our present form of civilization cannot stand the great strain of military preparation much longer. The World War was a terrific strain on civilization. The next war will be very much worse. Fear is the basis of war preparation. This is a business proposition and we should determine whether there is any real basis for the fear that causes these great military and naval programs. I do not care what the Cabinets of the world think. The masses of the people, who pay the taxes, have the vital interest in this subject.

Bliss did not favor the slightest move towards unilateral disarmament, but said, on the basis of his experience at the peace talks, that the world looked to the United States to get disarmament talks going. Once the invitations to such talks were issued, a major power that declined to come would be revealed as "the next Germany," according to the general.[359]

The same day that Bliss testified Secretary Daniels appeared. He testified as to the strengths of the three main naval powers, the United States, Great Britain, and Japan. When all three had completed the planned building programs the United States would be superior to the Royal Navy in tonnage and gun power of battleships, though not in number. The British outnumbered American light cruisers by more than 3 to 1, which was the biggest imbalance among the classes of vessels, though the total tonnage and total number of vessels of all kinds would be about the same. Japan was far behind these two, but after completion of her building program in 1927 the United States-Japan ratio in battleships would be 1.4 to1 rather than the current 2.5 to1.

[358] "Spring Styles in Armament," *Independent*, Feb. 21, 1921, 105:3759, 189.
[359] "Daniels Shows Navy's 1925 Lead Over All Powers," *New York Times*, Jan. 13, 1921, 1.

President Wilson and Secretary Daniels were still advocating the completion of the 1916 naval building program and their motives were questioned by some. Professor Amos Hershey of Indiana University was a questioner. The Wilson Administration had claimed that since the United States hadn't signed the Versailles Treaty and there were no disarmament negotiations in the offing, the US had no choice if it wished to stay ready for any eventuality. Hershey, however, wrote that he compared the present to the pre-World War I situation, when Germany began its large building program to challenge Great Britain, the leading maritime power. Now, however, it was we who were challenging Great Britain by continuing to build warships when they had suspended their program, and refusing invitations to participate in disarmament talks (under League auspices.) Our national budget reflected the stress we were putting on preparedness, since "during the last fiscal year ending in June 1920, over 90% of our total national expenditures were for war purposes, past, present and future."[360]

Passing the Trident

Professor Hershey wrote that if the United States and Great Britain continued their current policies the "trident will pass" from the British to the American Navy by 1924. Policies could change, of course. The British were considering whether new undersea and aerial weaponry might dethrone the battleship as the queen of the fleet. Most of the admirals in both navies, however, still thought the battleship to be the essential component of naval force. Secretary Daniels agreed: "Now comes our pacific Secretary of the Navy in wolf's clothing" to ask for an additional naval building program, which would add 88 new vessels, including four battleships. A naval competition between the United States and Britain could ensue, which would eventually ruin both nations economically and ruin chances for world economic recovery and peace immediately. There was also Japan to consider. She did not have current plans to increase her navy, but was questioning why the United States was continuing to expand its fleet. We should stop the "blind, reckless and wasteful policy of continuing to squander money on naval construction long after all excuse for it is over...It should be one of the first tasks of the incoming administration to call a conference of the leading naval powers to take counsel on this important matter."[361]

Japan wanted negotiations as well. Premier Hara called the idea that Japan was plotting against the United States "fantastic nonsense;" Admiral

[360] Hershey, Amos S. "The United States, the Main Obstacle to the World's Peace," *Independent*, 105:3759 (Feb., 1921,) 183.
[361] Ibid., 184.

Kato said it was "absurd and preposterous" to think that Japan would plan to attack America and made a pointed reference to Japan's joining the League of Nations as evidence of her good intentions. He also stated that Japan was ready to halt all naval construction if the United States and Great Britain would reciprocate. The political situation in Japan was, however fluid. A member of the Japanese parliament had issued a statement claiming that the nation spent more than half its budget on the military and that this could not but fuel suspicions that Japan was a "militaristic nation." Yet when he put forth a resolution in the legislature calling for armament reductions it was overwhelmingly defeated. A professor at the Imperial University in Tokyo was not surprised; he was quoted that "Elder Statesmen and militarists" would do all in their power to prevent others from making decisions about the Navy and Army. Other Japanese press comment agreed that nothing much would happen to reduce armaments until the United States took a first step.[362]

Senator Borah did all he could to encourage that step, going so far as to filibuster a naval spending measure to try to force an amendment calling for an arms reduction conference. According to Arthur Henning Davis, the *Chicago Tribune* Washington bureau chief, Borah's "mulish" action caused the Republican Senate leader, Henry Cabot Lodge, to call for a highly unusual closed session in order to lay out the perilous situation that Japanese actions had caused. Davis' take on the session, which he seemed to have no problem in penetrating, was reported the following day in an "exclusive dispatch" to the *Los Angeles Times* and a remarkably similar bylined report in the *San Francisco Chronicle*. The problems with Japan were their "imperialistic designs in the Pacific, menacing attitude in the California land controversy, breach of faith in the Yap affair [controversies between the US and Japan over commercial rights and possible fortification of the island of Yap in the Caroline Islands chain], and general sharp practice and double-dealing in relations with the United States."

President Harding and his Secretary of State Charles Evans Hughes agreed that things were at an impasse. Congress would not fund the navy that the admirals and the Navy Department wanted. If the Japanese or the British decided to build more ships then a naval arms race similar to that leading up to World War I might result. They decided to call for an arms limitation conference to meet in Washington in the fall of 1921. The invitations specified that the conference would deal with arms limitation and with the balance of power in the Pacific.

---

[362] I. Kawakami and Sidney Gulick, "The Government, Public Opinion, and the Press," *Outlook*, Jun. 1, 1921, 220.

Delectable Pink Teas

The cause of the World War, according to *The Nation*, was militarism. It was also the cause of the present difficulties. The upcoming conference's aim should be to work for a solution to militarism and *The Nation*'s commentator Rome G. Brown (1862–1926) believed that "It is not too much to say that if the Conference does not control militarism, militarism would control the Conference."

Conference planning did not inspire optimism. The conferees would arrive the following week with their military advisers. Would not these military advisers carry militarism with them, wouldn't they be vectors of the disease of militarism? We had our military advisers as well, surely we weren't immune? One way to assess militarism was the size and cost of the military establishment. The Army was, as of 1921, more than 50% larger than it was in 1916. Authorized expenditures had increased by the same ratio; its authorized strength was more than 50% larger. These increases indicated a growing militarism, especially since they occurred "without apparent reason or justification." Naturally the General Staff of the Army has grown in size and influence as well, and "that body of militarists has probably controlled Presidents and certainly Secretaries of War and Congresses."[363] Secretaries of War, even if they might have "strong pacifist inclinations," are co-opted by the smartly uniformed and seemingly subordinate generals who make it seem like the Secretary is the master of the arts of war. Congress, too, is furnished with young military aides who supply them with important information and make sure they are "honored with invitations to many delectable pink teas of a military flavor."[364]

Then there was the size and nature of the officer corps of the army. Adding together Regular Army, National Guard and Reserve officers the total was 100,000. This was enough to command and staff an army of 2 million men. *The Nation* noted darkly that Congress could only specify the total number. The appointing authority was technically the President, but in actuality the leadership of the Army would be selecting and promoting officers: "Naturally officers who differ with the Chief of Staff in matters of military policy will not be appointed or will not retain their commissions."

One hundred thousand officers was a lot for a nation at peace. However, the US Army General Staff knew some history, particularly the history of

[363] Rome G. Brown, "Militarism in the United Sates and the Conference," *The Nation*, vol. 113 no. 2940, November 9, 1921, 526.

[364] Ibid., 527. A "pink tea" is defined by Merriam-Webster Online as "1: a formal afternoon tea usually marked by a high degree of decorum 2: a decorous or namby-pamby affair or proceeding.

General Gerhard von Scharnhorst (1755–1813): "That Prussian soldier-statesman was the real father of the idea that converted an entire nation to militarism. To protect Prussia he would begin with the schoolhouse." Was this going to happen in America also? Already new regulations freed Army officers to serve as training officers in the nation's colleges and universities. They would also staff the Citizens Military Training Camps that were held across the country every summer. These and other assignments would produce even more officers for the Army.

Most of the 100,000 officers were not career military, but long service was not required to develop certain attitudes: "We have evidence of many instances in which brief military authority begot militarism in the individual." One piece of evidence was a story about an American Legion meeting held in a hotel. A high-ranking Legion official said that while he was standing in the hotel lobby he 'saw civilians jostling; mind you, actually jostling officers in combat uniform. If any of them had jostled me I should have knocked them down." This was the same type of arrogant militarism that had required civilians to step aside into the gutter if a group of Prussian officers walked towards them on a sidewalk.

It was agreed in the Navy and in the State Department that the most reasonable way to limit navies was to limit the number of battleships. The Navy thought that a ratio of 10:10:6, United States: Great Britain: Japan would be workable, if the United States could build up to a total of one million tons worth of battleships. The admirals were stunned to hear in Secretary of State Hughes' opening address to the Conference, on November 12, 1921, that the recommended ratio was as they recommended, but the total of battleships allowed for each nation was much lower.

Hughes began his talk by explaining that President Harding and he would like to have invited more nations than the U.S. Britain, Japan, France and Italy to the conference, but in order to speed the proceedings those five would negotiate on arms limitation. They had been allies during the war and between them controlled the bulk of naval power in the world: "The opportunity to limit armament lies within their grasp."[365] The other main issue for the negotiators, the Far Eastern Question, would be discussed by the five plus Belgium, China, the Netherlands and Portugal. The naval matters were to be dealt with immediately, but Hughes suggested that work on the Far Eastern Question also proceed, since the two problems were interconnected.

The Secretary pointed out that the task before the conferees was not a new one. Czar Nicholas, in issuing the call for the 1899 Hague Convention,

[365] Charles E. Hughes, *The Pathway of Peace, Representative Addresses Delivered During His Term as Secretary of State*, New York, Harper & Brothers, 1925, 20.

had noted that competition in armaments was creating economic hardship on all nations and was more likely to end in war than in a secure peace. That Convention had not limited arms, nor did a second that met in 1907, and war broke out in Europe 7 years later. Now we should feel impelled to avoid another war and it was imperative to repair the economic damage that had been done by the Great War and its aftermath.

But why deal only with the navies of the powers? Hughes stated that the naval issue was

> The question, in relation to armament, which may be regarded as of primary importance at this time and with which we can deal with most effectively and promptly, is the limitation of naval armament... the core of the difficulty is to be found in the competition in naval programs, and that, in order to appropriately limit naval armament, competition in its production must be abandoned. Competition will not be remedied by resolves with respect to the method of its continuance.[366]

And what portion(s) of a navy should be limited? Hughes stated that American admirals had told him the largest, or capital, ships (battleships and battle cruisers) were the logical choice. Navies wanted balanced fleets and the number of capital ships decided how many smaller vessels would be needed.

Four basic principles were listed that the Americans believed should govern the talks:

1. All capital-ship building programs, either projected or actual, should be abandoned.
2. Further reduction should be made through the scrapping of certain of the older ships
3. General regard should be had to the existing naval strength of the powers
4. Capital ship tonnage should be used as a measure of strength for navies and a proportionate allowance of auxiliary combatant craft prescribed.[367]

Getting down to numbers, Hughes proposed that the US scrap 15 capital ships under construction and 15 older battleships, for a tonnage of 847,720; Great Britain would scrap 19 for a tonnage of 583,375. Japan would scrap 10 older battleships and abandon its building program, for a total of 448,920 tons.

[366] Ibid., 26.
[367] Ibid., 27.

An observer commented that "Mr. Secretary Hughes sank in thirty-five minutes more ships than all the admirals of the world have destroyed in a cycle of centuries."[368]

The conference resulted in six treaties being signed. The Four-Power Pact, signed on December 21, 1921, called for consultations between Great Britain, the United States, Japan and France if a dispute in the pacific area arose between any two members. Its main effect was to replace the 1911 Anglo-Japanese alliance treaty as a means maintaining order in the Pacific. The other five treaties were signed at the close of the Conference on February 6, 1922. They were

> 1. The Five-Power Naval Limitation treaty. This defined capital ships as those displacing more than 10,000 tons and/or carrying guns with bores larger than 8 inches. In the 1920s this meant battleships, battle cruisers and aircraft carriers. A total tonnage ratio of 5:5:3:1.67:1.67 applied to Great Britain, the United States, Japan, France and Italy. There were tonnage limits such that the signatories would have to scrap some existing vessels and some under construction.
>
> 2. Another 5-power treaty that regulated the use of submarines in warfare, but did not limit their number or size. It also outlawed the use of poison gas.
>
> 3. A Nine-Power Pact agreed to by the five powers plus the Netherlands, Portugal, Belgium and China. This treaty affirmed China's status as an independent and sovereign nation. The non-Chinese signatories agreed to equality in commercial relations with China.
>
> 4. Another nine-power agreement established a commission to evaluate Chinese tariff policies.[369]

H.G. Wells in Washington

Press from around the world attended the conference. Noted British author and social critic H.G. Wells (1866–1946) came and wrote dispatches that were published in American and European newspapers. His reports from November and December 1921 were collected and published as *Washington and the Riddle of Peace*, which had its first publication in January, 1922. Wells believed that arms limitation was pointless unless the nations of the

[368] Baer, *One Hundred Years*, 96-97.

[369] https://www.britannica.com/event/Washington-Conference–1921–1922, accessed 4/1/2017.

world could develop an association that would work towards eliminating war. He cited some arms limitation ideas of the London League of Nations Association, which was considering a recommendation that all modern armaments should be eliminated, and offered some helpful suggestions of his own:

> As for example, that no hostilities should be allowed to continue except in the presence of a League of Nations referee, who shall be marked plainly on the chest and pants with the red cross of Geneva, and who — for the convenience of aircraft — shall carry an open sunshade similarly adorned. He shall be furnished with a powerful whistle or hand trumpet audible above the noise of modern artillery, and military operations shall at once be arrested when the whistle is blown. Contravention of the rules laid down by the League of Nations shall be penalized according to the gravity of the offense, with penalties ranging from an hour's free bombardment of the offender's position to the entire forces of the enemy being addressed very severely by the referee and ordered off the field.[370]

The London League of Nations Association might be rather ineffectual, particularly when faced with the supporters and employees of a strong armaments industry. H.G. Wells observed that if arms were to be drastically reduced, it would be over the objections of the armaments industry, which "supplies substance, direction and immediate rewards to the frothy emotions of patriotism; it rules by dividing us and it realizes that its existence in its present form is conditional upon the continuation of our suspicions and divisions. It does not positively want or seek war, but it wants a continuing expectation of and preparation for war."[371] In spite of this, he did not think that the arms industry would be an implacable enemy of the Conference. He wrote they were aware of the burden of arms expenditures, which contributed towards the economic and social collapse that he feared was coming.

When Secretary of State Hughes made his speech the effect was "dramatical." Wells estimated that the proposed strength ratios meant that in the event of war between America and Britain, neither side could be assured of victory, even with Japanese help. Japan could not expect to defeat either, and if they combined against her she would be crushed. "It puts Japan to so definite and permanent disadvantage that it amounts to the abandonment by Japan of the idea that fighting a war in the Pacific except as the last desperate defensive resort under the pressure of an unavoidable attack, and Japan can abandon that idea only if she can see her way clearly without a war to all that

[370] H.G. Wells, *Washington and the Riddle of Peace*, New York, Macmillan Company, 1922, 21-22.

[371] Ibid., 30.

she holds vitally necessary."[372] As to whether Japan would accept the proposed conditions, Wells was cautious. He knew that there was a "military caste in Japan loving war and not even dreading modern war...due to both ancient traditions and recent experience. Japan had most of the fun and little of the bitterness of the Great War and her people may conceivably have a lighter attitude towards aggressive war than any European nation."[373]

Negotiators for Japan and the other four powers wanted security, which Wells thought was a code word for freedom of action. France wanted only peace, but for its security must have the largest army in Europe, keep Germany and the Soviet Union weak and unrepresented, bring large numbers of African colonial troops to the Continent to control white Europeans, and have a large fleet of submarines which Wells believed could only be aimed at the British. For her security, Britain would require the largest fleet in the world and a system of efficient naval arsenals. Japan would only need control of East Siberia, privileged access to raw materials in Manchuria and extension of its concessions in China. With these intentions made clear, Wells wrote, these nations would be not "...so much disarmed as stripped for action...They do not so much propose to give up war as to bring it back by a gentlemanly agreement within the restricted possibilities of their austere bankruptcy."[374]

As a defender of free speech Wells was aware of those other than the five powers who were at the conference but whose voices were not heard. He had dinner with some Koreans who wanted freedom from Japanese occupation and discussions with Syrians who wanted the French mandate over their nation removed. He acknowledged that British policy in India was ill-advised and self-defeating and yet asked men from India if they were ready for self-government. He noted that on the first day of the conference there had been banners outside calling for the release of his fellow Socialist Eugene Debs and he related the case of Charles Ashleigh, a young Englishman who had done some publicity for the I.W.W and received a ten-year prison sentence for his efforts. Yet he believed that the Conference was beginning to attack the main problems of aggression and war, the fears of which were contributing to these and many other problems in the world.[375]

He was a supporter of the League of Nations and had been greatly disappointed that the Versailles treaty was defeated in the U.S. Senate. He hoped that the treaty negotiated at the Conference would be accepted by all the powers and thought it a great step forward, noting that it was essentially a peace treaty between Japan and the US, with the assistance of the English

[372] Ibid., 75.
[373] Ibid., 107.
[374] Ibid., 113.
[375] Ibid., 231-232.

and the French. President Harding had referred several times to an association of nations to work on problems of war and peace and Wells enthusiastically supported that idea. He thought such an association should be composed of the more "advanced" nations and should be extended to others when they were ready for it. The major task of such an association would be to continue and expand the "wearisome yet hopeful" work of the Washington Conference, so that true peace could be attained.[376]

Ida Tarbell at the Conference

Ida Tarbell (1857–1944) was a well-known author, journalist and muckraker, though this last term annoyed her. She also attended the Conference and her interpretation of its events differed from Wells. At first she was not happy with an agenda which gave precedence to limitation of armaments. There had been so much talk of reducing the burden of armaments expenditures that Tarbell asked, "Was the Conference merely to be a kind of glorified international committee on tax reduction?" She believed solving serious disputes between nations should come first: it was unsolved problems that caused arms races, not the other way around. This seems a denial that militarism is a serious problem, a position Tarbell retreated from later. [377]

Probably the most important goal for the Conference was to improve relations between the four powers so that international problems in the Pacific would not escalate into a war-making crisis. Tarbell saw a domestic analogy in the proceedings of a national conference on employment, which concluded just before the arms limitation meetings began. That report of that conference had stated that the time to act on serious economic challenges was before they became crises, a reasonable enough idea that would not become a partial reality until after the next global war. In the end, as previously related, Secretary Hughes did direct most attention to arms reduction, but had the Conference work on Pacific problems at the same time.[378]

Mr. Hughes' opening speech impressed Tarbell as deeply as it did H.G. Wells, but she was struck by what was left out of its recounting of the history of arms control efforts. The Secretary had, as noted above, recounted that history beginning with the Czar's call for a Hague conference in 1899. He made no mention of the Paris Peace Conference of 1919, which produced the Versailles Treaty, the League of Nations, and some stringent arms limitations—if only of the defeated Central Powers. There had been considerable

[376] Ibid., 296.

[377] Ida M. Tarbell, *Peacemakers-Blessed and Otherwise*, New York, The Macmillan Company, 1922, 17.

[378] Ibid., 21.

discussion for the next two years, under League auspices, of what might be done to limit arms and the trafficking in arms. Tarbell thought that Hughes may have called attention to the League by so studiously ignoring it. He also may have wanted not to lessen the dramatic impact of his opening speech's presentation of the specific outcome that the U.S. aimed to achieve.[379]

Tarbell admired the work of Secretary Hughes but not that of H.G. Wells. She was more understanding of French attitudes, perhaps because she had lived and worked in Paris for a time before the war. She sarcastically referred to Wells as "that ardent advocate of the brotherhood of man," then commented that his charge that a French submarine fleet could only be intended for use against England wasn't very brotherly. Further negative comments by him about the French were noted but not characterized, until it came time to discuss an idea broached by President Harding for an Association of Nations.[380]

This happened at the end of the second week of the Conference, when Harding made another address to a plenary session. The proposal was for an Association of Nations to be established, to continue the work that the Conference had begun. Tarbell confessed to be uncertain as to the motive for the suggestion. She thought it possible to be an attempt to jolt the Conference out of what she saw as distractions, one of which was a speech by M. Briand of France which was seen as obstructionism by some, including H.G. Wells. Another, "unamiable," explanation was that President Harding wanted to bask in the spotlight which had been shining brightly on Charles Evans Hughes, who had the Conference firmly in hand and spoke out often and directly. Tarbell contrasted him with former Secretary of State Elihu Root, who always began his statements with "The President instructs me to say." This was not the style of Mr. Hughes. Here Tarbell was reporting what others were saying and did not necessarily agree. She thought if the President craved attention it would have been evident in other of his actions, both before and during the Conference. It was not the Harding style, she wrote, quite the contrary: "Possibly the wisest thing Mr. Harding has yet done as President has been to let the members of his cabinet do their own work." In the cases of Secretary of State Hughes and Secretary of Treasury Andrew Mellon, this was true. In the case of Interior Secretary Albert Fall it would lead to the Teapot Dome scandal and disgrace.[381]

H.G. Wells' reaction to the President's idea gave Ida Tarbell one last chance to take a swipe at him. Wells was enthusiastic. He believed the proposed Association of Nations should continue the work of the Conference

379 Ibid., 48.
380 Ibid., 75, 99.
381 Ibid., 107.

and that further conferences to deal with economic affairs and limiting land armies should be planned. At its beginning, the Association should consist of the nations that signed the Nine Power Treaty concerning China and other "advanced" European and English-speaking countries." Later on, other nations who achieved stability and government based on liberal ideals could join.[382] Again, Ida Tarbell doubted Wells' commitment to the brotherhood of man and wrote that excluding such countries as Russia, India and practically the whole of Africa was not the best way to unify the nations of the world.[383]

It might seem that unity was possible in pursuit of a common goal like peace, but how each nation saw its security needs had always made agreement difficult. Tarbell was in full agreement with Wells on "security." The United States hadn't joined the League of Nations because it wouldn't give up its isolation from "entangling alliances," which isolation it believed made it secure. Isolation did not necessarily mean a reluctance to go to war: "If it was a question of war or [un]restricted immigration," I asked a Californian in the course of the Far Eastern discussion, 'which would you choose?' The look of surprise at the question answered me—'War.' I received the same reply from a Canadian—from an American labor leader—and they were all 'pacifists!' "[384]

Britain wanted to remain the power with the most powerful navy for its security, France wanted the most powerful land army, and Japan wanted a powerful navy *and* a powerful army. Japan had learned its militarism from the master, Prussia, and developed not only militarism but a sense of the weaknesses in the militarisms of others. She saw how corruption and overgrown bureaucracy had weakened Russian militarism and how liberalism and pacifism undermined militarism in England and France. When the war began the Japanese took the opportunity to wrest Germany's Asian possessions from her and make harsh demands of China.[385] Yet most of her gains from the war were taken away at the Paris Peace Conference and this did not make her withdraw. She would not withdraw from the Washington Conference either: "...Japan is, like all nations to a degree, a dual nation; there are two Japans—one clinging to the old, militaristic, autocratic notion of government, the other struggling to understand and to realize the meaning of a united, cooperating world in which each man and each nation shall have a chance at peaceful, prosperous living."

There was another nation that "alienated her best friends by her persistent militarism." That was France, which would not limit its army unless

[382] Wells, *Washington*, 292.
[383] Tarbell, *Peacemakers*, 224.
[384] Ibid., 165.
[385] Ibid., 181–182.

it was guaranteed against attack from Germany by the United States and Britain. "Having no guarantees, France kept her arms. Keeping her arms, the military spirit spread, and the military group grew stronger. How strong recent events have shown." This last may be a reference to the continuation of full conscription by the French, announced at the end of 1921.[386]

Yet in the end Tarbell thought the Conference a success. It "boldly and nobly attempted to do in a limited field something of what the Paris Conference attempted to do for the whole world. The limitation of armaments it proposes rests, like world disarmament, on unionism, standing together. Unionism requires faith; have we enough of it? It requires, too, men of good will. Have we enough of them? In the final analysis it is with them that "peace on earth" rests."[387]

The Navy was unhappy with the result, which was a rejection of their firm belief in the doctrines of sea power developed by Admiral Mahan. For them, the basis of national security and the means to influence the behavior of other nations, particularly potential opponents, was sea power. Another name for such a doctrine is navalism.

In the end the conference limited little. Signatories to the final agreement did agree to the numbers of capital ships, battleships and carriers, that they would have, but there were not limits on any other type of ship. A naval arms race was hardly prevented. There were also many exceptions and some rather strange rule interpretations, which provided some face-saving for parties unhappy with the overall balance of power that the treaty established.

Whether or not the country was happy with the treaty, the US Navy was not. Its leadership believed that the State Department didn't understand the situation in the Pacific and put too much trust in the good intentions of Japan. Rear Admiral Pratt, who strongly supported the agreement, was almost alone among the flag officers. A particularly sore point was the fact that the US had to scrap more ships than the other signatories—we had to "build down." Others were allowed to "build up," and thus add new, modern ships, including some battleships, to their navies in order to reach treaty limits.[388]

Captain Dudley W. Knox USN, Ret., was also critical of the Treaty. In his book he opened the argument by stating that America was the only nation pursuing peace from high motives. We were altruistic and wanted peace because we felt it was best for the world. Other nations, most especially the British and the Japanese, had more traditional aims of negotiating in their national interests. They felt, according to Knox, that they could not afford the expense of naval competition and so wanted navies to be limited in size.

[386] Ibid., 214.
[387] Ibid., 226-227.
[388] Baer, *One Hundred Years*, 107.

Not being as high-minded as we were, they wanted arms limitation to preserve their economies.[389]

Captain Knox saw other problems with the Washington Conference process. There was the press. Anywhere but in America reporters could get information from naval officers. Such information was of course the best and most reliable, since it came from the experts on naval affairs. The problem was that American naval officers were reticent about publicity, partly because of "many years of officially imposed repression." There was another reason; "...a seeming belief in many quarters that American naval officers differ from other Americans, and from officers of other nationality, in that they place selfish interests above their patriotism."[390] One would think that naval officers of any nationality would be "repressed" from stating thoughts and opinions contrary to their government's official line and that such "repression" would be the rule rather than the exception. It is also seems doubtful that supporters of disarmament thought American naval officers the only ones who would put the needs of their service above all else, "selfish" though that may be.

Anti-Militarists and Pseudo-Economists

The *New York Times* saw a danger in reductions in armaments beyond what had been agreed to at the Conference and was critical of those who "call themselves anti-militarists as soon as the last shot in a war has been fired and they can breathe freely...the condition of the navy as the first line of defense little concerns these pseudo-economists." The anti-militarists and pseudo-economists that the newspaper was referring to were members of the National Council for the Reduction of Armaments, an umbrella organization that had been formed in October 1921. It had issued a statement calling for a 50% reduction in military expenditures. The *Times* thought a partial list of members of the Council was "pertinent" and the first three organizations listed were the National League of Women Voters, the General Federation of Women's Clubs and the National Congress of Mothers and Parent-Teachers Association. Ten of the eighteen organizations listed were women's groups and the *Times* may have thought this indicated a weakly idealistic approach to matters of national defense. Other named organizations, such as the National Milk Producers' Association, probably did little to correct this impression. The editorial concluded that Congress must not "play fast and loose with the fleet. All but three of the ships of the three-year

[389] Dudley W. Knox, *The Eclipse of American Sea Power*, New York, J.J. Little and Ives Co., 1922, 5-6.

[390] Knox, *Eclipse*, 15.

program are to be scrapped. Whatever economies are effected in the navy, other capital ships must not be scrapped. The Washington Conference did not abolish war. Preparedness is still a duty."[391]

Sneering Civilians

Although the Conference did propose to end competition in the building of capital ships, supporters of the navy were quick to point out this need not, and should not, mean the end of competition in other areas. Indeed, some observers felt that it would "put a premium on the preparedness of personnel and material for instant effectiveness in the event of war. Then the battle will go, not necessarily to the largest force, but to the best prepared..." The US Navy, however, had never in the past been well prepared to fight a war; it had only been successful due to the courage of its personnel. This should not be allowed to continue, for the Conference would not end war or change the "underlying elements of human nature that make war possible." Robert Emery's article in the *New York Times* had several suggestions as to how preparedness could be enhanced. One was to continue giving its young officers a "fine sense of naval tradition, so important to a military organization though often sneered at by uncomprehending civilians." Another would be to close some naval shipyards, of which there were too many. Every coastal state congressman that had a "mud creek" in his district wanted a shipyard; two of the most unnecessary were the yards at Portsmouth NH and Charleston SC. Other suggestions were that Annapolis midshipmen should have a period of service as enlisted men and that navy recruit training should be centralized at one facility.[392]

President Harding was more hopeful about the possibility of human beings changing than Robert Emery was: "The President said that once he believed in armed preparedness. He went on, 'But I have now come to believe that there is a better preparedness in a public mind and a world opinion made ready to grant justice as precisely as it exacts it. How simple it all has been!' One might wonder if Mr. Hughes was ready to assent to that." The President concluded by thanking all the delegations individually and expressing the hope that there would be more such conferences in the future. Departure dates for all the dignitaries were listed and the Japanese delegates were said to believe that they were "taking home powerful weapons with

[391] "Preparedness Still a Duty," *New York Times*, Feb. 28, 1922, 17.

[392] Robert Emery, "A Navy Ready to Fight," *New York Times*, Feb.19, 1922, 97. Many of Emery's recommendations came to pass, but it took a while. The Charleston Naval shipyard closed in 1996 and naval recruit training was centralized in 1994. The Portsmouth facility continues in operation..

which to check the efforts of the militaristic party to build up a national bogey of an American aggressive war in the Far East."[393]

There were hopes that militarism in Japan could be contained. The new prime minister was Admiral Kato, who had been the chief negotiator at Washington. Though a military man, he was a close friend of his predecessor, Prime Minister Hara. Hara had taken over the Navy Ministry from Kato when the Admiral left for the Conference, becoming the first civilian head of that agency. Therefore, the "fact that Admiral Baron Kato is now Prime Minister does not indicate a return toward militarism...it is expected that the new Premier will adopt the ratification and carrying out of the Washington treaties and will cut down the expenses of the government, particularly for military purposes."[394]

Not everyone was so optimistic. As a *New York Times* editorial rather tentatively put it, "According to what is called in Washington 'the very latest' naval intelligence survey of the programs of the five signatory powers, Japan is outbuilding her associates and this is 'viewed with alarm.'...naval officers are 'convinced' that Japan is gaining an advantage over the United States with respect to light cruisers and submarines." The editorial writer did seem to be convinced that the situation should be viewed with alarm. For one thing, Japan or any other signatory had a perfect right to build as many light cruisers and submarines as she wished. If the US Navy was concerned about this, they could ask Congress for appropriations to build more ships to offset the Japanese advantage, if any. For another, the US had a three-to-one advantage in destroyers, most of them equal to or better than any others in the world: "The United States is so much stronger than Japan in this type of vessel that too much may be made of her light cruiser and submarine program."[395]

An émigré Russian military officer saw Japan's situation in geopolitical and racial terms more than in numbers and types of ships. General N. Golovin's book, *The Problem of the Pacific in the Twentieth Century*, was reviewed by the *New York Times* in December 1922. The General thought that Japan's situation was untenable. Japan was small in area but had a large population for its size. It would have to expand, and southward was the best way to go—that direction was better suited by "climate and other conditions...This will make it necessary for her to seize and occupy permanently those island lands, including the Philippines, that stretch down the Western Pacific to-

[393] Elmer Davis, "Harding Sees Dawn of a Better Epoch," *New York Times*, Feb. 7, 1922, 1.
[394] "An Admiral-Premier with Anti-Militaristic Policies," *Outlook*, June 21, 1922, 1.
[395] "Japanese Naval Construction," *New York Times*, June 29, 1922, 11.

wards Australia. And he [General Golovin] can see only war as the result of any attempt on the part of Japan to thus assuage her needs."[396]

General Golovin did not think that the US and Great Britain would be able to prevent war. He theorized that Japan's first move would be to occupy China and proclaim a policy of "Asia for the Asiatics." He was skeptical about the agreements reached at the Washington Conference, since they did not address the core issues, which he saw as "...the race problem—the friction, the rivalry and the hatred between the white and yellow races—and Japan's need for more territory...Militarism in present times is not measured exclusively by the size of armies and navies...the important factors must be considered of how far the state can mobilize all its living and material forces for war and how far it can prevent economic disintegration."[397] He did not recommend scrapping the treaty, recommending instead to strengthen the nations who had not participated in the Washington Conference but who were interested in resisting any Japanese expansionist move on the continent of Asia—that is, Russia and China. The unnamed reviewer of the book for the Times thought this unrealistic and possibly counterproductive. Trying to have everyone oppose Japan and isolate it was treating Japan like "the bad boy of the family of nations who must be shut up in the attic for the protection of the rest. Perhaps the solution could be made a little easier if more attention were paid to how the bad boy could earn his supper without interfering with the rest and less to putting new padlocks on the attic door."[398]

Our Militarism

Not only was Japan not the bad boy, it was one of the two nations best equipped to contribute to peace in the world, the other being the USA. Raita Fujiyama, President of the National Federation of Japanese Chambers of Commerce addressed the United States Chambers of Commerce at a meeting in New York in the spring of 1923. He asserted that the "militarists and bureaucrats" of Japan no longer held sway. Now the Japanese were only interested in peaceful development of their economy. He acknowledged that some Americans feared Japanese militarism. What they feared, however, only seemed to be militarism:

> Our militarism, however, was not intended as a threat to the world, but was the result of the situations which confronted us and menaced our national existence. Primarily the problem of the Far East grew out of the internal weakness of China. Every nation interested in China

[396] "Prophet of War," *New York Times*, December 17, 1922, 24.
[397] Ibid., 26
[398] Ibid.

> was aggressive and militaristic. Could Japan afford to allow any power, or concert of powers, to set up a militaristic regime at her very door? It is a pity that Japan, in order to get a square deal, was compelled to adopt the policy which caused her to be mistaken for a menace to the peace of the world.[399]

Concerning the present day, Fujiyama asserted that Japan's aim in China was not conquest or domination, but economic cooperation. He considered that the Washington Conference had settled the issues between the USA and Japan. These two nations were internally united and stable. Europe still had problems with wars, internal dissention and violence. It was up to the USA and Japan to serve as models of national harmony, to show Europeans how to live in peaceful prosperity.

Down with Militarism!

Japan may not have been as unified as Raita Fujiyama thought. In May 1923 a group of high-ranking military officers went to Waseda University in Tokyo to attend the inaugural meeting of the Society for the Study of Military Affairs. The American weekly *The Nation* issue of July 11, 1923 quoted the *Japan Chronicle* [An English-language newspaper published in Japan from 1900 to 1940] account of what happened:

> At the entrance of the university was hanging a flag with the characters: "Down with Militarism! Capture the Meeting Hall! Anti-Society for the Study of Military Affairs." When the military officers were entering the hall of meeting, one of the anti-society members cried "Behold those human butchers!" At the appointed time there was, besides the professors and seventy members of the society, an audience of nearly a thousand students.
>
> Professor Aoyagi, the president of the society, took the rostrum and began "I——"A student from the audience completed the sentence with "——am a militarist." Loud laughter greeted this sally, which was followed by: "Be ashamed of yourself, Aoyagi!" "He feels no shame; he has sold his soul to the militarists." Professor Aoyagi turned pale, says the *Asahi*, [*Asahi Shimbun*, major Tokyo daily newspaper] but he courageously said that liberty and discipline never were in conflict. They (the members) were not proclaiming militarism, but nationalism. The rest of his speech was drowned in the noise. The military officers compressed their lips and looked darkly at the disorder. "Who

[399] "Says World Hangs Upon Us," *New York Times*, May 9, 1923, 7.

> admitted these swashbucklers into the students' school?" one cried. "Drag them out!" shouted others.

Dr. Shiozawa then took the rostrum and said the audience misunderstood something. "Nothing whatever!" shouted the students.

"Was not Marquis Okuma the president of the Soldiers' Friends Society?" asked Dr. Shiozawa. "Don't misrepresent the spirit of the Marquis!" shouted the students. The doctor concluded his speech saying that militaristic national defense was international. Look at Russia. Look at America. They were devoting all their might.

> Dr. Takeda (the new president of the university), who had been fidgeting in his chair with impatience, betook himself to the platform and gazed on the students fixedly. "Reflect, Takeda!" the students shouted. "Have you forgotten the 16th year of Meiji?" (when Takeda stoutly attacked militarism.) Dr. Takeda turned scarlet with anger and cried that a nation constitutionally governed should respect the liberty of speech at public meetings...If there were militarism actually, it should be destroyed as soon as possible. It must be part of the business of society. But, he cried, the Waseda University ought to be ashamed of their conduct. He returned to his seat trembling with excitement.

The Nation related that several military officers attempted to speak after Dr. Takeda, but were treated the same as the academics. The meeting ended in confusion, but this was not the end of the controversy over the Society for the Study of Military Affairs. The protesters scheduled a meeting of their own for May 12. That meeting brought out pro-military activists, fist-fights broke out, and six students were seriously hurt. The next day a group of mostly younger professors held a meeting supporting the anti-militarists. They issued a statement, which read, in part, "The Society for the Study of Military Affairs invited militarists, including General Shirakawa, the Vice Minister of War, to the inauguration ceremony. We have reason to suspect that the society has joined hands with the military clique, and has been made the cat's-paw of the militarists. The society should be accused." As it turned out, no indictments were required, because the society was disbanded a few days later.[400]

Militaristic and Imperialistic Policies

The Washington Conference, it will be remembered, dealt with naval arms limitation and some of the military and political issues in the Pacific

[400] "Japanese Students Show Their Opposition to Militarism," *The Nation*, July 11, 1923, 44.

area. Meanwhile, there were ongoing issues beyond naval arms that affected peace and security in Europe.

No matter what Japan or any other nation did with its military, Senator Borah wanted everyone to understand that the United States would not form a political alliance with or against any state. That went against a basic tradition of American foreign policy and there was no chance for it to happen. However, we stood ready to talk and to render assistance to solve economic and financial problems where and when appropriate—as in talks about war debts and the activities of humanitarian agencies such as the American Relief Administration headed by Herbert Hoover. Many European attitudes and actions, however, had made it difficult for America to act:

> Her militaristic and imperialistic policies after the armistice diminish our hopes and destroy our faith. Europe today has greater military establishments than before the war. Such a policy is utterly brutal and insane. While debts increase and taxes mount higher and higher and human misery spreads, governments pile up burdens in the way of armaments. While the people of Europe are praying for peace their governments are preparing for war.[401]

Borah made clear his conviction that as long as European nations were maintaining large military establishments there could be no adjustments in the war debts they owed to the United States.

Around Armistice Day 1923 two clerics took a longer view of problems of war and militarism. In the case of Methodist Reverend George MacAdam it was a very long view indeed, back to classical Greek and Roman times. He was interested in the differences between the ways in which the Greeks and Romans viewed their gods of war. He noted that at the beginning of the twentieth century, with more than a half-century of peace between the powers of Europe, men were beginning to think, or perhaps dream, that peace could last indefinitely. Those thoughts and dreams were shattered in August 1914 when "The world aroused and looked up to see the resurrected, bristling form of old Ares the war god throwing his somber shadow over all the earth...And because the war god brought this time almost the entire planet to his worship, and because he dragged civilization to the very verge of ruin and left her there...There are many people who contend that he is deathless...War has hypnotized us with a sense of its inevitability."[402] MacAdam cited some contemporary evidence for beliefs in the persistence of war: a man-on-the-street poll in Chicago found 80% of respondents thought that wars would

[401] "Borah Tells Europe Why We Do Not Help," *New York Times*, January 10, 1923, 2.

[402] George MacAdam, "The War God," *The Methodist Review*, vol. 39 no. 6 (November 1923,) 852.

always occur. MacAdam, however, believed that this was somewhat of an automatic response, given without much thought. Given the recent ordeal of war and the slow, painful recovery from the devastation, some reflection on the history of war gods could be useful.

MacAdam wrote that the Greeks had in effect two war gods, Ares and Pallas Athene. Pallas wore a helmet and had a shield on her left arm. She was the goddess of battles. Athene, the goddess of wisdom, would support the Pallas side of her nature if the cause was just. Despite the fact that the Greeks, like every other nation old and new, considered all of their wars to be just, at least justice was considered. Their other war deity was Ares, who was rather disreputable. According to MacAdam this god was an import from Thrace and Scythia, and not at all popular amongst the Greeks. He was not concerned with justice but only with encouraging and sustaining war. He had few temples and statues in Greece, unlike Pallas Athene and other goddesses and gods. He was mocked by Greek satirists and playwrights and portrayed as scorned by Zeus. Just as there is a difference between Pallas Athene and Ares, MacAdam saw a difference in the way Greeks and Romans treated their war divinities. Mars, the Roman god of war, was one the most important gods of Rome, with many temples and festivals throughout the Empire. He was worshipped and revered, not made fun of and satirized. Perhaps this reverence was one reason why the Romans experienced centuries of constant war.[403]Perhaps, also, we did not have to follow the Roman path:

> It is strange that we do not realize that "toting a gun" is the almost certain condition of having to use it; that going about with "a chip on the shoulder" is the surest way of getting into a brawl; that the possession of an immense and efficient war machine is the almost certain guarantee of needing it and a continual suggestion and temptation to use it...The militarist will of course characterize this as an impractical pacifism, but is it? Is it not the commonest kind of common sense?[404]

Dr. Herbert Booth was more direct in his 1923 Armistice Day sermon, delivered over KHJ, then the radio station of the *Los Angeles Times*: "I want to say five things about war. First, war is contrary to the teachings of the Scriptures. Secondly, war is based on a wrong theory of the State. Thirdly, war is a criminal waste of money and settles nothing. Fourth, war in the twentieth century means the suicide of civilization. Fifth, war can be ended by the United States of America."

[403] Ibid., 856.
[404] Ibid., 862.

The Exaltation of Armed Force

Dr. Booth explained his second point, the about the theory of the state. He believed that militarism and a "wrong" theory of the state were connected: "Militarism is the doctrine of reliance upon and exaltation of armed force...Now, back of militarism lays a wrong theory, a wrong conception of the state. That theory is that the state is not a moral entity." Booth stated that everyone believes that the people of the state are "moral and responsible people." Yet put millions of these responsible moral agents together, and suddenly we have a state, which may or may not act in a moral and responsible way—but must further its own interests no matter how these actions affect other states. And, some thought that economic strength should be developed no matter the consequences. Booth countered this thinking by quoting the astronomical costs of the World War, and noting that "Ninety-three per cent of the taxes of the United States are going for war purposes." The Reverend regretted that we had missed an opportunity to try to eliminate war by not signing the Versailles Treaty. We had another chance, though, since he believed that "Europe is saying to us, 'You are free from the curse of militarism and are in a position to exercise moral suasion and leadership.' God grant that we may."[405] In the *Times* summary of Dr. Booth's remarks, no specifics were given about who in Europe was asking for our leadership.

The Navy League

One of the bitterest opponents of Josephus Daniels was the Navy League, which had been founded in 1902. The League did not see Daniels as the kind of naval partisan that was needed. The success of the Navy in the war, however, resulted in Daniels besting them; membership declined during and after the war. Naturally they did not see the end of the war as the end of all wars. They noted that the US now had over half the merchant vessel tonnage in the world and a strong navy was needed to protect it. [406]

The League was also bitter about the Washington Treaty, which they saw as a cave-in to the British, but they did not formally oppose the treaty. Instead, they conducted a nationwide campaign in support of maintaining a navy of 86,000 men. This figure was below what they thought was necessary, but Daniels' successor Navy Secretary Edwin Denby advised the league that it was the best that could be done and that he would try to do better in the future.

[405] "Pastor Asserts War is Civilization's Suicide." *Los Angeles Times*, November 12, 1923, III8.
[406] Armin Rappaport. *The Navy League of the United States*, Detroit, Wayne University Press, 1962, 79.

The League moved on. Ever since its founding some members had wanted to have a day set aside for celebrating the Navy, similar to Britain's Trafalgar Day. League President Robert W. Kelley suggested to Acting Navy Secretary Theodore Roosevelt Jr. that a Navy Day be established "on which the country would be reminded, through the concerted efforts of numerous patriotic organizations, of the Navy and its value to them." The Department agreed to cooperate and October 27, 1922 (the birthday of the late President Roosevelt, a champion of the Navy) was the first Navy Day. It was preceded by heavy publicity and with support from such organizations as the American Legion, Daughters of the American Revolution, and Military Order of the World War. The day was a big success all across the nation and

> A great amount of hostility was allayed by the careful emphasis on the defensive functions and peacetime duties of the Navy. Many critics were silenced by the League's endorsement of the limitation treaties. The absence in the celebrations of a jingoistic note or aggressive tone went a long way towards cutting the ground from under pacifist opponents...Only the extreme anti-Navy journals, such as the *Christian Science Monitor*, disapproved.[407]

The following year and 1924 were also successful, large crowds visiting ships and shore installations, watching parades, and listening to patriotic speeches. In 1923 the League wanted to stress the importance of building up to treaty limits and in particular to address the lack of cruisers in the Navy. The US had fewer cruisers than either England or Japan, to the extent that the ratio for cruisers was 1:5:3, US: England: Japan. When the Navy Department proposal for building 8 new cruisers reached the Senate floor in December 1924, the League had prepared the way with all the publicity it could muster, telling the public that the eight were vital as a first step, since the actual need was more than twenty. The League had the support of many newspapers, but the small navy advocates continued their opposition, claiming that there was no substantial threat to the United States and there was a real danger of creating a naval arms race. These critics claimed the League was in "conspiracy with naval officers, shipbuilders and nationalist societies...raising false scares to stampede the public into supporting increased appropriations."[408]

[407] Ibid., 94.
[408] Ibid., 101.

What Militarism Is

Japan was constantly under observation for signs of militarism, but the situation in Europe also caused concern. The British Army was small, but the Royal Navy was the largest in the world and caused some in the United States to question English motives. France had come in for some criticism during the Conference, because it refused any move towards negotiations on reducing land armies. The critics did not stop when the Conference ended and a French general replied to them in a 1922 article in *Current Opinion*. General Emil Taufflieb noted a previous article in the magazine had accused the French of desiring military domination over Europe. That was claimed to be the purpose of maintaining an 800,000-man army. The General disputed this and thought it necessary to explain the meaning of the word "militarism." The explanation, he wrote, is not best found in a dictionary. For true understanding, "it must be lived, it must be felt, as Alsatians under German rule have lived and felt it." Lacking that experience, however, militarism exists where the military are in ultimate charge of the civilian population and can overrule whatever decisions nonmilitary authorities may make. This was the situation in Alsace, which was ceded to Germany after the French defeat in the war of 1870: "A genuine dictatorship taught our brothers in Alsace what militarism is. France may have been militaristic under Napoleon I or Napoleon III, but that France is not the France of the Third Republic." The large French army was solely for defense against Germany, which General Taufflieb believed was ready psychologically, if not physically, to make war upon France again. It was true that the Germans had been forced to disarm and then limit their army to 100,000 men. But they had recently signed the Treaty of Rapallo with the Soviet Union and "what prevents her new friend Russia from providing her with guns and ammunitions?"[409]

Perhaps, though, militarism in France had developed long before the World War. Perhaps there was a "...peculiar combination of French royalism, clericalism, and militarism, about which Americans know so little, but which all republican Frenchmen dread..." If so, a demonstration might be French actions concerning the events in Hungary in 1919. A Hungarian government set up after the defeat of 1918 was swept aside by Hungarian communists led by Bela Kun. The party began hunting down and executing its enemies. Opponents of the new regime were assisted by Hungary's neighbors, especially Rumania, to topple the communists in turn. The neighboring countries were members of the Little Entente organized by France after the war, and some believed that France assisted in the attack on Hungary. Not,

[409] Emil Taufflieb, "French "Militarism" Defined and Explained," *Current Opinion*, vol. LXXIII no. 2 (Aug. 1922,) 179, 181.

however to support a return to democracy, but to assist in the re-imposition of monarchy in the person of Admiral Miklos Horthy, who served as Regent of the Kingdom of Hungary from 1919 to 1944. A French general had made the armistice with the Hungarians, separate from the November 11 1918 agreement, which paved the way for the dictatorship of the Admiral: "For French militarism is a living fact, and like German militarism before it, does not regard itself as altogether responsible to the civil authorities."[410]

Another way they were similar was that "French militarism, like the German militarism of 1914, cares not a fig for the public opinion of the world. It seizes upon an inexcusably loosely drawn provision of the Treaty of Versailles as a pretext for seizing German cities on the east bank of the Rhine..." The forces occupying those German cities, largely from colonial African contingents of the French Army, were considerable and well-placed to invade the Ruhr valley, the industrial heartland of Germany. The Versailles Treaty provision referred to stated that the forces occupying German territory would be withdrawn when Germany complied with all provisions of the Treaty. It did not specify what constituted compliance and how such compliance was to be determined. Germans believed that they had done everything required, but the French believed that full compliance meant payment of reparations in full. With postwar Germany still in political turmoil between pro and anti-government forces the French occupation of German cities strengthened the hands of radicals and communists as well as right-wing nationalists. But "What is that to the French militarists?" Increasing disorder in Germany might allow annexation of the territories occupied and French politicians would likely collaborate in such an annexation scheme. If the other signatories to the Treaty and the United States were opposed to France annexing German territory, that would make little difference. The only restraint on the militarists and the politicians was the "...good sense of the French people, who must sooner or later awaken to the dangers of a policy that threatens to leave France as morally isolated as Germany once was."[411]

The cost of the French military was high. According to author and journalist Robert Dell (1865–1940) in 1920 France spent on its military nearly three times their entire government expenditures of 1914. "This is the result of aggressive militarism and vainglorious imperialism." Though the nation was in a fiscal crisis, France had added to its budgetary problems by adding to its colonial problems. Dell believed that the French empire was already costing more to operate than it was producing revenue. Even so France had taken on new mandated territories from the League of Nations. One of these

[410] "A Disgrace," *The New Republic*, vol. XX no. 250, (August 20, 1919,) 74.
[411] "The Week," *The New Republic*, vol. XXII no. 280 (April 14, 1920,) 193.

mandates, Syria, was already in armed rebellion against French administration. "Then there is the occupation of German territory which the French militarists want to extend. All of these grandiose schemes make an enormous army essential." Conscription was still in force in France and had been extended to the French African colonies. This took young men out of the work force when they were at their most productive and was a drag on the French economy. Dell believed the situation was desperate and saw no possibility of solutions so long as expenditures of the French military loomed so large.[412]

Historian and foreign correspondent for *The Nation* William Macdonald (1863–1938) reported from French-occupied Frankfurt in May 1920. His article, datelined April 17, 1920, was entitled "What French Militarism Means." It was, however, critical of both French and German attitudes towards the Versailles Treaty and its implementation. He did not believe that French rule in the Rhineland was harsh. Many of the rules originally imposed had been relaxed and although soldiers were seen everywhere German civilians could go about their daily routines without interference. The French African soldiers so resented by the Germans were no longer on guard duty.

However, "With perfect frankness, France has returned to militarism." Macdonald meant that France did not believe that policies of conciliation and negotiation would get them what they desired and thought that the Treaty granted them. The Germans, however, believed that if they complied with every detail of the Treaty there would never be any negotiation—simply more demanded of them. It was an impasse, but "for the moment France is the militaristic Power of the world." However, use of that Power would only destabilize Germany and encourage the German "Monarchist and militarist party which knows what it wants and plots day and night to get it."[413]

A Terrible Militarist Miscreant

Foreign observers may have seen militarism in French policies, but what did the French think? According to the *Literary Digest* of August 5, 1922, the French "semi-official" *Les Temps* made two sets of comparisons in order to determine the truth or otherwise of accusations that France was a "terrible militarist miscreant." The first set was between French expenditures pre-and-post war. These showed that France spent about 90% more in 1922 than it did in 1913. However, counting expenditures in gold francs rather than in

[412] Robert Dell, "The Coming Crisis in France," *The Nation*, vol. CX no. 2862 (May 8, 1920,) 616.

[413] William Macdonald, "What French Militarism Means," *The Nation*, vol. CX no. 2863 (May 15, 1920,) 650-651.

paper money, i.e. correcting for inflation, expenditures in 1922 were 16% less than in 1913.

The other set of comparisons was with foreign countries. Not correcting for inflation, there was only one country that had a lower percentage of increased expenditure than France—that was Switzerland, which spent 73% more in 1922 than in 1913. Every other country's percentage increase in that time period was higher than France's 90%—the United States 174%, Great Britain 181%, Japan 290% and Italy 390%. Again correcting for inflation and converting them into amounts of "francs gold," the military budgets for 1922 are France 1.8 billion, the United States 6.1 billion, Great Britain 4.3 billion, Japan 1.9 billion and Italy 970 million.[414] These figures do show that France was not the only country to spend a lot of money on its military, but some facts are ignored, such as the fact that France, alone among the nations considered, had a conscript army in 1913—and in 1922.

Andre Tardieu (1876–1945,) was foreign affairs editor of *Les Temps* during the 1920s and was premier of France three times between 1929 and 1932. He may have written the article referred to above, "French 'Militarism' ".He did write an article in the April 1922 issue of *Foreign Affairs* which used some of the same numbers, but began by stating

> If, in speaking of French militarism, one wishes to insinuate that France dreams of adventures and conquests and even of a new war, one has to re-read my estimate of the crushing burden left on our shoulders by our victorious war. We want only peace, and we want it more intensely than any other people in the world. We have almost died of war. If, on the other hand, as I have read only too often in English and American newspapers, it is claimed that France is militaristic because it is devoting to armaments more money than any other country, I say—and I shall prove—that such a statement is contrary to the truth.

Tardieu's first point was a comparison between the military budgets of 1918 and 1922. In 1918 France spent 36 billion francs, in 1922 5 billion, a seven-fold reduction. Considering the increase in war expenditures from 1913 to 1922, Tardieu wrote that it was an increase of 266%. However, the cost of living had increased more than 300%. To Tardieu this represented a decrease in military spending.

And, in comparison, percentage increases for the United States were 340%, Great Britain 274%, Japan 332% and Italy 372%—France, again, was 266%, the least among the Allied Powers. "Yet the [four] countries which

[414] "French 'Militarism' ", *The Literary Digest*, vol. LXXIV no. 6 (August 5, 1922. 26.)

have passed her have never had to face the accusation of militarism which is now dinned into her ears.[415]

Reviving Militarism

And what of the new regime in Russia, which had the other large army in Europe? During the height of the Red Scare in the United States there had been considerable talk about the military power of the Soviet Union. In 1919 the Red Army was estimated to be 750,000 strong and, while the rest of the world was disarming "Lenin and Trotsky are reviving militarism." Though Trotsky was Minister of War it was claimed that Bolshevik victories in the ongoing Civil War were due to leadership of Czarist officers, whose obedience to their Communist leaders was only maintained by threats of death for any sign of disloyalty.[416] A 1920 report put the strength of the Red Army at 400,000, but acknowledged that it had decisively defeated one of its two major opponents, the White Army forces in Siberia that had been led by Admiral Kolchak. This was "being heralded by the Reds as a great victory for Bolshevist militarism over Russian nationalism." It seems more likely that the Bolsheviks would have called it a triumph of the working class rather than of militarism, but there is no doubt that it made them confident enough to predict more victories in the near future.[417]

These developments were "regarded by allied officials and diplomats as constituting the threat of a possible invasion of Europe and a serious menace to the peace of the world." They had happened for two main reasons. First, the Communist program in areas under their control was a failure and they had decided to build a "powerful military machine" to solidify and extend their control over Russia. Second, the western allies had failed to send the aid that they had promised to the White Armies. Now, unless the allies were willing to admit defeat and submit to Communism, they must "fight the Bolshevist military menace to save what is worthwhile in the world from the Communist terror...Governments must fortify themselves for a real fight against Bolshevik militarism."[418]

By the end of 1920 talk of the danger of Soviet militarism abated. For one thing the Red Army, which had been engaged in a war with Poland, had been decisively defeated before Warsaw and forced to retreat from Polish territory. Their victory over Kolchak in Siberia had not forced a Japanese evacuation there; Japanese troops would remain until 1925. The Red Scare in

[415] Andre Tardieu, "The Policy of France," *Foreign Affairs*
[416] "Bolshevist Army Grows to 750,000," *New York Times*, Feb. 15, 1919, 4.
[417] "Now See Red Terror as Peril to World," *New York Times*, Jan. 11, 1920, 3.
[418] Ibid

the United States dissipated after the fall elections. Some, however, still felt that Soviet militarism endangered Europe.

One of those was Senator Borah, but his analysis differed strongly from that of anti-communists and most conservatives. He saw militarism as a response by those who are excluded from the affairs of the world. We had not recognized the Communist regime, now firmly in power, due largely to propaganda about its hostile intentions toward us. The current example was a message from the head of the Communist International to the Workers' Party in the United States, which was claimed to include instructions to work for raising the red flag over the White House. The red flag phrase apparently was in a Soviet government newspaper article, but translations differed widely. Borah thought the claim "miserable fustian and futile trash" and was for recognition of the current government of Russia. He suggested that a payment schedule for money that was owed to the United States by Russia could easily be arranged after recognition. Once this was negotiated trade between the two countries could be resumed. Borah thought the Soviets would feel secure enough to reduce their army by at least half once they were welcomed back into the community of nations.[419]

Other observers were concerned with more than the Soviets. The delay in ratification of the treaties ending the World War, which process was not completed until the summer of 1923, seemed demonstrate a lack of enthusiasm for arms limitation. Current figures showed that 6 million men serving as soldiers in Europe, which was an "armed camp." The Soviets were increasing both their army and their munitions factories, the Turks could call on 1.5 million men if needed, the French had a million man army, the "new government in Italy" (Mussolini and his Fascists had just come to power) had about 400,000 men and British Empire forces totaled more than 700,000 men. Germany, although restricted by the Versailles treaty, could assemble a million men in "a few days" and Japan was increasing her land forces. The impact here was that "war preparedness drums are being brought from their hiding places." There would again be volunteers to beat those drums. The American Defense Society, which had "practically unlimited financial backing" and had done such "splendid work" in the run-up to World War I was active again: "The people of the United States must be educated along the line of preparedness for war."[420]

General Pershing too thought Americans could use more education about our military needs. In his opinion we should make more efforts to strengthen our army, at least to fulfill the "meager" program laid out in the National

[419] William E. Borah, "Borah States the Case for Russia," *New York Times*, Dec. 30, 1923, XX1.
[420] "Peace Ideas a Chimera?" *Los Angeles Times*, Nov. 20, 1922, I1.

Defense Act of 1920. It was as dangerous to ignore the lessons of the war as it would be to

> ...permit the development of militarism in America...I am no militarist but just a plain practical citizen who would profit by the experience of the past and not indulge in daydreams. We have been leaders in advocating thorough understanding between nations and have decried militarism the world over. We are and have been in a practical state of disarmament and now only advocate a modest state of preparedness as a national insurance.[421]

Secretary of War Weeks believed that war would come again. It was no more reasonable, he said, to believe that the murder or robbery that we read about in our morning paper is the last that will ever occur, than to believe that the recently concluded war is the last one that will ever happen. His annual report for 1923 was characterized by the *New York Times* as "The answer of the Coolidge Administration to pacifists who would still further decrease the cost of our army, already cut below our vital needs...It challenges those who have been engaged in propaganda against the army on the ground that the nation cannot afford and does not need as large an army as the budget estimates contemplate." The Secretary made several comparisons between categories of national expenditures. He estimated, for instance, that if every taxpayer were to buy an Army Colt .45 for self-protection the total spent would be less than the yearly cost of the Army. Further annual comparisons included a reckoning that we spent "six times as much for soda and confections as we spend for military purposes, for tobacco nearly four times, for perfumery, jewelry and other items of adornment nearly five times, and for theatres, cabarets and similar amusements more than three times. Military preparations cost us, roughly, one-eighteenth of what we spend for luxuries, amusements, and mild vices." The report referred back to postwar allegations about the cost in lives and money of a lack of preparedness and military training and noted that the number of men in military units or in some type of training had declined since 1921 from 519,041 to 504,010.

Weeks also observed times had changed and we could no longer rely upon our "isolated situation." Transportation was becoming quicker and more efficient every year. International trade was much more important to us than it had been before the war and we were more aware of the need for a merchant marine to make us competitive in world markets. Not to maintain an effective defense would invite aggression and could bring war. He hearkened back to recent history and stated that some observers had noted Germany had prepared extensively for war and yet it had turned out disas-

[421] "Pershing Pleads for Preparedness," *New York Times*, Nov.12, 1922, 33.

trously for her. Obviously, though, more preparation might have changed the outcome, so this was not an argument against preparedness. In the case of France, if *she* had not prepared for war she might no longer be a free and independent nation.

Militarizing Professional Civilians

Moving back to statistics, the Secretary stated that there were 1.25 American soldiers for every 1,000 Americans and it would be ridiculous to imagine that "one professional soldier can ever militarize a thousand professional civilians...our present scheme is a compromise between compulsory military service and a large professional army." The nature of this scheme, which was the National Defense Act of 1920, and the small size of our army were such as to "completely eliminate the possibility of a growth of militarism."[422]

Earlier in 1923 Weeks had visited the West Coast and on May 24 he addressed a lunch meeting of the Chamber of Commerce and the Commercial Club of San Francisco. He called for support of efforts to strengthen the reserves of the army, telling his audience that the large forces mobilized for the Great War were rapidly dwindling and by 1935 only 20% of their wartime number would be available for service and this 20% would decrease to zero soon afterwards. Even though the Regular Army was quite small,

> One frequently hears protests against our new system of defense. A few rather prominent citizens are making severe accusations. Typical of such statements is one to the effect that the militarists of the nation are carrying on a far-flung campaign to Prussianize the nation. [The claim is made that] our reorganization act seeks the same end that the German militarism sought—to make every male citizen of military age a unit in the war machine. Those who think that the association of army officers with civilians will militarize the former should stop to think of what they imply. Even though our officers were seeking militarism, which they decidedly are not, is our plane of intelligence so low that these few, a mere handful in the midst of the civil population, can convert millions to an abhorrent doctrine?[423]

Still, there were anti-militarists who saw little value in any type of military organization. In Wisconsin, home state of one the leading anti-militarists of the Progressive Era, Senator Robert La Follette, the legislature attempted to disband the state's National Guard. The "Polakowski bill" to abolish the Guard passed the Wisconsin state assembly by a substantial margin in the spring of 1923. Proponents of the measure believed that the

[422] "Weeks Defends Cost of Our Army," *New York Times*, Dec. 1, 1923, 1.

[423] "Weeks Pleads for Reserves," *Los Angeles Times*, May 25, 1923, I4.

Guard would never be needed to maintain order within the state. It also was a "standing provocation to take part in foreign wars," expensive and liable in peacetime to deteriorate into a "sham force." And, according to a scornful *New York Times* editorialist,

> There was much maudlin talk about the sacrifice of Wisconsin boys who served in France. Lame and hypocritical as these arguments were, it required all the vigilance of Governor Blaine to stem the tide running in the legislature in favor of the bill. The Governor sent an emergency message to the legislature in which ...he attacked the idea that the Guard was an encouragement to militarism..."The National Guard of Wisconsin has no relationship whatever to the causes of war." He explained that the Guard was a peace organization, to keep order and protect property on occasions of menacing domestic violence.

The *Times* editorialist was confident that the measure would not pass the State Senate, but

> While the action of the Assembly is sinister, indicating that in Wisconsin there is a combination of Socialists and labor agitators bent upon the disbandment of the National Guard, and no doubt opposed to the maintenance of the regular army, it is a satisfaction to know that the National Guard...has shown steady improvement since the National Defense Act became a law, a condition that is largely owing to the cooperation and assistance of the War Department.[424]

More Peace in the Pacific, More Militarism in Europe

The end of the First World War did not mean the end of great-power military competition, though it did mean the end of gunfire between them. Succeeding Administrations would be concerned that America be in the first position in the power rankings of navies. Most Americans were willing to share this position with the Royal Navy, but none seemed willing to have the Japanese Imperial Navy be in the first rank. To Japanese observers, this seemed unfair and demonstrative of American militarism-and navalism. There were American critics of America as well. We were continuing our naval building program, when Great Britain and Japan had suspended theirs.

Conclusions

Whatever the influence of critics of militarism on military and naval policy, there was the factor of prime importance-money. Adjustment to peace-

[424] "The Wisconsin Attack on the Guard," *New York Times*, March 5, 1923, 14.

time economies had been difficult everywhere and armies and navies were by far the largest shares of national expenditures. An increasing number of voices in the press of the naval powers called for negotiations to prevent competition in naval arms, seen as not only damaging economically but a major cause of the late war.

President Harding's Secretary of State Charles Evans Hughes had a surprise in store when he opened the Washington Conference on the Limitation of Naval Armaments on the day after Armistice Day, November 12, 1921. The U.S. would be recommending not only limitation of arms but reductions in number of vessels in service and/or under construction. The work was done remarkably quickly and five treaties implementing the agreement were signed at the final session on February 6, 1922.

The Conference had two main objectives, to limit the size and relative sizes of great power navies, and to provide a means of settling current and future disputes in the Far East. The agreements signed accomplished these goals. The agreements were time-limited and Japan would opt out when the time came. They did, however, provide peace for their time between potential adversaries. Since it limited without any thought of eliminating armaments, both anti-militarists and their detractors could support it, to varying degrees.

Controversies over what constituted dangerous militarism were not limited to the navies of the world. European armies the size of the French or the Soviet were also criticized as the product of militaristic policies. As always, defenders of those armies explained that they were completely and solely for self-defense. The size of the Regular Army of the United States certainly did not put it in the same league as the Soviet Union or France. This fact did not deter anti-militarists, who could point out that 48 National Guard contingents and the organized reserves made for a more imposing number—especially seeing as how we did not border on any nation that had the capability or the desire to fight us. Mobilization Day, 1924 would provide a chance for both sides in the US to re-state their cases.

8. Mobilization Day, 1924

> "For the first time in its history the national land defense force of the United States will be mobilized on a peacetime basis on Sept. 12, the anniversary of the battle of St. Mihiel and the day before General Pershing retires as Chief of Staff."
>
> *New York Times*, May 15, 1924.

Nineteen twenty-four was an election year. The place of the military in national and international affairs would continue to be debated and the debate sharpened for a time over plans for a national mobilization day event planned for September. Before those plans were announced, however, commentators like Jane Addams continued to speak out about militarism in America.

Addams spoke at a meeting of several hundred members of the Women's International League for Peace and Freedom in New York, on March 23, 1924. She told attendees that she believed it was easier for women to become pacifists than men. This was because women were not as afraid of failure as men. Pacifists, then as now, face an uphill struggle and must be philosophical about defeat. She also indicated a belief that women were not only tolerant of failure, but more tolerant of a diversity of opinion. While other organizations had to ban discussion of politics and religion, the Women's International League for Peace and Freedom discussed any topic in an "agreeable manner." The League's first meeting was in The Hague in 1918, but women had been active in working for peace before then:

> While the rest of the world was entirely absorbed in the terrible realities of modern scientific warfare, this group went steadily ahead...Today, with the same high courage with which the women of the League faced militarism of ten tragic years of history, [meaning 1914–1924] they lead the way to reorganization and fresh development of the political and economic and spiritual forces which underlie human relations, national and international.[425]

Jane Addams very likely would have had differences with Mrs. Calvin Coolidge on supporting military training for civilians. In April 1924, the First Lady announced her sponsorship of a contest.

> She proposes to give three "national trophies" from the White House on Flag Day, June 14. To the girls and young women [between the ages of 13 and 19] who write the best short essays on why their young men friends should attend the citizens' military training camps which are conducted each summer by the War Department. This contest is sponsored by the Women's Overseas Service League, has been approved by the Secretary of War, and Mrs. Coolidge is lending herself to the scheme.

The *Herald of Gospel Liberty* was not offended by this plan. It was outraged:

> Never before in the history of our nation, so far as we know, has any prominent official of the Government or any one closely associated with a President undertaken in times of peace to put war ideas and aspirations into the minds of our school children. And this effort becomes all the more repugnant to thinking people because it is done by women, and for girls, to plant in the minds and hearts of the girlhood of this land the war germ and the military ideals and even to connect it all in the lives of these young girls, with their warm personal attachment for some one of the opposite sex...And it becomes altogether distressing when the wife of our Chief Executive plays the leading figure of the scheme, and uses the White House and our national Flag Day to further this effort of the militarists...However much she might deny or deplore it, this step throws the power of her tremendous example and influence to the side of militarism and in behalf of the war system.

A great opportunity had been lost, lamented the *Herald*. How much better, they opined, to have had a contest for essays against the "pagan system and practice of war." But the project she supported was so harmful that "We feel keenly that the censure of Christian America should be very plainly felt by the much-honored wife of our Chief Executive for having loaned herself

[425] "Jane Addams Spurs Hopes of Wars' End," *New York Times*, March 24, 1924, 4.

to this project, which aligns her and her influence alongside the whole war system and uses her to further a most insidious propaganda for great military preparedness."[426]

Life magazine took a much lighter view of the problems of war and militarism. That was its purview as a humor magazine similar to the British *Punch*, from its founding in 1886 until it was sold to Henry Luce in 1936. In 1924 it ran a contest, asking its readers to send in their ideas on how to achieve bigger and better wars:

We Want Bigger and Better Wars

> LIFE's great War Prize contest has ended in a veritable blaze of glory and the judges are now feverishly wading through the vast mass of contributions. The four prize-winners will be announced in the May 8th issue of LIFE, and the public will then learn the identity of those heroes who are to be personally responsible for the next war. In the weeks that intervene we shall continue to publish representative war plans, selected from the thousands of manuscripts that have been submitted. Among them are these:

Old but Good

> Send an American battleship to a Japanese port. Blow up the ship. Blame it on the Japs. Remember the Maine.

Liberty or Death

> Cultivate the spirit of our ancestors. They started a war rather than have TEA forced upon them. This generation submits to less than one per cent in its beer.

The Power of the Press-Bureau

> As a starter I suggest a disarmament conference in order that all Armies and navies may be reduced to good fighting trim. Then some hero of the last war (George Creel?) to be chairman of a committee on public misinformation. Within a month he could have us believing that we were threatened by the Swiss Navy. Then, when the next American tourist tumbles off a mountain in the Alps, blame the Swiss Government and the row is on.

Oil and Trouble

[426] "The Wife of the President Encourages Militarism." *Herald of Gospel Liberty*, vol. 116 no. 15 (April 10, 1924,) 339.

> Do something mean to the Standard Oil Company. Our Government has shown (at Smyrna, Tampico, in Java and other places) how sensitively it resents slights put upon the Standard Oil Company. Let four men, disguised as (a) Austrians, (b) Russians, (c) Frenchmen, (d) Albinos (all or each), drive a Ford up to a Socony [Standard Oil Company of New York] service station in Hoboken, or other convenient locality near a telegraph office, and obtain five gallons of gasoline, presenting in payment a lead dollar or a fistful of German marks. This is what is known, in international fin—I mean, politics, as "confiscation" and "interference with American interests," and it never fails to get quick results. Preferably, the man in the white uniform who tends the service station should be rapped smartly on the wrist. This is "indignity and injury to an American citizen" and is simply awful. Remember that "American citizen" and "American property" are technical terms. Make sure (1) that there's oil on the premises; (2) that it's Standard Oil; (3) that the victim is a Standard Oil employee. Others don't count.[427]

The Bugle Will Sound

The Army's plans for a national mobilization exercise were announced in May 1924. As the *New York Times* put it "the bugle will sound the assembly in cities, towns and hamlets throughout America and the three fold army, the regulars, the National Guard, and the organized reserves will be called out." The date selected was September 12, the sixth anniversary of the American victory at St. Mihiel and the day before General Pershing was to retire from the Army. On May 14 President Coolidge authorized Secretary of War Weeks and the Army to proceed with the plan. It was later revealed that the President did not know about the project prior to the Army's issuance of the initial order, dated April 26. The scope of the exercise was to be broad and to include industrial mobilization, planning for troop movements to ports on both coasts and transfer of heavy railway guns to points along the coasts. The *Times* stated that moving the railway guns might require the strengthening of some bridges and construction of new spur lines. It was noted that opposition had developed. "Efforts to prevent Mobilization Day have met with no success, as far as the War Department is concerned." An unnamed organization referred to it as "goosestep day" and inferred that it was a going-away present for General Pershing. The newspaper somewhat oddly stated that now that the planning had begun Secretary Weeks was helpless to stop it, since the law "requires that the Army always be in a state of readiness"[428]

[427] J. Randle Menefee, "We Want Bigger and Better Wars," *Life*, vol. 83 no. 2163 (April 17, 1924,) 13.

[428] "Army to Mobilize Land Defenses," *New York Times*, May 15, 1924, 32.

Weeks certainly had no interest in stopping Mobilization Day. He continued to try to build support for the military—and its expenditures. He sent a letter to the nation's newspapers that was published in the May 25, 1924 *Los Angeles Times*, attacking those who were claiming that war expenditures totaled 85.8 % of the federal budget. Weeks considered that some people who believed these "incorrect and misleading" figures were well-meaning citizens who were honestly confused. Some of these believers, however, were of a much different ilk: "These people include those forces in America who are preaching revolution and the establishment of a Communistic government and also those who seem to believe that any army or navy is unnecessary."

Weeks figured that expenditures for the military totaled 13.5 %, quite a difference from the National Council for the Prevention of War's number of 85.2 %. The difference arose because the Council included military pensions, veterans benefits, service and retirement fees on the national debt and some other non-current expenses—payments for wars "past and future." Weeks considered some these not part of the Army's budget, and he had a point there. He did not have a very good point about how small federal expenditures were in relation to state, county and municipal expenditure totals for the nation. It also doesn't seem that it accomplished much for his case to complain that critics never suggest saving money by reducing pensions or veteran's benefits, but only by cutting the "relatively small expenditure for military defense of the country." Finally, Weeks warned Americans who were asked to "...support reductions in the appropriations for the nation's defensive services, on the plea that the 'cost of militarism' is a direful burden on the American people, would do well to inform themselves of the facts and to examine into the character and patriotism of those who are promoting the pacifist campaign before taking a step that may readily align them with the enemies of the republic."[429]

It only took three days for Mobilization Day to become, officially at least, Defense Day. Pershing addressed a group of 1,000 officers at a dinner in New York on May 17. In his opinion the history of the United States was "marked by strife...young Americans of every generation had been called upon to defend their homes." He said that in the last sixty years there had been "four great conflicts that were none of our making." Apparently he saw the United States as the victim of aggression in the Civil War, the Spanish-American War, the Philippine-American War and World War I. He pointed out that we had only a "semblance" of an army in 1917 and it had taken us more than a

[429] John Weeks, "Foes of America Gnaw at Defense Structure," *Los Angeles Times*, May 25, 1924, 7.

year to engage in combat in France with a sizeable force. The upcoming exercise's main goal was to stir interest in preparedness by both those connected with the Army and the citizenry at large. He hoped that the public would learn about the local military units and join ranks with them in celebrating the American Army's first large victory in France, at St. Mihiel. Pershing described what a typical captain in the reserves might do by way of planning for the mobilization of his unit, calling this an "expeditious and economical means of providing for the common defense and at the same time of improving our citizenship."[430]

The Army sent letters to all the state governors, asking them to help in observing the day. Governor Percival Baxter of Maine wrote a letter to newspaper editors, in which he made his objections known. Leaving open the possibility that he might approve of such an exercise in the future, he averred that the "present time" was not right. He believed that a mobilization exercise might be seen as an aggressive move by some other nations and might give them an "excuse for similar mobilizations. The race for supremacy might be begun anew, with another and far more terrible war as its result." Baxter stated that he was not a pacifist and supported expansion of the Maine National Guard and the operation of the Citizens Military Training Camps: "I, however, do not believe in parading our strength to the world, or in calling attention to the fact that the US is the most powerful nation." He noted further that Secretary of State Hughes had been quoted as saying "We know that in no power or combination of powers lies any menace to our security... There is no reason to demonstrate our ability to take care of ourselves, for no-one doubts it."[431]

Governor Charles W. Bryan (Democratic nominee for Vice-President and younger brother of William Jennings Bryan) put his disagreement with Mobilization Day on a different basis than the Maine Governor. In a statement sent to newspapers the Governor said he would comply and have the National Guard assemble, but would not call upon civilians to participate, as it would be an "economic waste" to take all adult men away from their farms, jobs and businesses. To Bryan this amounted to a draft, compulsory military service, and he was dead set against that. The commander of the Nebraska Guard, General Duncan, told the Governor that he believed the National Defense Act of 1920 provided for such a civilian mobilization. The Governor said he saw nothing in the Act to support that. Bryan reported that Duncan said the US has lost many men in the First World War through a lack of preparedness. Bryan replied that "...we had saved [being involved in] several

[430] "Pershing Outlines Defense Day Plans," *New York Times*, May 18, 1924, 14.
[431] "Maine Governor Against War Show," *New York Times*, June 27, 1924, 16.

wars by not being prepared to fight." In agreement with Baxter and Hughes, the event would tend to "...impress upon the people the importance of war when there is none in sight...lead foreign countries to believe this country is preparing for war and keep the military spirit rampant when we all want peace."[432]

President Coolidge made no comment on the subject—he was, after all, noted for saying little. In July, however, Frederick J. Libby, Executive Secretary of the National Council for the Prevention of War, succeeded in getting a rise out of Silent Cal. The Council was planning a demonstration in Washington to mark the tenth anniversary of the outbreak of the Great War and asked for his support. In his reply Coolidge stated he was happy to endorse the Council's efforts, but noted that the Council had been referring to Mobilization Day as "militaristic." He totally rejected this characterization. He repeated an earlier claim that the Government had never called the upcoming event Mobilization Day, its proper name was National Defense Day or just Defense Day. It was not a mobilization for war but a test of readiness, required by the National Defense Act of 1920. It would show that we relied upon the volunteer spirit and patriotism of Americans in time of war, and not upon a large standing army. It was "utterly unfair" to condemn it as a mobilization for war.[433]

Mr. Libby did not retreat an inch. He replied thanking the President for his support of the Council's observance and then wrote that he would like to correct a "misapprehension," this being that the Government had never called it Mobilization Day. He had some examples, but still this was somewhat of a quibble since it had been referred to by the Government as Defense Day a few days after the initial announcement. As far as the National Defense Act requiring such a demonstration, he observed that the relevant provisions of the Act were very general and certainly do not specifically *require*, by any stretch, what was being planned. Libby continued by stating that the plan might provoke similar actions by other nations. It could also damage the effort, supported by the President, to adhere to the World Court, and influence the nation's youth in a negative way. Libby concluded by objecting to a statement by General Pershing that "every patriotic citizen will be expected to participate." He and many like him "believe that the wise national policy for our country at this juncture is to avoid "national defense tests," and to express in concrete and practical forms of cooperation a spirit of audacious friendliness. They, too, count themselves as patriots."

[432] "Gov. Bryan Attacks Mobilization Day," *New York Times*, Jul. 29, 1924, 1.

[433] "Coolidge Condemns Attempt to Hinder Defense Day Aims," *New York Times*, Jul. 27, 1924, 1.

On the same day that the *New York Times* published its story about letters exchanged by Coolidge and Libby there was a story about observance of No More War Day the previous day, July 26, 1924. This event was sponsored by the Women's Peace Society. Their flyers noted that we were spending "more for militarism" than in 1913, and it would be better to mobilize for peace rather than for war. C.M. Penfield, of the American Defense Society, wasn't fooled by the Women's Peace society sponsorship of the event. He knew who was behind it: "The demonstration held today is directly in line with the wishes and commands of the Third International, whether the persons holding the no-more-war celebration are connected with the communist party or not." This was so because the Third International had called, according to a *Times* article of July 13, for anti-war demonstrations during July 22-August 4, 1924. Mr. Penfield further pointed out that the Soviet Union had an army of around 750,000 men. [434] The combination of being interested in peace demonstrations and having a large army was more than suspicious to him.

Questioning opponents' backing and motives is common in political and social controversies, but *The Independent* thought it had gone too far. "With that passion for the *reductio ad absurdum* which is the disease of American thought, Pacifists are now busy calling advocates of preparedness Prussians, Goose-steppers, and Militarists; and the Preparedness Cohorts are equally busy describing the Pacifists as treasonable fanatics in the pay of the Soviets." Issues were many and widespread; a group of 183 Protestant churches in Philadelphia felt that young men should be advised against enrolling in military schools and against attending the civilian military training camps operated every summer.

On the other hand, the "Militarists" publish charts to demonstrate that the women's clubs of America are controlled by agents from Red Russia, and that Dorcas societies (a Dorcas society is a Christian women's group organized to make or otherwise provide clothing for the poor) and needlewomen's guilds (perhaps a reference to the International Ladies' Garment Workers' Union) are subtle disguises in which American institutions are attacked and undermined.

Be reasonable, *The Independent* exhorted. "Balance is required. Don't beat or abuse your horse or dog, but don't worry about the ant crawling around beneath your feet. Oppose war, but not self-defense. It was right and proper to outlaw aggressive war and punish those who disobey." It was also right and proper for America and all nations to maintain "...an armed force suffi-

[434] "Observe No More War Day," *New York Times*, Jul. 27, 1924, 13.

cient to protect them from aggressive attack. Such a force must be modern in equipment and training. If this be militarism, make the most of it."[435]

The Military Virus has Been Eating into the Heart of America

If *The Independent* thought that use of terms like "Prussian" and "Militarist" was extreme, the Herald of Gospel Liberty thought it was extremely accurate. They came out opposed to the idea on all levels on July 24, 1924. The weekly did not take the announcement seriously at first, thinking that it was a journalist exaggerating some sort of routine War Department exercise. Now, however, in late July, it appeared as though the "War Department really intends to 'mobilize' all military and civil forces to show the Government and the world how quickly and efficiently the United States can get ready to fight." The regular army, the reserves, and the state national guards would all participate and "certain factories and lines of business are to be marshalled into line as though war were actually declared. And it is the hope of the War Department to make this day an annual occurrence!" It was difficult to believe this could happen in America. The plan went completely against American values and traditions, and demonstrated "...the extent to which the military virus has been eating into the heart of America since the war began. Ten years ago America was boasting to the world of its freedom from the militarism which has damned Europe for centuries."[436]

The editors of the *Herald of Gospel Liberty* had three main objections to the mobilization plan. First, they did not think that the War Department should be proposing such an event without at least the involvement of Congress. The plan was introduced by the War Department completely on its own. Only Congress could declare war and approve military budgets. They, as representatives of the people, should be the ones to originate such a far-reaching measure. It seemed as though the military and civilian supervisors in the War Department were committing the nation to actions that were unpredictable at best and very likely disastrous. "And already the military authorities and the militaristic press of America are assuming that to question this plan or to refuse to enter heartily into it is to be unpatriotic and an object of censure." It was positively dangerous to give the War Department such a sweeping authority.

Second, it went against the common sense of traditional American military. Americans (and Canadians) saw no need to fortify the long border between us, a fact of which both nations were proud. We maintained the smallest possible regular army and criticized those European nations who

[435] "Pacifist and Militarist," *The Independent*, vol. 113 no. 3873 (July 19, 1924,) 32.

[436] "Shall the United States be Prussianized?", *Herald of Gospel Liberty*, vol. 116 no. 30, 699.

conscripted large armies and had widespread military training. That was before the Great War. Now the War Department wanted a much larger regular army. It also strongly supported the Civilian Military Training Camps (CMTC) and expansion of the Reserve Officers Training Corps (ROTC.) As a crowning absurdity, it was going to be annual event; we would mobilize every year. This was a procedure "that would delight the souls of the old Prussian warlords as an entering wedge that will inevitably fasten the military system and military manipulation upon this nation in a degree that would have been considered incredibly preposterous a few years ago." Preposterous because there was no one that wanted to fight us—no enemies meant no possible war. Mexico and Canada were not going to invade and there was absolutely no military threat from any European country. Even if there was a war with Japan, which wasn't going to happen, neither nation would be crazy enough to try to land an army on the shores of the other.

Finally, there was the "cherished principle...of world leadership in all the finer lines of idealism." With our ideals of democracy and liberty we were an example to the world and a powerful force for good. All this, however, was before the war. At the end of the war, with the peace negotiations and the defeat of the Treaty of Versailles in the US senate, a great opportunity to lead the world had been lost. Perhaps, if America had joined with the other nations of the world in the League of Nations, we would still be a real leader and positive example to humanity. Perhaps, if we had shown moral leadership, we would not have had "...an unprecedented debauchery of political sordidness and delinquency in high places," epitomized by scandals like Teapot Dome. Because we had no real enemy, the other nations of the world must "doubt our good sense or our good intentions."

There were also the strictures of the Christian religion, which was a message of peace and good will. The churches of America were engaged in effort to lead the nation and the world into an era of peace and freedom. If the War Department was successful in holding and repeating Mobilization Day, this would destroy belief in the sincerity of American purposes, no matter what its religious leaders may claim.

The *Herald* scoffed at the claims of some about the objectives of the event, such as desires to show respect to General Pershing upon his retirement or to commemorate the sacrifice of those killed in the St. Mihiel offensive. The General and the dead deserved all honor, but Mobilization Day was the brainchild of militarists; it did not come from everyday Americans, who wanted no more of war. "And as we love our living heroes and cherish the memory of our honored dead, every American...should vigorously protest to the President and other governing officials at Washington to save our nation from such an egregious blunder as that which the War Department proposes."[437]

The *Herald* was not the only religious publication that opposed mobilization day plans. *Literary Digest* surveyed opinion in church outlets and asserted "If its anathemas are sufficiently potent, 'Defense Day,' as planned by the War Department for September 12, will fail under the Church's assault." The *Digest* quoted *The Christian Century* as asserting that "American churches are in the full tide of a mighty movement against the whole war system. Deliberately, we say, the Government of the United States seems to be forcing the issue to discover the extent to which the churches are prepared to back up their recent brave words for peace...[September 12 will be] a day when a portion of the country will be forced to choose between Christ and Mars."

The Unitarian *Christian Register* was also unequivocal in its condemnation:

> For a nation whose resources of defense are incomparable among all the nations of the earth to play the braggart and the bully is, as the wise of this world already rightly say, so mean as to make us hang our heads and then rise up and resolve to put decent ideas and idealists in charge of our government. The reason we have pacifism is to be found in the unspeakable militarism whose agents flood the press with the venom of fictitious hates and imaginary alarms. It is the law of action and reaction. If pacifism arouses our opposition for its lack of depth, militarism arouses our wrath for its rape of our priceless spirit of reasonable trust in human nature everywhere in the world.[438]

The controversy over whether Mobilization Day was militaristic continued into August. John W. Davis, Democratic nominee for President (no smoke-filled rooms for Democrats—it took 101 ballots to select the 1924 nominee), agreed with Governor Bryan. He did not involve himself in the details, merely stating that he thought the time and effort could be better spent in "getting the world back to work and peace."[439] Governor Bryan, however, seems to have been a detail-oriented man. He managed to obtain a copy of a letter from Army General George B. Duncan to former draft board members in Nebraska, requesting their assistance to identify men of military age in their locales and encourage them to participate in the observance. The Governor repeated that he did not object to the Nebraska Guard and volunteers from the American Legion and other patriotic organizations participating; in

[437] Ibid., 700

[438] "The Churches' Wrath at 'Defense Day'," *Literary Digest*, August 9, 1924, 30

[439] "Davis Chimes in with Running Mate," *New York Times*, Aug. 1, 1924, 6.

fact, he had directed the Guard to do so. He did object to "a plan to appoint military committees to mobilize civilians in the State."[440]

The *Literary Digest* examined newspaper editorial opinion about the plan after the party conventions.

> [With the President and his administration supporting the project, Republican newspapers naturally favored it.] But speaking for the Democrats, one paper denounces Defense Day as "an incendiary holiday," another would rechristen it "Goose-Step Day," and still another cries "Don't ape the Kaiser," while many papers agree with the *Boston Post*'s assertion that "the people of these United States have had about all the militaristic provender they desire" ... According to the *Louisville Post* "what Mobilization Day really means is War Day. It is a psychological preparedness that is desired. If every year the people can be brought together to glorify war the militarist will have succeeded beyond his wildest expectations...Before the World War William of Prussia, then Emperor of the German Empire, reviewed his troops each year and staged sham battles for the maintenance of their discipline and morale, and to stir up militarist ambitions in the hearts of his people. We know the result, but not even William had the temerity to mobilize industry and agriculture, the whole civilian strength of the nation. We want nothing of the spirit of hate in this country. Governor Bryan is right. Mobilization Day is not needed."

The New York *World* was also strongly opposed. Their editors claimed that

> Something of the spirit in which September 12 is anticipated in at least one State may be gathered from an announcement, the first to be issued on the subject, of the program to be followed in Maryland: 'An enemy is coming...The country must use its military manpower. Its men must spring to arms by millions. They must drive the enemy out in man-to-man combat. They, with the organized branches of the 'one big army,' will be asked to join the big gesture that means America is ready.

The *World* noted with approval Governor Bryan's objections that mobilizing large numbers of civilians along with all the armed forces was economically wasteful and might well be viewed as threatening by other nations. In Europe a full mobilization usually led to war, "Therefore, mobilization is something not to be undertaken lightly and carelessly and in a half-holiday spirit. If it is absolutely necessary, the date and the manner should be determined not by the War Department but by the men responsible for the conduct of foreign affairs. In this case the matter has been handled most ir-

[440] "Bryan Charges Defense Day Draft," *New York Times*, Aug. 29, 1924, 2.

responsibly." The reason why the *World* thought it irresponsible was that on the very day that America was mobilizing the League of Nations would be in session in Geneva. By September 12 it was hoped that Geneva meetings between England and France would result in more non-military treaty provisions for French security. If that were accomplished then perhaps France would feel secure enough to rely less on conscripting a large army. But what kind of message would be sent "...by a continental mobilization of manpower. To any European, even the most moderate and peaceable, it will amount to saying: America, in no danger of invasion, puts its only trust in armaments; France, in actual danger, would be a fool to put its trust in anything else. That is why, in spite of the President's denials, the mobilization will seem to Europe, as Governor Bryan said, a militaristic gesture."[441]

The Hartford *Times* quoted Democratic presidential candidate John W. Davis, who quite agreed that this was not the time for America to mobilize:

> It is one thing to keep the military organizations of the country in adequate practice, it is quite another to encourage demonstrations which can be nothing else at a time when every energy should be bent on getting the world back to peace and to work, calming the prejudices and passions growing out of the World War and encouraging fruitful trade and commerce. In all these America should take the lead.' Mobilization Day must stand upon its merits. Thus far it has not demonstrated sufficient to support it.

Nonsense, Mr. Davis, replied the New York *Sun*:

> It is a great pity that a man of Mr. Davis's history should not have said something to curtail the mischief that one section of the Bryan statement may create. Governor Bryan warned that this 'mobilization' would be viewed with alarm by the 'war-sick peoples' of the world. Perhaps Governor Bryan believes that; he is no close student of foreign affairs. But Mr. Davis cannot possibly believe it. He knows that countries which have compulsory military service and extensive annual maneuvers will not worry over this very publicly prepared-for day. If anyone anywhere is worrying over it the fact is curiously unknown to newspaper correspondents. But it will be strange indeed, if Governor Bryan's talk, like the *World's* editorials on an 'incendiary holiday,' should not give mischief makers a chance to say that the plan is the creation of jingoes. If such use is made of the partisan utterances that Governor Bryan and Mr. Davis have made, the blame rests with them. Mr. Davis, at least, knows that mere common sense and not jingoism

[441] "Defense Day as a Campaign Issue," *Literary Digest*, vol. LXXXII no. 7 (August 16, 1924,) 5.

has inspired this 'defense test' on the part of a country which has the smallest per capita military force in this world.

Common sense or not, the Columbus *Evening Dispatch* thought our actions shouldn't worry any other country:

> We have nothing in existence which if massed together could create such a display of military strength as to give outside powers an uneasy suspicion that we are preparing for imperialistic domination or for actual military conquest. Much less can we make any such show of strength as to turn the heads of our own rising generation, and fill it with desire for war, and a passion for glory to be won on the field of battle. Anyone who has allowed the announcement of the proposed 'defense test' to arouse fear that any result of this kind could follow has been dreaming the idlest and most unreasonable of dreams.[442]

And what kind of people were these idle and unreasonable dreamers? Pacifists, according to the Chicago *Tribune*:

> If it is left for the United States to provoke a war the chances are the world has seen its last battle-field. The real dementia Americana is in our locoed pacifists. They are in a peaceful land which never properly attends to its defenses, and there they rave as if America were walking in armor, rattling the saber, and threatening the peace of the world.

Insane pacifists were a problem, agreed the Troy (NY) *Record*, but there were more sinister forces at work—pro-Germans:

> This element is still in existence; and a strong arm of defense, even though it does not point toward militarism and takes no one from the pursuits of ordinary life, is obnoxious to them. They want no militarism—except in Germany. These elements, largely associated with the La Follette movement, think they can hurt President Coolidge by calling him a militarist and making his admirable plan to test our present system an indication of his warlike attitude. National Defense Day is a splendid barometer of a chief element in assuring our safety.

Norman Thomas objected to the entire plan. Thomas, long-time leader of the Socialist Party USA and perennial candidate, was running for the governorship of New York in 1924. He was also a National Committeeman of the Conference for Progressive Political Action, which had been established by Progressive Party presidential candidate Senator Robert La Follette. Thomas stated on August 1, 1924, that Democratic opposition to all or part of the Mobilization Day plan was "purely partisan." He believed this because The Democrats didn't declare their opposition "...until the storm of American

[442] Ibid., 6

protest against this affront to all efforts for world peace..." developed. Thomas accused the Democrats of not fighting a war to end war, as President Wilson claimed, but a war to make the world safe for "great investments." By "great investments" he was referring to the billions of dollars of loans made to England and France by the US during the war. And now, as opposed to opportunistic Democrats, "Behind the La Follette advocacy of peace is the guarantee of his personal opposition to international war and the clear-cut declaration of the Cleveland platform and resolution not only against Mobilization Day, but against all those forces of militarism and imperialism that make for war."[443]

Of course, Mobilization Day had its 100% supporters, who were not in favor of half-measures. Army General Robert Lee Bullard, who commanded II Corps from Governors' Island in New York, told the New York Times about plans to "revive the old 'draft boards' that functioned so well in 1917." Bullard also recommended that other supporting committees be established, so that observance of the day could be organized in every city, town and village. He did not speak of mobilizing civilians and only desired that "all patriotic citizens" attend at least one Mobilization Day event.[444]

In the same article that quoted General Bullard there was information about the activities of the Advisory Board to the Army's Chief of Ordnance. This Board had been established after World War I to help the Army with matters of industrial preparedness—to make sure that if the nation had to mobilize for a real emergency, American industry would be ready to begin supplying the newly enlarged forces with the arms and equipment that they would need. The chairman of the board was E.H. Gary, Chairman of the Board of Directors of U.S. Steel, industrialist and founder of Gary, Indiana. Mr. Gary spoke rather belligerently about peace: "Mere expression of a pious wish for peace had never prevented the outbreak of war. Unless we distrust our own motives, proper preparedness means only that we mean to repel invasion of our inalienable rights and compel continued peace by maintaining our ability to command it."[445]

Brainsick and Hysterical

In his statements quoted above, General Bullard expressed no opinion about those who were opposed to the whole idea of Mobilization Day. A few days later he made up for this omission. Opponents of the project were "...a few brainsick, hysterical pacifists...Let each and every one of us, every

[443] "Davis on Defense Scored by Thomas," *New York Times*, August 2, 1924, 2.
[444] "Bullard Describes Defense D ay Plans," *New York Times*, Aug. 11, 1924, 15.
[445] Ibid.

citizen, stand himself up before his looking glass and ask himself what he is going to do to contribute to the national readiness to maintain our American rights and liberties, and if he say 'nothing,' then count himself a 'slacker.'" He concluded by blaming pacifists for American unpreparedness for the Great War, and gave his opinion that "Only stern repression of the pacifists and great devotion of our people saved us the last time."

Other commentators took a more tolerant view. *Outlook* magazine observed that it was natural during a war to not question the sacrifices being made. After the war, however, the sacrifices may seem huge and the gains quite small. Pacifism will probably increase and this was no bad thing. A certain amount of antiwar agitation was understandable and even commendable—but it wouldn't do to disarm the nation: "One of the lessons which ought to have been learned in the World War is that when war comes the Nation ought to have under its control all its resources—not only its man power for the battlefield but also its industrial power. In response to that lesson Congress passed the National Defense Law, and now September 12 has been designated as National Defense Day." This was not a mobilization. Assembling the armed forces of a nation to engage in battle, that was mobilization. This was a "reminder" to the people that in times of emergency the nation will call upon them.

According to *Outlook* there were only two ways America could go. One was to have a massive standing army. "The other is by the organization of the whole citizenry for self-defense. There ought to be no question in the mind of anyone who values civil liberties as to which is the better method." President Coolidge agreed. In the aforementioned exchange of letters between Coolidge and Frederic Libby of the National Council for the Prevention of War, the President had claimed that September 12 was a "non-militaristic gesture for the purpose of keeping down to its lowest possible point the professional military organization of the United States."

As a matter of fact, "American citizens who detest militarism (which is the determination of national policies by the military branch) should not obstruct, but encourage such undertakings as National Defense Day and the maintenance of civilian military training camps." Pacifist policies would be self-defeating. When war erupted it would be long and expensive in lives and treasure, because of a lack of preparation. If citizens did become involved in events like Defense Day and military training was widely available and seen as a citizen's responsibility, the nation should be secure. Once again the example of Switzerland was cited. The war raged all around them but they were not attacked. This was because the Swiss had military training for all adult males and a national militia system.[446]

Current Opinion of Sept. 1, 1924, took turns on the issue, first quoting those who pooh-poohed any feeling that the day was some sort of plot by warmongers. President Coolidge and the Department thought the event could be compared to a fire drill, "whose sole object is to keep our military machine well oiled, thereby rendering unnecessary a huge permanent army and furthering the cause of peace and economy." Opponents would have none of this. They thought the President was protesting too much when he objected to the name "Mobilization Day" and thought it should be called "Defense Day." But why did the War Department call it a "mobilization test" if it was not testing mobilization for war? Why did the War Department choose Sept. 12, the sixth anniversary of the St. Mihiel offensive, biggest American operation of the war? And why, with the rest of the world still war-weary, were we holding nationwide fire drills in case a war came along? It was as useless as a "life boat drill in the prairies...We may not believe all our neighbors say when they talk of peace. But it is an act of questionable politeness to interrupt them by rattling our saber." Finally, opponents pointed out that on Sept. 12 the League of Nations Assembly convened in Geneva. Just a coincidence, or...?[447]

Defense day plans moved a Japanese educator to organize a Peace day observance in Tokyo for September 12. Professor Sawayanagi, a member of the upper house of the Japanese Diet, recruited about one hundred fellow educators and academics to distribute a pamphlet criticizing Defense Day. It stated that Japanese people felt that the exercise was directed against them. The pamphlet stated that "Peace based on armaments is a frail peace; real peace is realized by extended education and enlightened thought." The Professor said in an interview that his group also wanted to educate the Japanese public about the danger to international peace of increasing armaments. It was noted in the article about the Professor's initiative that Japanese military and naval circles were thought to be keenly interested in the outcome of Defense day.[448] Several days after the event Japanese General Kameji Wada gave his evaluation of September 12, 1924: "America is more militaristic than Japan. No people are more interested in military matters than Americans. Mobilization Day is merely one of the evidences of this." The General wanted Japanese to pay more attention to national defense and not be "misled by false ideas of peace."[449]

[446] "Peace and Defense," *Outlook*, vol. 137 no. 14 (August 6, 1924,) 532.
[447] "Defense Day Under Fire." *Current Opinion*, Sept. 1, 1924, 277.
[448] "Japan Celebrates Peace Day Today," *New York Times*, Sept. 12, 1924, 23.
[449] "Calls Us Militarists," *New York Times*, Sept. 15, 1924, 23.

The day before the event the War Department was optimistic, putting it mildly. They claimed that opposition by such figures as Governor Bryan actually did supporters a favor, by stimulating "widespread discussion that has helped rather than hindered it." All nine Army corps in the country were enthusiastic too, as was the American Legion. The Department thought that 50,000,000 participants was a reasonable estimate. The American population in 1924 was 114,000,000, so the day would be memorable indeed if the prediction was borne out.[450]

The September 13 edition of the *New York Times* stated that "While the reports say that 16,792,781 citizens in 6,500 cities and towns took an active part, further returns may increase the number materially." The "reports" were reports received by the War Department from the nine Army corps areas in the United States. "Active part" seems to include both participants and observers. Several of the corps estimates are two or three million, perhaps what we might call guesstimates. Some cities did more than others; Philadelphia had "50,000 men, women and boys paraded down Broad Street with 100 floats symbolic of America's traditions." The *Times* noted that the day was observed throughout Nebraska, whose Governor Bryan had "made an issue" of Defense Day.[451]

In Los Angeles the city "exceeded its quota" of 14,000 volunteers to devote the day to the parade and patriotic observance—15,700 signed up. The parade announcer was KHJ (The L.A. Times station) radio personality Uncle John, who exhorted the crowd to join the choruses of patriotic songs sung by marchers. The crowd's biggest reactions were to the Grand Army of the Republic, Disabled Veterans of the World War (some on crutches) and the Gold Star Mothers and Widows. Secretary of the Navy Charles Wilbur made an address, passing along the word from Washington. He pointed to a recent announcement from President Coolidge. The President had said that "as soon as his son returned from school he would be sent immediately to a reserve training camp."[452]

The President also reviewed the parade held in the capital, where the marchers were said to total 30,000, civilian and military marching together. The President was joined on the stand by Secretary Weeks, General Pershing, Secretary of State Charles Evans Hughes, and other high ranking military officers and government officials. The President and other civilian men

[450] "50,000,000 to Answer Defense Day Appeal," *New York Times*, Sept. 11, 1924, 8.

[451] "Cities and Towns Everywhere Observe Day; 50,000 March in Philadelphia," *New York Times*, Sept. 13, 1924, 2.

[452] "City Exceeds Defense Quota; Thousands Cheer Paraders," *Los Angeles Times*, Sept.13, 1924, A1.

wore top hats and frock coats in the late summer afternoon heat. Volunteers were assigned to march with the unit deemed most suitable for their background. A group of cabdrivers was very logically assigned to the motor transportation unit. The civilians marched in the middle columns of formations and military men on the outside. Not everyone was in step, "...but they marched with heads erect, eyes to the front and with the spirit of men ready to respond to any call for military duty."[453]

An Un-Uniformed Army

The march began at the Capitol and ended at the Ellipse just south of the White House. The Associated Press reporter covering the event seemed mightily impressed by the "...un-uniformed army... [that] flowed up Pennsylvania Avenue with the orderly, steady, unbroken movement of a great river." The expressions on the marchers' faces were "serious." Onlookers were serious too. Most of them stayed for the whole parade and with "grave reverence" saluted or raised their hats every time the American flag passed. At the Ellipse the men listened to Secretary Weeks and General Pershing express their thanks for their participation. The Secretary thought the day's events were a big defeat for the "pacifists." According to Weeks they had predicted that Mobilization Day would be the greatest setback to peace efforts in Europe that had ever happened. Not so, the Secretary claimed—in fact, there had been increased talk of peace and disarmament in Europe recently. The day had been so successful that he wanted to make it a regular event. General Pershing also thought that any ideas that the day was intended to make a threat against anyone was "baseless, not to say childish." Anyone could see that that what came to be called the force in being was small and not capable of aggressing anyone. The day was a demonstration, however, of a readiness to rally to the colors if attacked, and an indication that we would not "soon drop back into our prewar attitude of inaction and neglect."[454]

The day was concluded with evening speeches by General Pershing and Secretary Weeks, over a national radio hookup. This included, for the first time, radio stations on the West Coast, and it was estimated that a record 25 million tuned in. The General expounded on the peaceful nature of the day's events and ridiculed the idea that anyone could think that they demonstrated militarism or an aggressive attitude towards the rest of the world. He invoked what must have been his own experiences of weather as a support for the need of testing defense readiness—even though there was no threat on the horizon, he said, "storms often appear out of a clear sky." After his speech

[453] "Coolidge Reviews Parade of 30,000," *New York Times*, Sept. 13, 1924, 1.
[454] "Stalwart Hosts Rally to Banner of America," *Los Angeles Times*, Sept. 13, 1924, 1.

Pershing made a series of telephone calls to four Army generals stationed in different parts of the country. These were broadcast also, another first in radio, so that listeners could hear both sides of the conversation. Readers of the *New York Times* were assured that although the same system would be used by the military in the event of an emergency, those conversations wouldn't be on the radio. These dialogues had two purposes—to hear reports on Defense Day and to mark General Pershing's retirement from active duty, which was to be effective the following day at noon. When General William Bullard came on the line from New York and was asked by Pershing how the day had gone he replied "Bully, bully...I should say that about 1,000,000 civilians turned out." The other three generals were equally happy with the results.

Military officers and Republicans were not the only ones who approved of the events of the day. Democratic presidential candidate John W. Davis did too, though the *New York Times* reporter covering Davis in Colorado on September 12 characterized his approval as "mild." In his speeches that day he criticized the Coolidge Administration for not paying enough attention to the Navy. We had fallen seriously behind both Great Britain and Japan in the number of modern cruisers and other vessels not limited by the Washington Treaty. Davis said that Americans are not militaristic and did not want or need to be. Our main defense was the expanse of ocean that separated us from anyone who might want to harm us. We needed a powerful navy to prevent the barrier from becoming a highway. It was fortunate, he said, that there were not historical examples of a large navy becoming a danger to the rights and liberties of the nation that built it. The same could not be said for large standing armies.

Outside the big cities there does not seem to be much criticism, if any. In Brazil, Indiana, the day was "well observed," even though the weather was bad: "Weeping skies" and sodden streets failed to spoil the patriotic enthusiasm which marked the observance of Defense Day in this city last evening." The parade was headed by the "Legion firing squad" [i.e., the color guard,] the police, American Legion, post office employees and speakers and committees riding in cars. Several bands and citizens in their cars brought the rear. The parade ended in the Forest Park auditorium, where "close attention was paid to the exercises." Civil War veteran and former congressman E.S. Holliday was the first speaker. Although "well along in years, his voice was strong as he...defended the purpose of Defense Day and denounced its critics...'Whenever you attack Defense Day or question the right of our country to prepare for defense then you are attacking your country and are not a good citizen.' "The second speaker was Judge Sydney S. Miller of Indianapolis, who was a major in the Army reserves and had served with the 42d division in France. Judge Miller quite agreed with E.S. Holliday, stating that "Defense Day was not a military demonstration and no war-like gesture was being made—that it was simply a day of patriotic demonstrations from a purely defense standpoint." In concluding his address the judge stated that "When a man refuses to take up arms to defend his country, he ceases to be a man, so let us pledge ourselves here tonight that if we are ever forced to go into another war we will go prepared."[455]

The Escanaba (Michigan) *Daily Press* ran Associated Press reports from around the state. In Saginaw, Congressman Bird J. Vincent said that "Defense Day is not a militaristic demonstration, but an effort to show the nation that its greatest security in time of peace rests in an adequate preparation." As for Defense Day activities in Escanaba itself, the *Daily Press* described the evening's events in the high school auditorium. The main speaker was Fr. Alphonse Coignard of Perkins, Michigan. According to the unnamed reporter, the priest spoke at length about empires destroyed by pacifism, going from the Persian Empire conquered by Alexander the Great to the Second Empire of Napoleon II demolished by Otto von Bismarck, who "had not listened to pacifist doctrines occasionally." In addition, Father Coignard asserted that "National Defense Day is not an act of militarism, but an act of peace. It may prevent international crime, just as the placing of locks on doors and the use of bank vaults in the bank prevents robberies."

Martian Instincts

An unimpressed and occasionally sneering reporter for the Sandusky Ohio *Register* wrote that:

> If there has been any shadow of doubt lurking in the minds of Sanduskians as regards the significance of Defense Day, it was dispelled by the address of Chaplain H.F. MacLane of the Soldiers' Home delivered from the steps of the court house on the occasion of Sandusky's observance of the movement on Friday afternoon...the oration of Chaplain MacLane explained the exact meaning of Defense Day. His arguments were based, not on any hypothetical reasonings and theories, but on an intimate knowledge of the Martian [the capital M shows the reporter hadn't confused Martian with martial] instincts and inclinations of the world, and were pillared and bolstered by a formidable and convincing array of antecedents that brand unpreparedness as a vicious and criminal assault on the nation.

[455] "Defense Day Well Observed," *Brazil Daily Times*, September 13, 1924, 1.

The Chaplain said that America was usually unprepared for war—and unpreparedness had serious consequences: In the World War our armies in France had to use artillery supplied by our allies.

> And the chaplain asserted that many of our boys died in the field needlessly because they did not understand the mechanism and operation of these strange weapons. The chaplain's address was heard without a murmur, save now and then an occasional burst of applause as some *trite* [emphasis mine] remark struck home. Then followed the playing of the Star Spangled Banner by the band during which all, even those in the remotest corners of the assemblage, stood with heads reverently bared. Then the bugler sounded 'retreat' and the assemblage dispersed. So drew to a close Sandusky's first observance of the Nation's Defense Day.[456]

Estimation of the size of crowds is more a matter of art and purpose than science. Challenging the size estimate of a crowd is common nowadays. Even in 1924, however there was a minimum of one skeptic who had thoughts about the figure of 16,782, 791 participants in the event nationwide. Mr. Bradley Stone of Boston wrote the New York Times:

> One would like to know how these figures were arrived at, with a promptness and exactness surpassing anything ever known in election returns. Was the process something like that of Artemus Ward, who, when he mentioned the total number of rats in the United States, said that he "spoke simply from memory"? What was the nature of the participation? Did it cover the persons who stood on the sidewalks to see the processions go by? Without exacter detail the wicked "pacifists," although so vociferously assured that the whole thing was a "peace gesture," are sure to suspect that this emanation from the War Department is "tendez" literature...the "more than" implies that the returns were not all in, as they hardly could be at so early an hour; in Massachusetts, for instance, Chicopee and Longmeadow may not have been heard from.[457]

Not all potential participants were welcomed to the parades. In Wilkinsburg, near Pittsburgh, the local Ku Klux Klan demanded to march in the full regalia, hoods and all. When they were denied, an anonymous caller to the parade marshal threatened to break up the parade if the Klan was not allowed to march. The parade was cancelled rather than risk violence.[458] This makes the suggestions made by the Chicago Defender pertinent then and

[456] "Lack of Preparedness Scored by Chaplain at 'Defense' Observance," *Sandusky Register*, September 13, 1924, 1.
[457] "The Defense Day Figures," *New York Times*, Sept. 21, 1924, X12.
[458] "Town forced by Klan Threat to Cancel Parade," *New York Times*, Sept. 12, 1924, 1.

now. They proposed a sort of internal Defense day—to defend the constitutional rights of American citizens from attack by racists such as the Klan: "Let us have a Defense day against the unwritten law that makes every white man a law unto himself...Let us face together the real enemies of our country's welfare here at home and there shall be no needless worry about the enemy afar off. Let us have a Defense day that will in every true sense defend all that is near and dear and essential to the future destiny and propagation of this government, which must be without prejudice of race, religion and color."[459]

"A More Appropriate Day"

Those who were able to have their parades and celebrations seemed mostly to consider the events a success. The War Department proposed that the next Defense Day be on November 11, 1925, Armistice Day. The President replied to the Acting Secretary of War Davis on May 25, 1925 that he did not approve of the date and suggested Independence Day "as being a more appropriate day." An account of the selection of the date noted that July 4 was the President's birthday. It was further observed that the original date for 1924 was September 13, General Pershing's birthday, and was chosen to honor him on his retirement. The General wanted September 12, in memory of the Battle of Saint Mihiel, however, and that was the day of the 1924 event.[460]

The selection of Independence Day on May 25 did not leave much time for preparation. On June 3 six state governors' replies to a War Department request for cooperation were noted. Four replies promised cooperation, one said we'll get back to you. Governor Trumbull of Connecticut advised that "I am in favor of the principle of a defense test, but feel it would be more representative of what this state can do if undertaken at a time when it would not be at the expense of the workingman's holiday." In 1925 the event was on a Saturday, and Saturday was still a work day for most people. Governor Trumbull thought many in Connecticut would be away for the weekend, thinning the crowds in his state.[461]

What Would You Do?

Army Chaplain Joseph Hunter of Fort McArthur thought there might be citizens that didn't understand what the purpose of Defense Day was—or was not. It was not a "military gesture," a recruitment effort, or a means "to acquire munitions of war or train citizens for fighting." No, it was a method

459 "Defense Day," *The Chicago Defender*, Sept. 13, 1924, 12.
460 "July 4 to be Defense Day," *Los Angeles Times*, May 26, 1925, 1.
461 "Governors Promise to Aid Defense Test," *New York Times*, June 3, 1925, 25.

of ascertaining who and what was available for national defense-an "inventory." As a way of understanding why such an inventory was necessary, the Chaplain proposed a thought experiment:

> Let us consider a concrete case which is as probable as our sending troops to Europe appeared to be when that war started. It is possible that an enemy battleship fleet might have command of the Pacific, and be within a day's sail of the harbor of Los Angeles, with the probable intention of making it a base for the invasion of the United States. In such a specific case, what would you do? Defense Day is a fitting time to get a census or inventory of our personnel [personal?] and community willingness to defend our homes and loved ones; to maintain American ideals and institutions, and to promote the national security.[462]

It would also separate the sheep from the goats: "If our citizens think more of personal pleasure on July 4, than of a patriotic celebration of the day, linked with an inventory of our loyalty to the principles for which our Revolutionary War was fought, it is time for us to awake to that fact."[463]

The End of Militarism

Far from being militaristic, Defense Day would be the end of "talk and fear of militarism." Colonel Dwight M. Greene, commander of the Los Angeles Defense Test Forces, wrote that Defense Day was in the American grain—we would continue to maintain a small standing army and depend upon the citizens to rally to the colors in the event of a large war. The Army was capable of handling smaller problems requiring military force—there were more than 100 of these since the founding of the republic, against "less powerful foes." Rather than turning to "...European sources for our military system," Defense Day would be "...the muster day each year upon which the physically fit patriotic men of the nation are asked to turn out so that the organized leaders in the Officers' Reserve Corps may test out the patriotic strength in each community and witness the manifestation of public interest showing endorsement of the American principle of a great, ready citizen army of patriots, rather than an expensive, militaristic, large standing army."[464]

Major Ford A. Carpenter put it even more strongly: Defense Day was the "...most potent means to dissipate the fear of militarism that is so strong in the minds of some people and to eliminate any menace of militarism in the

[462] Hunter, Chaplain Joseph. "Defense Day Aim is Told by Chaplain," *Los Angeles Times*, June 23, 1925, A3.
[463] Ibid.
[464] Green, Col. Dwight M. "Patriots Asked to Give One Day," *Los Angeles Times*, June 25, 1925, 20.

United States." Carpenter defined militarism as the control of the government by the army. Our small standing army was, he thought, in no position to dominate civil authority. Some critics of the exercise had claimed that it would be seen as aggressive in intent by other nations. Nonsense, according to the Major: "...no foreign nation could possibly misunderstand the defense or be concerned in any way, unless it was regarding our wealth with covetous eyes. All foreign governments had known since 1776 that we would use ...the full force of our citizenry for national defense," so no one should be upset if we tested that use once a year. However, there was something else behind foreign critics besides covetousness: "Only the insidious foreign forces which seek to destroy the nation itself, as the world has witnessed in the Communistic movement in all quarters, are the ones that combat this appraisal of American citizens of the nation's power."[465]

No Blatant Bands

In Los Angeles the center of activity was the campus of the "University of California, Southern Branch," today's UCLA. There citizens of military age could indicate their availability and willingness to defend the nation, by putting their name on a list. Several hundred reserve officers, the "nucleus of...a war time army of hostility," signed in. Several hundred more registered by mail. The event was said to have participants from all walks of life, from "mule skinners to divisional commanders." At the campus there were posts for all professions to report to—one account listed 64 types of workers, in alphabetical order from armorers to wheelwrights. When everyone had reported, there was a parade, a "...silent parade around the athletic field of the university. No blatant bands preceded the march. No cheers accompanied them on parade. It was a peacetime parade, composed of fighting men who place peace ahead of conflict, but who are ready to throw off their robes of peace if the nation calls." This being Los Angeles, "One of the features of the parade was a car containing a group of film actresses, enlisted to serve in the nursing and entertainment corps...The girls, dressed in summer attire, made a striking picture and included Maryon Aye, Barbara Bedford, Joyce Compton, Lolita Lee, Clara Horton and Ethel Grey Terry." There was of course a speech, by Attorney Frank G. Terrell, to cap off the day. "Attorney Terrell declared that no guarantee against invasion and everlasting peace is as enduring as preparedness for war. All those nations that would look with cov-

[465] Carpenter, Maj. Ford A. "Defense Day is for Civil Army," *Los Angeles Times*, June 30, 1925, A9.

etous eyes upon the United States as a place to attack and invade he advised to keep away."[466]

During the day Army corps commanders called in counts of the number of enrollees. The total came to 8,040,359. This was about half the number that participated last year. Army spokesmen noted that, as the governor of Connecticut had said, the fact that July 4th was on a Saturday may have reduced attendance, since the workweek then included Saturdays and many people may have used the rare two day break for recreation rather than mobilization. In the evening there were speeches by General Pershing, his successor General Hines, Vice-President Dawes, Acting Secretary of War Davis and W.S. Gifford, president of the American Telephone and Telegraph Company. They "...talked to the country through the medium of the most pretentious [portentous?] program of radio broadcasting ever undertaken..." All cited the need for preparedness as a war prevention measure. Mr. Gifford came last and concluded the proceedings by stating that

> The well-being and opportunity here to enjoy life and the pursuit of happiness are greater than can be found anywhere else in the world. They are beyond the promise held out in any other nation in the world. To safeguard them is our only desire and our solemn duty...Unpreparedness is not protection against war but may be an invitation to war. While steadily planning and striving for peace let us see that our national household is in order and that we are ready to strike quickly and surely if need be, for national freedom and integrity.[467]

Major General Amos Fries, head of the Army's Chemical Warfare Service, seemed to think that the national household was in some disorder. He gave a speech to the Oldest Inhabitants Association of Washington D.C. on July 4. In it he "...denounced pacifists as representing groups of people who praise everything in the world except that which is American." He added "They have fine words for murderous Soviet Russia and for this Government and that Government in foreign lands, but never a word for America and her wonderful traditions and ideas. Many are men and many are women who are posing as leaders of thought and lovers of our country, but he who hath no respect for his ancestors cannot expect respect from his descendants or contemporaries." General Fries mentioned the Women's Peace Union of New York City, declaring that an affirmation on the letterhead of the union, pledging signers to withhold aid from either defensive or offensive war, was "treasonable."[468]

---

466 "City Joins for Test," *Los Angeles Times*, July 5, 1925, 1.

467 "8,040,395 Muster in National Test of Defense Power," *New York Times*, July 5, 1925, 1.

468 "General Fries Assails Anti-War Drives," *New York Times*, July 5, 1925, 16.

In Los Angeles there may not have been blatant bands, but in New York's Central Park "Flags waved, bands blared and Mayor Hylan made a speech." The Mayor did not speak directly about Defense Day, but did state that "The history of all nations has shown that liberty can only be preserved by the exercise of eternal vigilance and that those who are prepared to defend their country in time of peril must be conspicuous in the ranks of those who work for the good of the country during times of peace." Major General Charles P. Summerall, Second Corps Commander, put the matter much more strongly. He condemned "indifferent patriots" who did not participate in the proceedings and said that "Those who are not with us today are against us...What value would there have been in the Declaration of Independence had those who signed it not been able to give life and force and effect to their words? Their words mean war, and have meant war ever since they were penned. If we wish to preserve our independence today we must be just as ready as they were to pledge our lives, our fortunes and our sacred honor."[469]

Conclusions: Evaluating the Event

It would be interesting to know which US Army officer came up with the idea of a Mobilization Day event. Associating it with the retirement of General Pershing was something of a feint which collapsed when the General declined the honor. Within the space of a few days after the plan was made public the name was changed to Defense Day. Shortly thereafter it was usually referred to as "the defense day test," minus the capital letters. Thus anti-militarists forced the Army to retreat at the beginning of the battle. As all good strategists do, they attempted to press their advantage.

The Army, regained its footing, however, and began to promote the event more in terms of patriotism than of any sort of military preparation. When the program was attacked as displaying militarism, President Coolidge denied that it was in letters made public in July 1924, though he did not praise it much. Coolidge, so far as is known, was not informed of plans for the event prior to its announcement in May. His policy goal as regards the Army was to keep it as small and inexpensive as possible—even to reduce expenditures on it, if possible. A national celebration of the Army and its role in the life of the nation was unlikely to ever get better than lukewarm support from him.

Nineteen-twenty four was an election year. Possibly the Army and the War Department thought that with claims of true and undying patriotism arising everywhere no one would question the raison d'être of the observance. They were wrong. The Democratic candidate, John W. Davis, didn't

[469] "Summerall Scores Passive Patriots," *New York Times*, July 5, 1925, 17

see a need that a Mobilization Day/Defense Day/defense test day would meet. His disapproval was mild compared to that of some other Democrats and after the event he was mildly approving of the effort.

The Army and the War Department pronounced themselves well satisfied with the turnout that they reported on September 12, 1924, the day of the event. They never did say what constituted participation in the proceedings—did their total include observers as well as those who actually signed up? No one in authority seemed interested in explaining the numbers.

The original plan was to have the event be an annual observance. President Coolidge continued to seem little interested in it. The Army had planned for the 1925 date to be November 11. At the end of May the President rejected that date and selected July 4, Independence Day, leaving little time for preparations. This time the Army reported a little over 8 million participants, about half the 1924 count. Searches of online newspapers from around the country for 1926-28 revealed no articles about Defense Day.

It seems like the Army won a battle but lost the war. In 1924 the event was massively covered by the press and observed throughout the nation in cities, towns and villages. But the same questions asked by anti-militarists about a larger army and more military training applied here: Who was the enemy? How would he invade? *Why* would he invade? There were no good answers.

9. Militarism in the New Era

The 1920s are often referred to as the "New Era," distinguishing them from the preceding two decades of the Progressive Era and the following New Deal of the 1930s. There were several things that were new about the 1920s. One was the confidence of the Republican leaders that they had solved problems of business and government by fostering a close cooperation between the two. Not for the last time, many people were predicting prosperity that would stretch far into the future.

Before this confidence could develop, however the problems of modern war had to be dealt with. Within a matter of weeks after the outbreak of the First World War influential Americans, led by Theodore Roosevelt, were calling for the nation to arm itself in case war came. Soon support of military expansion became "preparedness." By January 1915 TR was calling for intervention against Germany, but opposition was forming—the American Union against Militarism was organized in that same month. Nineteen-sixteen was an election year and both candidates supported neutrality and condemned militarism. However, both supported preparedness, which anti-militarists claimed was militarism in disguise. When war was declared on April 17, 1917, the debate over militarism was stifled, but only until November 11, 1918.

The war was short and victorious for America, though the casualties for the last few months were horrific. Supporters of keeping an enlarged military after the war pointed with pride at the accomplishments of American servicemen, all done without a hint of militarism. Anti-militarists didn't argue a lot about what had happened during the war, but were strongly opposed to an expanded military now that peace had broken out—that, they claimed, would obviously be militaristic.

Most of the supporters of larger armed forces also supported various schemes for universal military training, which would be a continuing issue. Everybody should want to serve their country, supporters claimed. This was patriotism in action, not militarism. Just because the Great War was over didn't mean there would never be another—and American troops were still deployed in the Soviet Union and on the east bank of the Rhine. Antimilitarists, in the absence of enemies who had the capability and desire to attack us across an ocean, saw no need for anything beyond a small regular army.

The National Defense Act of 1920 set the maximum authorized strength of the Regular Army at 250,000. The Act also provided for regular army reserves and regulation of the state national guards. Pro-military groups had wanted an army of 500,000, provisions for universal military training and a reserve of trained soldiers up to six million. What they got was much less and the opposition of antimilitarists in Congress undoubtedly influenced the outcome. Even more than the opposition of anti-militarists, however was opposition of both Republicans and Democrats to the expenditure of more tax money than was absolutely necessary. Army generals professed themselves satisfied, but the sincerity of their claims may be doubted, particularly since the actual strength of the Army was usually less than 120,000.

Cost-cutting was a major motivation behind the Harding Administration's 1922 initiative for a conference to limit naval arms. It was successful, since by the terms of the Treaty of Washington the signatories were limited in the tonnage of capital ships they could have. This meant stopping the naval construction programs and scrapping ships that would exceed the limits set for the United States, Great Britain, Japan, France and Italy, in the ratio 5:5:3:1:1. For the United States this meant the end of its 1916 naval construction program, which had continued after the war. The admirals, unlike the generals, made no pretense of being pleased. They and their supporters continued to press for more non-capital ships of types not restricted by treaty—specifically, cruisers, the largest and most powerful type of vessel that the Treaty did not limit as to the number a signatory could have. Anti-militarists had reason to celebrate the Treaty of Washington and continued to oppose new naval construction.

Militarism had been something of an issue in the 1920 presidential nomination contest, with the participation of Army General Leonard Wood as a candidate. It became an issue in the 1924 campaign when early in the year the Army announced plans for a National Mobilization Day. Anti-militarists erupted and within a few days the Army said what we meant was...National Defense Day. Nevertheless, Democrats ended up opposing the idea, if rather quietly. President Coolidge's support was lukewarm at best. His plans for the following year's observance seem designed to make it go away, and it did—by 1927.

After the First World War, those who opposed the idea of a large army were largely successful. Opposing a large navy, however, was mostly unsuccessful. The opponents of expanded land forces would shift their emphasis to opposing military training in schools, colleges and summer training camps for civilians. Those who wanted to limit the size and composition of the navy supported each attempt at diplomacy to limit—and someday hopefully reduce—the navies of the world powers. Neither supporters nor opponents of strong military forces were content with the status quo. The political battles would continue until the next great war ended them.

Bibliography

Addams, Jane. *Women at The Hague: the International Congress of Women and Its Results*. New York, Macmillan Co., 1915.

Allen, Frank Edward. *Keeping our Fighters Fit for War and After*. New York, Century Co., 1918.

Angell, Sir Norman. *America and the New World State; a Plea for American Leadership*. New York and London, G.P. Putnam & son, 1915.

Baer, George. *One Hundred Years of Sea Power: the U.S. Navy, 1890–1990*. Stanford, Stanford University Press, 1994

Baker, Roscoe. *The American Legion and American Foreign Policy*, New York, Bookman Associates, 1954.

Borah, Senator William E. *Modern Militarism*. Washington D.C., Government Printing office, 1916.

Borah, William E. Closing Speech of Hon. William E. Borah on the League of Nations in the Senate of the United States, November 19, 1919. Washington, Government Printing Office, 1919.

Coletta, Paulo E. *The American Naval heritage in Brief*. Washington D.C., University Press of America, Inc., 1980.

DeBenedetti, Charles. *Origins of the Modern American Peace Movement, 1915–1929*. Millwood N.Y., KTO Press, 1978.

Deming, Seymour. *From Doomsday to Kingdom Come*. Boston, Smart and Maynard, 1916.

Duffield, Marcus. *King Legion*. New York, Jonathan Cape and Harrison Smith, 1931.

Ekirch, Arthur A. Jr. *The Civilian and the Military*. New York, Oxford University Press, 1956.

Ferguson, George Oglethorpe. An Answer to the Rev. Newell Dwight Hillis' Sermon Recently. Washington. D.C., 1915.

Finnegan John Patrick. Against the Specter of a Dragon: The Campaign for American Military Preparedness, 1914–1917. Westport, Connecticut, Greenwood Press, 1974.

Fiske, Bradley A. *The Art of Fighting*. New York, Century Company, 1920.

Gray, Justin. *The Inside Story of the Legion*. New York, Boni & Gaer, 1948.

Hawley, Ellis W. *The Great War and the Search for a Modern Order*. New York, St. Martin's Press, 1979.

Hillis, Newell Dwight. *Studies of the Great War, What Each Nation has at Stake*. New York, Fleming H. Revell Co., 1915.

Hobson, J.A. *Democracy after the War*. New York, Macmillan Company, 1918.

Hughes, Charles E. The Pathway of Peace, Representative Addresses Delivered During His Term as Secretary of State. New York, Harper & Brothers, 1925.

Jastrow, Joseph A. The Psychology of Conviction, a Study of Beliefs and Attitudes. Boston, Houghton Mifflin Company, 1918.

Jensen, Joan M. *Army Surveillance in America, 1775–1980*. New Haven, Yale University Press, 1992.

Johnson, Robert David. *The Peace Progressives and American Foreign Policy*. Boston, Harvard University Press, 1995.

Johnston, R.M. *Arms and the Race*. New York, Century Co., 1915.

Jones, Richard Seelye. *A History of the American Legion*. Indianapolis, Bobbs-Merrill Co., 1946.

Kawakami, K.K. *What Japan Thinks*. New York, Macmillan Company, 1921.

Keene, Jennifer D. *Doughboys, the Great War, and the Remaking of America*. Baltimore, Johns Hopkins University Press, 2001.

Kennedy, David M. *Over Here: the First World War and American Society*. New York, Oxford University Press. 1980.

Kirschbaum, Joseph. *The Naval Expansion Act of 1916: Planning for a Navy Second to None*. Dissertation UMI #3311364, George Washington University, 2008.

Knox, Dudley W. *The Eclipse of American Sea Power*. New York, J.J. Little and Ives Co., 1922.

Koistinen, Paul C. *Planning War, Pursuing Peace, the Political Economy of American Warfare*. Lawrence, University Press of Kansas, 1998.

Lane, Jack C. *Armed Progressive, General Leonard Wood*. San Rafael, Presidio Press, 1978.

Millis, Walter. *American Military Thought*. Indianapolis, Bobbs-Merrill Company, 1962.

Moley, Raymond Jr. *The American Legion Story*. New York, Duell, Sloan, and Pearce, 1966

Morgan, Ted. Reds: *McCarthyism in Twentieth-Century America*. New York, Random House, 2003.

Nasmyth, George William. *Universal Military Service and Democracy*. Washington D.C., American Union against Militarism, 1917.

Neiberg, Michael S. *The Path to War*. New York, Oxford University Press, 2016

Pietruska, David. *1920, the Year of Six Presidents*. New York, Carroll & Graf Publishers, 2007.

Rappaport, Armin. *The Navy League of the United States*. Detroit, Wayne University Press, 1962.

Roosevelt, Theodore. *America and the World War*. New York, Charles Scribner's Sons, 1915.

Ross, Edward Alsworth. *Principles of Sociology*. New York, The Century Co., 1920.

Rumer, Thomas A. *The American Legion, an Official History 1919–1989*. M. Evans and Company, Inc., 1990

Smith, Munroe. *Militarism and Statecraft*. New York, G.P. Putnam's Sons, 1918.

Sprague, Franklin Monroe. *Made In Germany*. Boston, The Pilgrim Press, 1915.

Tarbell, Ida M. *Peacemakers-Blessed and Otherwise*. New York, The Macmillan Company, 1922.

Tawney, R.H. *The Acquisitive Society*. New York, Harcourt, Brace and Howe, 1920.

Villard, Oswald Garrison. *Universal Military Training: Our Latest Cure-All*. Washington, D.C., American Union against Militarism, 1918.

Wells, H.G. *Washington and the Riddle of Peace*. New York, Macmillan Company, 1922.

West, Henry L., and Charles T. Hallinan. *Universal Military Training*. Washington D.C., American Union against Militarism, 1919.

Wheat, George Seay. *The Story of the American Legion*. New York, G.P. Putnam & Sons, 1919.

Wilson, Woodrow. *National Preparedness*. Washington D.C., Government Printing Office, 1916

Wood, Leonard. *The Military Obligation of Citizenship*. Princeton, Princeton University Press, 1915

Index

Printed in the United States
By Bookmasters